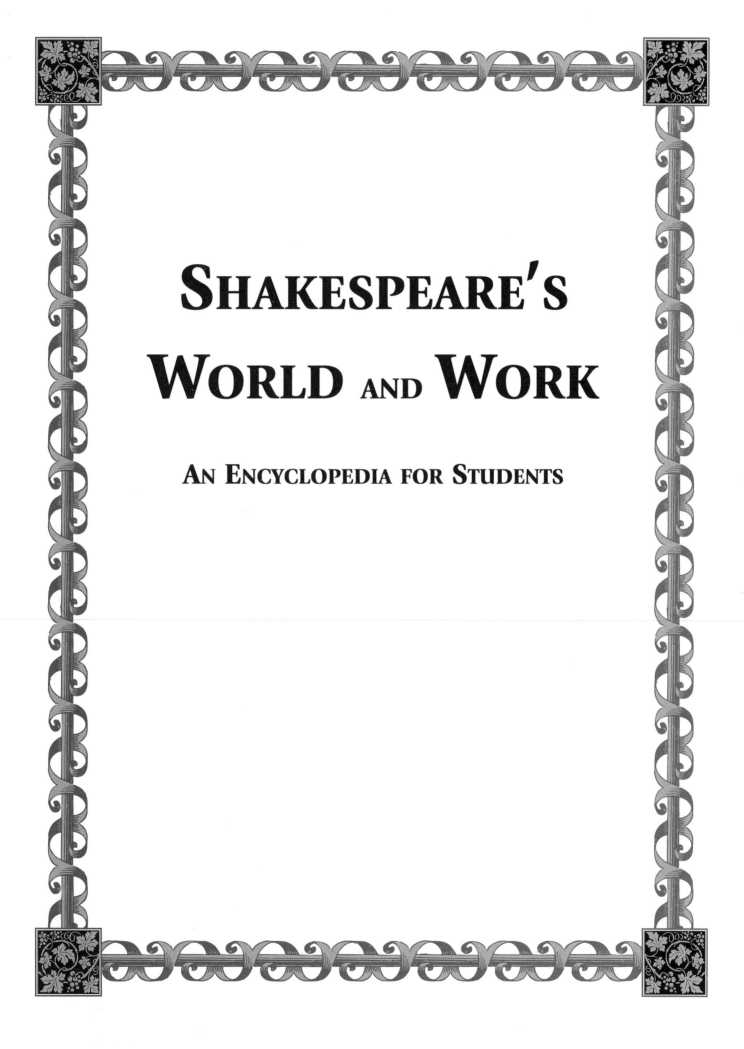

SHAKESPEARE'S WORLD AND WORK

AN ENCYCLOPEDIA FOR STUDENTS

JOHN F. ANDREWS
The Shakespeare Guild
Editor in Chief

WILLIAM M. HILL
The Peddie School
Associate Editor

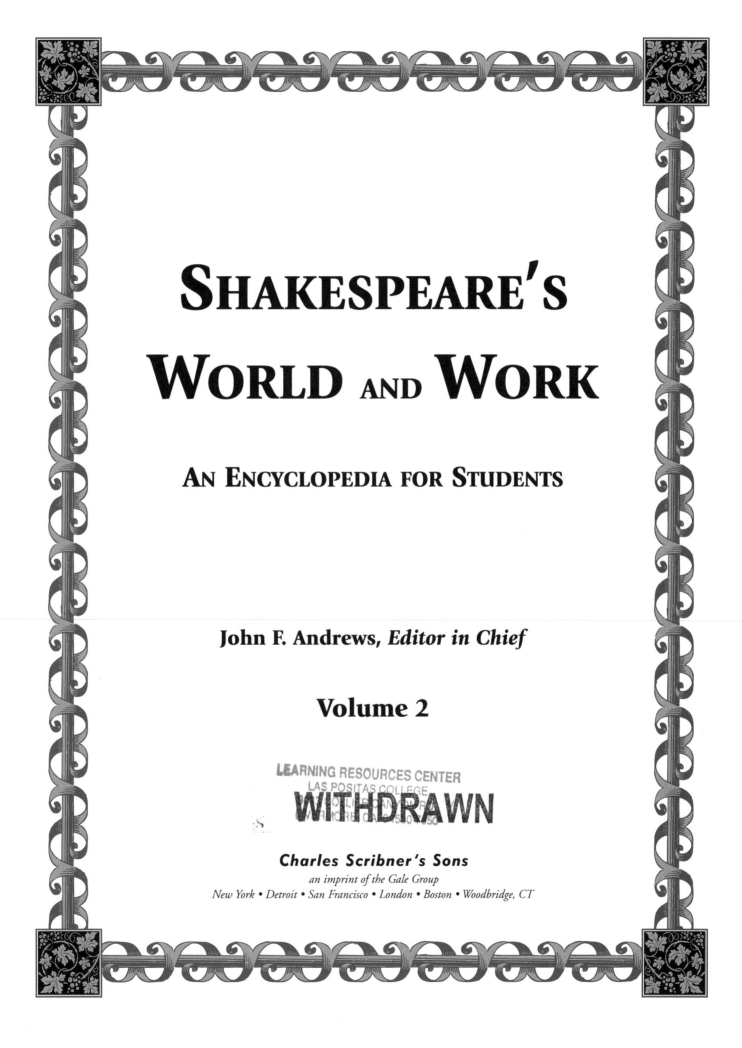

SHAKESPEARE'S WORLD AND WORK

AN ENCYCLOPEDIA FOR STUDENTS

John F. Andrews, *Editor in Chief*

Volume 2

Charles Scribner's Sons
an imprint of the Gale Group
New York • Detroit • San Francisco • London • Boston • Woodbridge, CT

Developed for Charles Scribner's Sons by Visual Education Corporation, Princeton, N.J.

For Scribners
PUBLISHER: Karen Day
EDITOR: John Fitzpatrick
COVER DESIGN: Jennifer Wahi

For Visual Education Corporation
PROJECT DIRECTOR: Jewel G. Moulthrop
WRITERS: Guy Austrian, Jean Brainard, John Haley, Mark Mussari, Rebecca Stefoff
EDITORS: Amy Livingston, Joseph Ziegler
COPYEDITING SUPERVISOR: Helen Castro
COPY EDITORS: Marie Enders, Eleanor Hero
INDEXER: Sallie Steele
PHOTO RESEARCH: Martin A. Levick
PRODUCTION SUPERVISOR: Paula Deverell
PRODUCTION ASSISTANTS: Susan Buschhorn, Brian Suskin
INTERIOR DESIGN: Maxson Crandall
ELECTRONIC PREPARATION: Fiona Torphy, Christine Osborne
ELECTRONIC PRODUCTION: Rob Ehlers, Lisa Evans-Skopas, Holly Morgan

Library of Congress Cataloging-in-Publication Data

Shakespeare's world and work : an encyclopedia for students / John F. Andrews.
    p.   cm.
    Includes bibliographical references and index.
    ISBN 0-684-80629-0 (set) — ISBN 0-684-80626-6 (v.1) —
ISBN 0-684-80627-4 (v.2) — ISBN 0-684-80628-2 (v. 3)
    1. Shakespeare, William, 1564–1616—Encyclopedias. 2. Dramatists, English—Early modern, 1500–1700—Biography—Encyclopedias. I. Andrews, John F.
(John Frank), 1942–

PR2892 .S56 2001
822.3'3—dc21
[B]
                                                                    00-068743

SHAKESPEAREAN CHRONOLOGY

Note: The dating of Shakespeare's plays is often uncertain. For simplicity, we have listed the *earliest* dates accepted by *The Riverside Shakespeare,* 2nd ed., 1997.

YEAR	EVENTS
1532	King Henry VIII breaks with the Catholic Church to marry Anne Boleyn.
1533	The future Queen Elizabeth I is born to King Henry VIII and Anne Boleyn.
1534	King Henry VIII becomes head of the Anglican Church.
1536	Anne Boleyn is executed.
1547	King Henry VIII dies. Edward VI is crowned.
1553	King Edward VI dies. Mary I assumes the throne and begins to reestablish Catholicism.
1555	Roman Catholicism is officially reestablished. Persecution of Protestants begins.
1558	Queen Mary I dies. Elizabeth I is crowned.
1559	Elizabethan Settlement reforms the Anglican Church. Strict sumptuary laws prohibit Elizabethans from wearing clothing above their station.
1564	William Shakespeare is born to John and Mary Shakespeare. Christopher Marlowe is born.
1566	John Shakespeare is appointed an alderman of Stratford-upon-Avon. King James VI of Scotland is born. Edward Alleyn is born.
1567	Richard Burbage is born. Thomas Nash is born.
1568	John Shakespeare is elected mayor of Stratford-upon-Avon. Mary, Queen of Scots, takes refuge in England.
1570	Pope Pius V excommunicates Queen Elizabeth I.
1571	John Shakespeare is elected chief alderman.
1572	Ben Jonson is born.
1573	Henry Wriothesley, 3rd earl of Southampton, is born.
1576	The Theater playhouse opens.
1577	The Curtain opens. Raphael Holinshed's *Chronicles* is published.
1579	John Fletcher is born.
1580	Sir Francis Drake completes circumnavigation of the world.
1582	William Shakespeare marries Anne Hathaway.
1583	A daughter (Susanna) is born to William Shakespeare and Anne Hathaway. The Queen's Men acting company is formed.
1585	Anne Hathaway gives birth to twins, Judith and Hamnet. First English colony is established in North America.
1586	Queen Elizabeth I outlaws printing presses outside of London, Cambridge, and Oxford. Philip Sidney dies.
1587	The Rose opens. Mary, Queen of Scots, is executed.
1588	Spanish Armada is defeated. Richard Tarlton dies.
1589	Shakespeare writes *Henry VI, Part 1.* Thomas Kyd writes *The Spanish Tragedy.* King James VI of Scotland marries Princess Anne of Denmark.

1590 Shakespeare writes *Henry VI, Part 2* and *Part 3*. Edmund Spenser's *The Faerie Queene* is published. Thomas Lodge's *Rosalynde* is published.

1591 Shakespeare writes *Richard III*. Philip Sidney's *Astrophel and Stella* is published.

1592 Shakespeare writes *The Comedy of Errors*. Robert Greene's *Groatsworth of Wit* is published. Philip Henslowe begins his *Diary*.

1593 Shakespeare's *Venus and Adonis* is published. Shakespeare writes *Titus Andronicus* and *The Taming of the Shrew*. Christopher Marlowe is killed in a tavern brawl. Theaters are closed throughout the year due to plague.

1594 Shakespeare's *The Rape of Lucrece* is published. Shakespeare writes *The Two Gentlemen of Verona, Love's Labor's Lost,* and *King John*. The Chamberlain's Men acting company is formed. Thomas Kyd dies.

1595 Shakespeare writes *Richard II, Romeo and Juliet,* and *A Midsummer Night's Dream*. William Shakespeare is named as one of the players paid for performing for Queen Elizabeth I. The Swan opens.

1596 Hamnet Shakespeare dies. John Shakespeare is granted a coat of arms. William Shakespeare writes *Henry IV, Part 1; Henry IV, Part 2;* and *The Merchant of Venice*.

1597 William Shakespeare purchases New Place in Stratford-upon-Avon. Shakespeare writes *The Merry Wives of Windsor*. Performance of *The Isle of Dogs* at the Swan theater results in the imprisonment of the playwrights and the temporary closing of all theaters. The Poor Law is passed.

1598 Shakespeare writes *Much Ado About Nothing*. War of the Theaters begins. Shakespeare acts in Ben Jonson's *Every Man in His Humour*. The Theater is dismantled.

1599 Shakespeare writes *Henry V, Julius Caesar,* and *As You Like It*. Robert Devereux, Earl of Essex, fails to quell rebellion in Ireland. The Globe opens. Edmund Spenser dies.

1600 Shakespeare writes *Hamlet*. The Fortune opens.

1601 John Shakespeare dies. Shakespeare's *The Phoenix and Turtle* is published. Shakespeare writes *Twelfth Night* and *Troilus and Cressida*. The Chamberlain's Men are hired to perform *Richard II*. Robert Devereux, Earl of Essex, is executed for revolting against Queen Elizabeth I.

1602 William Shakespeare purchases land in Old Stratford. Shakespeare writes *All's Well That Ends Well*. War of the Theaters ends.

1603 Queen Elizabeth I dies. King James VI of Scotland is crowned King James I of England. The Chamberlain's Men become the King's Men. Theaters are closed due to plague.

1604 The King's Men participate in King James I's coronation procession. King James ends war with Spain. Shakespeare writes *Measure for Measure* and *Othello*. Theaters reopen.

1605 William Shakespeare buys an interest in Stratford-upon-Avon tithes and writes *King Lear*. Gunpowder Plot is discovered. The Red Bull opens.

1606 Shakespeare writes *Macbeth, Antony and Cleopatra,* and *Pericles*. John Lyly dies.

1607 Susanna Shakespeare marries John Hall. Shakespeare writes *Coriolanus* and *Timon of Athens*. Jamestown, Virginia, is settled. Theaters are closed for three months due to plague.

1608 Mary Shakespeare dies. The King's Men lease Blackfriars.

1609 Shakespeare's *Sonnets* and *A Lover's Complaint* are published. Shakespeare writes *Cymbeline*. Theaters temporarily close due to plague.

1610 Shakespeare writes *The Tempest*. Ben Jonson writes *The Alchemist*.

1611 Shakespeare writes *The Winter's Tale*. The King James Bible is published.

1613 William Shakespeare buys Blackfriars Gatehouse and writes *Henry VIII* and *The Two Noble Kinsmen*. The Globe burns down. The Hope opens.

1616 Judith Shakespeare marries Thomas Quiney. William Shakespeare revises his will and dies.

1623   John Heminges and Henry Condell produce the First Folio. Anne Shakespeare dies. Sometime prior to this date a monument to William Shakespeare is placed in the Holy Trinity Church of Stratford-upon-Avon.

1625   King James I dies. Charles I is crowned.

1642   English Civil Wars begin. Puritans seize control of government. London theaters are closed.

1660   Ban on theaters is lifted. Women appear in plays on the English stage. Samuel Pepys begins his *Diary.*

1674   William Davenant produces a musical adaptation of *Macbeth.*

1709   Nicholas Rowe's edition of Shakespeare's works is published.

1725   Alexander Pope's edition of Shakespeare's works is published.

1729   Voltaire translates Shakespeare's works into French.

1730s   Drury Lane and Covent Garden acting companies are granted theater monopolies in London.

1741   David Garrick debuts as Richard III.

1765   Samuel Johnson's edition of Shakespeare's works is published.

1769   Shakespeare Jubilee is held in Stratford-upon-Avon.

1803   First Variorum edition is published.

1807   Thomas Bowdler's *The Family Shakespeare* is published.

1823   Charles Kemble stages *King John* at Covent Garden.

1826   Ira Aldridge debuts as Othello.

1838   William Charles Macready restores the original text of *King Lear* to the stage.

1843   Monopolies on London theaters end.

1849   Astor Place Riot erupts in New York.

1883   Samuel Taylor Coleridge's *Lectures and Notes on Shakespeare and Other English Poets* is published.

1895   Elizabethan Stage Society is founded.

1899   A scene from a Shakespeare play is captured on film for the first time.

1910   Herbert Beerbohm Tree stages an elaborate *Midsummer Night's Dream.*

1912   Harley Granville-Barker produces the first authentic Shakespearean production of modern times.

1920s   Barry Jackson introduces 20th-century costuming in Shakespeare's plays.

1930s   Theodore Komisarjevsky introduces mixed-period costuming.

1937   First production of a Shakespeare play is made for television.

1944   Laurence Olivier produces a film version of *Henry V.*

1948   Olivier's *Hamlet* is released, the first foreign film to win the Academy Award for best picture.

1957   Performances of Shakespeare's works begin in New York City's Central Park.

1961   Royal Shakespeare Company is founded.

1965   Peter Hall directs his influential production of *Hamlet.*

1970   Peter Brook directs a film version of *King Lear.*

1985   Akira Kurosawa directs *Ran,* a film based on *King Lear.*

1989   Kenneth Branagh directs and stars in a film version of *Henry V.*

1996   Baz Luhrmann directs *Shakespeare's Romeo + Juliet.*

1999   BBC audience survey names Shakespeare as Britain's "Man of the Millennium."

CHRONOLOGY OF SHAKESPEARE'S WORKS

Note: All dates are based on *The Riverside Shakespeare,* 2nd ed., 1997.

1 Henry VI	1589–92
2 Henry VI	1590–91
3 Henry VI	1590–92
Richard III	1591–93
Venus and Adonis	1592–93
The Comedy of Errors	1592–94
Sonnets	1592–1609
Titus Andronicus	1593–94
The Rape of Lucrece	1593–94
The Taming of the Shrew	1593–94
The Two Gentlemen of Verona	1594
Love's Labor's Lost	1594
King John	1594–96
Richard II	1595
Romeo and Juliet	1595
A Midsummer Night's Dream	1595–96
Henry IV, Part 1	1596
The Merchant of Venice	1596–97
Henry IV, Part 2	1596–97
The Merry Wives of Windsor	1597
Much Ado About Nothing	1598–99
Henry V	1599
Julius Caesar	1599
As You Like It	1599–1600
Hamlet	1600–01
The Phoenix and Turtle	1601
Twelfth Night	1601–02
Troilus and Cressida	1601–02
All's Well That Ends Well	1602–03
A Lover's Complaint	1602–08
Measure for Measure	1604
Othello	1604
King Lear	1605
Macbeth	1606
Antony and Cleopatra	1606–07
Pericles	1606–08
Coriolanus	1607–08
Timon of Athens	1607–08
Cymbeline	1609–10
The Tempest	1610–11
The Winter's Tale	1611
Henry VIII	1613
The Two Noble Kinsmen	1613

HISTORY IN SHAKESPEARE'S PLAYS: ENGLAND

When Shakespeare's plays were collected for publication in the FIRST FOLIO, ten of them—*Richard II; Henry IV, Part 1; Henry IV, Part 2; Henry V; Henry VI, Part 1; Henry VI, Part 2; Henry VI, Part 3; Richard III; King John;* and *Henry VIII*—were classified as "histories." These plays are similar in that they dramatize political events, such as wars and power struggles, during the reigns of seven English kings. Although *King Lear* and *Cymbeline* also depict events that occurred during the reigns of English kings, these plays do not qualify as histories because the themes they emphasize are personal or familial rather than political.

ELIZABETHAN HISTORY PLAYS

History plays were popular during Shakespeare's time for three reasons. First, they appealed to patriotic feelings, which were especially strong among the English during the years immediately following the defeat of the SPANISH ARMADA in 1588. Second, they were appreciated as a storehouse of useful lessons about kingship and successful leadership. Finally, they drew on two popular historical works that provided source material for characters and plots at a time when new plays were in great demand.

SHAKESPEARE'S INFLUENCE ON HISTORICAL DRAMA. Until Shakespeare began composing historical dramas, they were seldom if ever written. In fact Shakespeare is often credited with inventing the genre*. Because so few Elizabethan plays have survived, however, it is impossible to know whether Shakespeare was the first playwright to dramatize historical events for the purpose of exploring human experience—both personal and public—in the context of the passage of time.

Although scholars are uncertain about who invented historical drama, most acknowledge that Shakespeare gave the form its highest expression. His histories are remarkable because they provide a sense of the great political issues of the past while conveying an impression of what life may have been like under the rule of earlier monarchs. They enable audiences to see earlier periods through the eyes of a variety of characters, from kings and nobles to gardeners and foot soldiers.

The themes that Shakespeare explores in his histories may be the key to their timeless appeal. In these dramas he asks his audiences to ponder the qualities required in a good leader, which may or may not be the qualities one associates with a virtuous human being. He also examines the sometimes competing needs for individual freedom and for social order. Another recurring theme concerns how the actions of a ruler, such as declaring war, affect a nation and its people.

HISTORICAL SOURCES AND ACCURACY. For most of his history plays, Shakespeare relied on two main sources for information: Edward Halle's *The Union of the Two Noble and Illustre Famelies of Lancastre and York* (1548) and Raphael Holinshed's *Chronicles of England, Scotland, and Ireland* (1587). *King John* is Shakespeare's only English history play that is not based primarily on the works of Halle or Holinshed. Its source was an anonymous play called *The Troublesome Raigne of John, King of England*.

*** genre** literary form

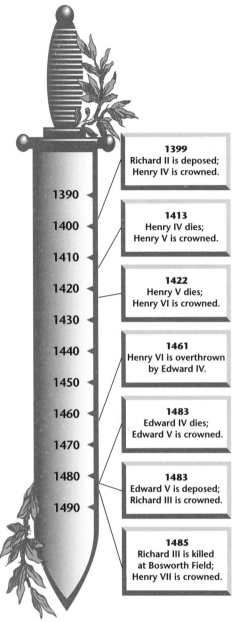

1399
Richard II is deposed;
Henry IV is crowned.

1390

1400

1413
Henry IV dies;
Henry V is crowned.

1410

1422
Henry V dies;
Henry VI is crowned.

1420

1430

1461
Henry VI is overthrown
by Edward IV.

1440

1450

1483
Edward IV dies;
Edward V is crowned.

1460

1470

1483
Edward V is deposed;
Richard III is crowned.

1480

1490

1485
Richard III is killed
at Bosworth Field;
Henry VII is crowned.

* **tetralogy** four-part series of literary or dramatic works

* **usurpation** seizing of power from a rightful ruler

Shakespeare altered some facts while crafting his history plays, and he sometimes rearranged the order of events. In *Henry IV, Part 1*, for example, the playwright lowered the age of Hotspur to make him more of a peer to Prince Hal. He could not, however, have Hotspur win the battle of Shrewsbury. In general, despite the artistic liberties he took, Shakespeare remained faithful to the larger patterns and outcomes of historical events.

SHAKESPEARE'S HISTORIES

Shakespeare's English histories are grouped according to the period they cover. Four of the plays—*Richard II; Henry IV, Part 1; Henry IV, Part 2;* and *Henry V*—deal with the fall of King Richard II and the rise of Henry Bolingbroke and his son Hal. Because Bolingbroke and Hal belonged to the house of Lancaster, these four plays are known as the Lancastrian tetralogy*, or the Henriad. Another quartet of histories—*Henry VI, Part 1; Henry VI, Part 2; Henry VI, Part 3;* and *Richard III*—focus on the decline and fall of the Lancastrian king Henry VI and the seizure of the throne by the house of York. These plays are known as the Yorkist tetralogy. The two remaining plays, *King John* and *Henry VIII*, are not closely linked to the others, but they share an interest in England's relationship to the papacy in Rome.

THE LANCASTRIAN TETRALOGY. The four plays that make up the Lancastrian tetralogy offer some of Shakespeare's most powerful writing. They examine Richard II's unsteady reign and his subsequent overthrow by Henry Bolingbroke, the duke of Lancaster. The action continues with the tumultuous reign of Bolingbroke (now Henry IV), which is marked by the misbehavior of his son Hal. The last two plays of the tetralogy focus on Hal's transformation from a seemingly irresponsible youth to Henry V, England's greatest king.

For centuries the English believed in the divine right of kings, an assumption that rulers were God's representatives on earth and received their authority to govern from him. In *Richard II*, Shakespeare poses the question of what is to be done with a monarch who perverts or fails to fulfill his duties. The playwright portrays Richard as a man who wastes money, fails to provide for the defense of his country, and is too weak to suppress revolts by powerful noblemen.

The rebellious Henry Bolingbroke is a decisive, capable leader. He is not, however, the man to whom the crown should legally be given. Shakespeare suggests that the only way to bring order to England is for Bolinbroke to seize the throne. To do so, however, and retain his power, Bolingbroke must have Richard killed. The irony of the play, and of history, is that to reestablish order, Bolingbroke first has to create greater disorder and commit an ungodly act.

In *Henry IV, Part 1*, Shakespeare dramatizes how much the usurpation* of the throne costs the new king. As Henry IV, he must struggle to keep his crown amid growing discontent among his subjects, who question his claim to it. This issue is temporarily resolved with the defeat of the rebel leader Hotspur at the battle of Shrewsbury, a clash as familiar to the Elizabethans as the battle of Gettysburg is to Americans.

The central character of *Henry IV, Part 1* and *Part 2* is the king's eldest son, Prince Hal. In these two plays Shakespeare reveals his genius for transforming historical events into art. The plots are structured on the principle of contrast. The activities of three major groups—the king and his court, Falstaff and his tavern cronies, and Hotspur and his rebel camp—are placed side by side to show their contrasting attitudes toward life. Three individuals provide models for Hal: the king for his devotion to duty, Falstaff for his wit and ability to detect pretense in others, and Hotspur for his raw courage.

Like many other Elizabethans, Shakespeare knew the stories of Hal's wild youth. In *Part 1* he depicts several rowdy tavern scenes to show the prince's fun-loving side. Eventually, however, he contrasts these scenes of drunken pleasure with Hal's victory on the battlefield at Shrewsbury, where he slays Hotspur.

The contrasts continue in *Part 2*, which deals with the last years of King Henry IV's reign and with the transformation of Hal from an irresponsible young man to England's most beloved king, Henry V. Trapped in his past, Hal learns to take control of events and emerges at the end of the action as a valorous and capable leader.

Henry V is, first and foremost, a study of kingship. Shakespeare portrays the young monarch as a firm ruler who is also capable of great compassion and humility. The play builds to a famous battle scene at Agincourt, France. The historical Henry had actually invaded France three times in five years. For dramatic purposes, however, Shakespeare condenses these battles into one memorable scene. Like the battle of Shrewsbury, the confrontation at Agincourt becomes etched in the minds of Shakespeare's audience.

One of the most interesting aspects of *Henry V* is its duality. The play may be read either as a celebratory epic or as a political satire. Some productions, especially when mounted during periods of protest or antinationalist feeling, have presented the play as a critique of war and of the scheming politicians who wage it.

THE YORKIST TETRALOGY. Although the events contained in the Yorkist tetralogy occurred after those in the Lancastrian tetralogy, Shakespeare composed the Yorkist sequence first. In poetic value these four plays pale in comparison to the Lancastrian tetralogy—at least until *Richard III*. The York plays illustrate the Elizabethans' high regard for political order. The tetralogy dramatizes a time when, because of Henry's weak leadership, disorder engulfed England and led to the WARS OF THE ROSES, a period of civil strife that dominated the second half of the 1400s.

The three plays that Shakespeare named after Henry VI cover 49 years, from the king's coronation when he was only an infant in 1422 to his murder at the hands of his Yorkist cousins in 1471. *Henry VI, Part 1* deals chiefly with England's political turmoil and the resulting loss of the empire that Henry V had won in France. The two main characters of *Part 1* are the English hero Lord Talbot and the legendary French leader Joan of Arc. Talbot is a war hero who captures French cities and avenges the deaths of noble Englishmen. He embodies the characteristics of a great

See
color plate 9,
vol. 2.

REHABILITATING RICHARD

Some people consider Shakespeare's depiction of King Richard III as a murderous hunchback to be totally unacceptable. Since 1924 the Richard III Society has endeavored to prove that Richard was framed for the murder of Prince Edward. Society members hold that Richard was a handsome and noble king. They sponsor historical research and publish several periodicals to promote their cause. Some admirers of the infamous king have even staged protests outside theaters presenting *Richard III,* asking cast members not to participate in "the monstrous lie perpetuated by Shakespeare about a most valiant knight."

leader, firmness and fairness. The French heroine, on the other hand, is portrayed as a devil worshiper. *Part 1* concludes with a dishonorable truce with France and the king's unwise marriage to Margaret of Anjou, a French noblewoman.

Part 2 and *Part 3* dramatize Henry's inability to preserve his nation's dignity and power. Impending civil war builds throughout *Part 2* as Shakespeare dramatizes the events that lead to the conflict between the houses of Lancaster and York. As Henry VI and his Lancastrian supporters weaken, the Yorkists—under Richard Plantagenet, the duke of York—grow more powerful. The conclusion of *Part 2* features one of Shakespeare's largest battle scenes, on the field of St. Albans. The play climaxes with York's victory and his promise to seize the crown from Henry. Elizabethans would have recognized in York's speech the destructive ambition that leads to social and political chaos.

Part 3 opens with a weak Henry VI proposing that he be allowed to continue as king in exchange for naming York, rather than his own son, heir to the throne. Shakespeare personalizes history by emphasizing Queen Margaret's dismay over her husband's decision to deprive their son of his rightful place. In protest she leads her own army into battle against the Yorkists. She succeeds initially, retaking the city of York and beheading the duke of York. But the Yorkists rally and defeat Margaret's troops. Eventually, York's son seizes the throne and is crowned Edward IV. Shortly thereafter, Richard, Edward's brother, murders Henry in the TOWER OF LONDON. Thus the Yorkists complete their triumph over the Lancastrians.

Richard III, the final play in the tetralogy, is considered one of Shakespeare's masterpieces and a haunting study of evil. Second in length to

Shakespeare's *Henry V* appealed to the audience's patriotism with its portrayal of the battle of Agincourt, in which the English won a decisive victory over a vastly superior French force.

See
color plate 12,
vol. 2.

* *soliloquy* monologue in which a character reveals his or her private thoughts

Hamlet, it is the only play that begins with a soliloquy*. Shakespeare opens the play by condensing 12 years of English history—from the projected marriage of Richard and Lady Anne in 1471 to the death of Edward IV in 1483—into the first six scenes. The playwright then dramatizes the three-month reign of the boy-king Edward V, a period that enables the conniving Richard to seize the crown. One of the play's most horrific scenes is the reported murder of 13-year-old Edward in the Tower of London. The last two acts cover Richard's bloody two-year reign, which ends with his death at the hands of Henry Tudor, the future King Henry VII.

KING JOHN AND HENRY VIII. The historical King John ruled England from 1199 to 1216. Shakespeare's play of the same name deals with the king's struggle to assert and defend the legitimacy of his reign. King John is best remembered for sealing Magna Carta at Runnymede in 1215. This historic moment, the granting of the charter, is considered the cornerstone of English law and civil rights. Yet it is never mentioned in Shakespeare's play.

Instead the play focuses on the dispute between John and the supporters of his nephew Arthur over who should occupy the throne. Although Shakespeare portrays John as a usurper, he also makes it clear that Arthur would be an unfit king. Shakespeare greatly altered the chronology of events of John's reign, and for that reason *King John* is considered to be the least accurate of all his histories.

Henry VIII is Shakespeare's only play about a Tudor monarch. The play's historical value rests on its depiction of Henry's divorce from his first wife, Katherine of Aragon, and his marriage to Anne Bullen (Boleyn). The action concludes with the birth of Elizabeth, who would become Queen ELIZABETH I and one of Shakespeare's most important patrons.

For many years scholars maintained that Shakespeare's historical dramas were reflections of the "Tudor myth," a belief that the ungodly crime of deposing Richard II resulted in nearly a century of political turmoil and that only the rise of the Tudor dynasty, begun by Henry VII, could resolve that conflict. Recent critics maintain that Shakespeare was not limited to that reading of England's past, and that the plays reflect the wealth of material that was available to the playwright. (*See also* **History in Shakespeare's Plays: Ancient Greece and Rome; Holinshed's Chronicles; Italy in Shakespeare's Plays.**)

HOLINSHED'S CHRONICLES

Elizabethan dramatists, including William Shakespeare, relied heavily on Holinshed's *Chronicles* for historical source material. First published in 1577, the *Chronicles* quickly became the most respected source on the history of Britain. In fact the book was so popular that it was enlarged and reprinted in 1587. It is this second edition, which contained more than 3.5 million words, that Shakespeare is most likely to have used. Along with Plutarch's *Lives*, the *Chronicles* provided crucial material for many of Shakespeare's plays.

Holinshed's *Chronicles* originally appeared as *The first volume of the chronicles of England, Scotland, and Ireland . . . containing the description and the chronicles of England from the first inhabiting unto the Conquest.* It was intended to be one book in a multivolume survey of world civilizations, covering "the histories of every known nation" and recounting events from the time of the biblical Flood to the reign of Queen ELIZABETH I. Only one other volume of the set, an atlas, was ever published.

The English historian Raphael Holinshed (ca. 1528–ca. 1580) organized the volume on England, Scotland, and Ireland and wrote the section on England himself. Edmund Campion wrote the history of Ireland. The history of Scotland was a translation by William Harrison of an earlier Latin work written by Hector Boece.

The *Chronicles* provided the information about the WARS OF THE ROSES that Shakespeare used to write eight of his English history plays. The *Chronicles* also served as the playwright's historical source for *King John, Henry VIII, Macbeth,* and parts of *Cymbeline* and *King Lear.* (*See also* **Plays: The Histories**.)

HOMOSEXUALITY

Elizabethan views of love and sexuality were very different from modern ideas, particularly with regard to relationships between men. The terms *gay* and *homosexual* did not exist, and Elizabethans did not think of individuals in terms of their sexual preference. King JAMES I was widely known to enjoy the company of attractive young men, but he also had a wife and several children. Sexual acts between men were technically illegal, yet intimate friendships between men were common. It was considered normal and desirable for a man to express his affection for his male friends, even in very passionate terms.

For a man to have sex with another man, known as buggery, was a crime that was punishable by death. It was, however, an offense that was rarely prosecuted. The definition of buggery was vague and general, referring also to sex with animals and to certain acts between men and women that were considered unnatural. (Curiously, there were no laws concerning sexual relationships between women.)

At the same time, expressions of love between Elizabethan men were quite common, as the literature of the period shows. Male characters in Shakespeare's plays, such as Antonio in *The Merchant of Venice,* frequently express a deep, heartfelt love for their friends. Shakespeare's *Sonnets* are also filled with declarations of love for an unnamed "fair youth," thought by many scholars to be the "Mr. W. H." to whom the editor dedicated the first quarto* version of the *Sonnets* in 1609. In some of these poems, Shakespeare's speaker urges his young friend to marry and have children. In other, apparently later, verses he makes it clear that he feels very jealous of those—both male and female—who appear to be rivals for the youth's affection. The most explicit mention of homosexuality in a Shakespeare play is a scornful reference to Patroclus as Achilles' "masculine whore" in *Troilus and Cressida* (V.i.17). (*See also* **Friendship; Love.**)

* *quarto* referring to the format of a book or page; a sheet of paper folded twice, yielding four leaves or eight pages

HOPE THEATER

* *bearbaiting* Elizabethan spectator sport in which dogs were encouraged to attack a chained bear

Built in 1613 by theater owner and manager Philip Henslowe, the Hope theater was situated on the Bankside, south of the original City of London. Hoping to attract audiences from the GLOBE, which had recently burned down, Henslowe had agreed to provide a theater for the acting company known as Lady Elizabeth's Men. He modeled the Hope on the Swan, another London playhouse. Like the Swan, the Hope was designed with a covered roof.

A bearbaiting* arena, called the Bear Garden, was located on the site Henslowe had chosen for his new theater. He demolished it in order to build the Hope. Because bearbaiting was a popular Elizabethan pastime, and one that Henslowe knew could be even more profitable than drama, he built the Hope with a portable stage that could be moved aside to make room for this moneymaking blood sport. He also added facilities for the animals. Henslowe made an agreement with the acting company, however, that the theater would be used for bearbaiting only one day every two weeks; the rest of the time it would be available for plays.

The Hope theater opened in 1614. That year and the next, Lady Elizabeth's Men staged many plays there. Because of the covered roof, however, the smell of animals lingered in the theater, and many of the people who came to see the plays found the odor offensive. The actors complained, moreover, that Henslowe was using the theater for bearbaiting more often than he had agreed, and they filed a series of lawsuits against him. These lawsuits continued beyond Henslowe's death, and no settlement was ever reached. After 1617 only minor acting companies staged plays at the Hope, which became increasingly associated with bearbaiting and eventually became known once more by its old name, the Bear Garden.

In 1642 the government closed all the theaters in England and outlawed the staging of plays. Although bearbaiting was also outlawed, it apparently continued at the Hope until about 1655. That year a child was killed in the bearbaiting ring. As a result of this incident, the theater was closed, and all the bears were shot. The building itself was torn down the following year to make way for apartment buildings. (*See also* **Acting Companies, Elizabethan; Elizabethan Theaters; Games, Pastimes, and Sports; Henslowe, Philip; Playhouse Structure.**)

HOTSPUR

See Henry IV, Part 1.

HOUSEHOLDS AND FURNISHINGS

During the Elizabethan era households and furnishings in England became more comfortable and luxurious than they had ever been. These changes resulted largely from the end of the WARS OF THE ROSES, the dynastic battles that tore England apart during the second half of the 1400s. The end of hostilities meant that nobles no longer needed to live in castles protected by thick stone walls. Instead, wealthy English families

Households and Furnishings

remodeled their residences into comfortable homes and then filled them with furnishings that displayed their wealth, power, and good taste.

THE GREAT HALL. The front entrance of a typical Tudor* manor led into the great hall, a massive room located in the center of the building and used for entertaining. During banquets, family members and honored guests sat at a 20-foot-long wooden table on the dais, a raised platform located at one end of the hall. The lord and lady of the manor sat on heavy wooden chairs, which were made comfortable and beautified by cushions embroidered with designs of flowers, birds, and other woodland creatures. Honored guests sat on stools, while the lower ranks sat on long benches.

An enormous fireplace—located midway between the dais and the other end of the great hall—warmed the vast room, which was made drafty by its many large windows. These windows let in light that illuminated rich tapestries* covering the walls. In addition the light revealed the hall's high ceiling, which in some homes was decorated with the 12 signs of the zodiac or semiprecious stones that reflected the sunlight. The windows themselves often contained stained glass that bore the family coat of arms. Sumptuous velvet curtains added still more color.

At the end of the great hall stood a grand staircase, a winding flight of stairs that was one of the characteristic features of a typical Tudor manor. The stairs, which had several landings to make climbing easier, were made of wood, and the newel* that supported them was carved with intricate figures, such as acorns or leopards.

The kitchen, located beyond the great hall, contained a huge fireplace for roasting beef, brick ovens for baking bread, and other cooking equipment—pots, pans, spits, knives, and cleavers—for preparing food. Servants washed the cookware in the scullery, where in some homes dishwater was carried away through pipes and expelled through the mouth of a gargoyle* on an exterior wall. Adjoining the kitchen were storage rooms, such as the dry larder (for meat), the wet larder (for liquor), and the pantry (for bread and pastry).

THE GALLERY. The most important room in a Tudor manor was the gallery. This immense chamber—sometimes more than 200 feet long—served to display the family wealth. The walls were decorated with richly carved panels separated by pilasters*, and the ceiling was adorned with geometric designs and biblical proverbs. The gallery contained the household's most valuable furnishings, including cupboards that displayed the family plate (household articles covered with gold, silver, or other precious metals).

The gallery also served as an exercise room during inclement weather. The room's length made it an ideal place for children to play and for adults to walk. In fact windows that stretched along one entire side of the room enabled walkers to look at the manor's gardens while staying dry and warm. The wall opposite the windows provided an ideal space to display painted portraits, which often depicted family members wearing their most sumptuous apparel. It was customary to cover portraits with drapery, such as green silk curtains fringed with gold, to prevent sunlight from fading the images. Shakespeare alludes to this practice in *Twelfth*

* **Tudor** referring to the dynasty that ruled England from 1485 to 1603

* **tapestry** heavy, handwoven cloth with multicolored designs or images

* **newel** support post at the center of a circular staircase

* **gargoyle** carved rainspout resembling a grotesque human or animal

* **pilaster** ornamental column or pillar set partially into a wall

THE CLOSET

One of the most fascinating rooms in an Elizabethan manor house was the closet. This room was the master's private sitting room. Its walls were lined with books and covered with family portraits and maps of the world. It was customary to burn perfume or spread rose leaves around the room—not only to deodorize the area but also to reflect the master's personality. The closet also served as a retreat for Elizabethans, a sanctuary away from the rest of the world. In *Henry V*, for example, the young king tells the French princess he is wooing that he knows she will gossip about him with her servants in the privacy of her closet.

* *pallet* thin, straw-filled mattress
* *Ionic column* pillar distinguished by a fluted shaft and upper sections resembling scrolls curving downward
* *canopy* cloth covering suspended above a bed

Night, when before unveiling her face, Olivia says: "we will draw the curtain, and show you the picture" (I.v.233).

BEDCHAMBER. Many of life's most important events—births, deaths, wakes—occurred in the bedchamber. Shortly before giving birth expectant mothers had their bedchambers decorated with silk hangings and colorful cushions in preparation for visitors. If the mother or child died in childbirth, a common occurrence, the chamber was draped in black and served as a mourning room.

Normally the bedchamber was relatively bare, with a chest (which doubled as a seat) and a few tables and stools as furnishings. Bedroom walls, however, were often decorated with tapestries that depicted scenes from Greek and Roman mythology or history. Shakespeare describes such items in *Cymbeline:* "her bedchamber . . . was hang'd / With tapestry of silk and silver; the story / Proud Cleopatra, when she met her Roman [Antony]" (II.iv.68–70).

The most important object in the room was the enormous four-poster bed. Crisscrossed ropes, which held up a straw pallet*, served as the bed's base. On top of this, soft feather mattresses were piled two or three deep. Linen sheets and woolen blankets were placed on top of the mattresses. Some bedposts were carved to resemble Ionic columns*, and their bases were inscribed with such words as *hope, faith, love,* and *truth*. Bedposts held up a canopy* and drapes to provide privacy and help shut out cold drafts.

Even luxurious bedchambers, however, did not have carpets on the floors. Instead the floors of all rooms were covered with rushes, a mixture of reeds and hay. Because mice and other vermin frequently infested the grassy floor coverings, rushes had to be changed at least once a month. When new rushes were brought in, the sweet smell of new hay filled the manor.

ORDINARY HOMES. Not every Elizabethan, of course, could afford to live in such luxury. The typical home of a laborer consisted of one room with a central fireplace. The windows, if any, were few and small, and the quality of the glass was so poor that it was barely transparent. As a result, these homes often were dark and damp. Packed-down dirt served as the floor, and the ceilings were usually undecorated plaster or wood. Straw pallets served as beds, and chests provided both storage spaces and dining tables. (*See also* **Architecture; Personal Hygiene.**)

HUMOR IN SHAKESPEARE'S PLAYS

Shakespeare was a tremendously innovative playwright, and even though the humor that was so much a part of his talent is most evident in his comedies, it is a key element in all of his plays. In fact some of Shakespeare's most entertaining scenes and characters are found in tragedies such as *Hamlet* and in histories such as *Henry IV, Part 1*.

INFLUENCES. Among the earlier writers whose work influenced Shakespeare's humor was Titus Maccius Plautus, an ancient Roman dramatist.

Humor in Shakespeare's Plays

* **genre** literary form
* **medieval** referring to the Middle Ages, a period roughly between A.D. 500 and 1500

SHAKEASPEARE'S SNUBS

Shakespeare is almost as famous for his words expressing disdain, revulsion, and hatred as he is for expressions of beauty and love. The following are some of Shakespeare's most powerful put-downs:

* "Would thou wert clean enough to spit upon!" (*Timon of Athens*, IV.iii.359).
* "Go thou and fill another room in hell." (*Richard II*, V.v.107).
* "Thou elvish-mark'd, abortive, rooting hog!" (*Richard III*, I.iii.227).
* "This sanguine coward, this bed-presser, this horse-back-breaker, this huge hill of flesh—" (*Henry IV, Part 1*, II.iv.241–43).
* "The tartness of his face sours ripe grapes." (*Coriolanus*, V.iv.17–18).
* "How tartly that gentleman looks! I never can see him but I am heart-burn'd an hour after." (*Much Ado About Nothing*, II.i.3–4).

Shakespeare was especially influenced by Plautus's use of informal language, puns, and other forms of wordplay. Shakespeare also borrowed situations and plot elements from Plautus's comedies, which usually featured secret love affairs, mistaken identities, and women disguised as men. The essential framework of *The Comedy of Errors*, for example, which depends on the confusion resulting from two sets of twins, came from two of Plautus's comedies—*Menaechmi* and *Amphitruo*.

Another significant influence on Shakespeare's humor was the commedia dell'arte, a genre* of comedic drama that originated in medieval* Italy. Commedia dell'arte was dominated by stock situations that featured improbable complications involving love and comical misunderstandings. It also featured standard character types, such as the pantaloon, a talkative old man who meddles in young lovers' affairs. The pantaloon tradition probably inspired Shakespeare's creation of Polonius, the long-winded lord chamberlain in *Hamlet*. One of the most popular stock characters from the commedia dell'arte was the foolish, boastful soldier, known as the *capitano* or *miles gloriosus* (from ancient Roman comedy). This character type served as the basis for such Shakespearean figures as Parolles, the blustering coward in *All's Well That Ends Well*, and Armado, the pompous Spaniard in *Love's Labor's Lost*.

FUN WITH PUNS. Like many Elizabethans, Shakespeare loved wordplay, especially puns. A pun is the clever use of words that sound alike but have different meanings. In *Julius Caesar*, for example, a cobbler, or shoemaker, plays on the words *sole* (the bottom of a shoe) and *soul* (the immortal essence of a human being): "I am but, as you would say, a cobbler. . . . A trade, sir, that I hope I may use with a safe conscience, which is indeed, sir, a mender of bad soles" (I.i.10–14).

His use of puns enabled Shakespeare to give multiple meanings to words. When King Claudius, the man who has murdered Prince Hamlet's father and married his mother, accuses the prince of looking gloomy, Hamlet responds, "Not so, my lord, I am too much in the sun" (I.ii.67). This simple statement can be interpreted both as Hamlet's way of saying he feels overly scrutinized by the king and as suggesting that he is too much of a devoted son to look happy so soon after his father's death.

ONE WORD, MANY MEANINGS. Equivocation, also referred to as quibbling, is the clever use of a single word that has more than one meaning. Shakespeare used this type of wordplay to create comical verbal banter. In *Hamlet*, for example, a grave digger continually pretends to misunderstand Prince Hamlet's words. When Hamlet asks him "upon what grounds" the prince of Denmark went insane, he is asking what caused the prince's insanity. The grave digger, however, interprets the word *grounds* literally and replies "Why, here in Denmark."

WORD ABUSE AND MISUSE. Shakespeare's characters often reveal their intelligence—or lack of it—by their words. One of the most humorous ways in which the ignorant display their lack of learning is in their tendency to use malapropisms, unintentional misuses of words. In *Much Ado*

About Nothing, for example, an inept constable named Dogberry, selecting the most sensible person for guard duty, says, "You are thought here to be the most senseless and fit man for the constable of the watch" (III.iii.22–23). Later, when departing from his watchmen, Dogberry reminds them to be vigilant. As usual, however, he misspeaks: "Be vigitant, I beseech you" (III.iii.94).

INSIDE JOKES. Shakespeare often included comic references to famous people, happenings, or fads of his day. Many of these topical allusions are

Shakespeare's usage of humor ranges from subtle, witty wordplay to coarse, physical slapstick—such as stuffing Sir John Falstaff into a laundry basket and dumping him in the Thames (in *The Merry Wives of Windsor*).

satirical ridiculing human wickedness and foolishness

incomprehensible to modern readers. Shakespeare scholars, however, have provided explanations for many of them. *The Merry Wives of Windsor*, for example, contains an inside joke about a group of Germans who have come to the town of Windsor to visit the royal court. This joke relates to the knighting of men who are being admitted to the Order of the Garter, the occasion for which the play may have been written in 1597. A few years earlier a German duke named Frederick Mömpelgard visited England. During his stay he was seized with the desire to be installed in the Order of the Garter. Shakespeare knew that Mömpelgard's ambition was familiar to the play's first audience, so he included an incident about German visitors that would surely have been recognized as satirical*.

Shakespeare also poked fun at Elizabethan fads. During the late 1500s the term *humor* was commonly used to describe a dominant aspect of a person's personality or behavior. In *The Merry Wives of Windsor*, a foolish character named Nym uses and misuses the word *humor* so often that it becomes ludicrous. When Sir John Falstaff asks him to deliver a love letter to Mistress Ford, a married woman, Nym uses this trendy word twice in his short reply: "I will run no base humor. Here, take the humor-letter" (I.iii.77–78).

DIRTY JOKES. Humor about sexuality is found throughout Shakespeare's plays. One of the most common subjects for such amusement is cuckoldry. In Elizabethan England a cuckold was the husband of an unfaithful wife. The name echoed cuckoo, a bird that deceives other species of fowl into raising its hatchlings. According to folklore a cuckold sprouted a pair of invisible horns on his head. Consequently, any mention of horns in the writing of the period is usually an allusion to cuckolds and is meant to elicit laughter from the audience. In *Much Ado About Nothing,* Benedick expresses the common belief that a married man is condemned to live the life of a cuckold: "if ever the sensible Benedick bear it [marries], pluck off the bull's horns, and set them in my forehead" (I.i.262–64).

Other jokes regarding sex were more direct. In *Titus Andronicus,* for example, there is a humorous exchange of words between Aaron (the secret lover of Tamora, the empress of Rome) and Chiron (Tamora's son). When Chiron discovers that Aaron has made Tamora pregnant he says, "Thou hast undone our mother," to which Aaron replies, "Villain, I have done thy mother" (IV.ii.75–76).

SLAPSTICK. Although most of Shakespeare's humor is verbal, he also entertained audiences with physical comedy. Because his surviving texts lack detailed stage directions, however, much of the stage business they contain must be inferred from clues in the script. Some of the funniest moments in *The Merry Wives of Windsor* rely on the audience's enjoyment of the physical woes of Sir John Falstaff. During Act III, for example, he is stuffed into a big basket of dirty laundry and then dumped into the muddy Thames.

CARICATURE. Like most humorists, Shakespeare used exaggeration to create comic situations. In several of his plays he parodies traits of recognizable foreigners. In *Henry V*, for example, Shakespeare presents a scene depicting a group of soldiers, among them Fluellen, a Welshman; Macmorris, an Irishman; and Jamy, a Scotsman. All of these characters are depicted as speaking in ridiculously heavy accents, especially Jamy, whose words are barely comprehensible. Macmorris is presented as hot-tempered, a characteristic that many Elizabethans associated with the Irish. While such stereotyping may be disquieting to modern audiences, it illustrates Shakespeare's fondness for using many different forms of humor. Most of his humor is quite sophisticated, but some of it is so broad as to approach farce. (*See also* **Characters in Shakespeare's Plays; Fools, Clowns, and Jesters; Language; Plays: The Comedies; Playwrights and Poets; Shakespeare's Sources.**)

HUNTING

See *Games, Pastimes, and Sports.*

IAGO

* *satanic* characteristic of Satan, or the devil

Iago is one of three principal characters in *Othello*. Many observers consider him the satanic* counterpart to "the divine DESDEMONA." By playing on Desdemona's husband's fears and doubts, Iago brings about the downfall of all the major characters in the play, including himself.

Iago is Othello's ancient, a type of military subordinate. He has a reputation for honesty, and in the course of the play others turn to him repeatedly for advice and help. He takes advantage of the situation and

One of Shakespeare's most fascinating villains, Iago seems to dominate the action whenever he is on stage. In this 1985 Royal Shakespeare Company production, Iago (David Suchet) skillfully manipulates Othello (Ben Kingsley) into believing that Desdemona has been unfaithful.

secretly mocks Othello, saying that he "thinks men honest that but seem to be so" (I.iii.400). Iago's soliloquies*, however, reveal to the audience that he is actually untrustworthy, suspicious, and filled with malice. Disappointed at having been passed over for the position of lieutenant to Othello, Iago influences his newly appointed rival, Cassio, to disregard his better judgment, drink too much, and engage in a foolish brawl. When Cassio loses his position as a result, Iago advises him to ask Desdemona to plead with Othello on his behalf. Iago then convinces Othello that Desdemona wishes to help Cassio because she is having an affair with him. Iago works on Othello's insecurities until he persuades him to murder Desdemona. When Iago's plans eventually unravel—as letters from Roderigo betray his guilt and his own wife, Emilia, reveals Desdemona's innocence—Iago finally displays his true nature by killing Emilia to silence her.

Iago's motives have been the source of much controversy. In his soliloquies and other speeches, he gives various explanations for his actions. He tells Roderigo of his anger at being passed over for promotion, but later he admits that he suspects Othello of having slept with Emilia and wishes to even the score "wife for wife." Other speeches suggest that he envies the virtues of the other characters, such as Othello and Cassio. In the final scene, however, Iago refuses to provide any explanation for his crimes, saying, "what you know, you know: / From this time forth I never will speak word" (V.ii.303–304).

Because Iago's stated motives keep changing, some scholars question whether his word can be trusted even when he is speaking only to himself. Because he appears to take great pleasure in executing his devious plans, moreover, Iago seems at times to be genuinely diabolical*. Some scholars have traced his dramatic ancestry to the character of the VICE, the traditional villain in medieval morality plays*. To Shakespeare's audiences, the evil deeds of such a figure would have required no explanation. (*See also* **Pageants and Morality Plays; Psychology.**)

See
color plate 14,
vol. 2.

* *diabolical* characteristic of the devil

* *morality play* religious dramatic work that teaches a moral lesson through the use of symbolic characters

IAMBIC PENTAMETER

See *Language; Poetic Techniques.*

IDES OF MARCH

In Shakespeare's *Julius Caesar*, a soothsayer* warns the title character to "Beware the ides of March" (I.ii.18). According to the ancient Roman calendar, the 15th day of March was known as the ides; during months other than March, May, July, and October, the ides fell on the 13th. The term *ides* comes from the Latin word *iduare*, which means "to divide," and the ides divided each month into two parts. Debts, interest, and other payments were often due on the ides, so it became known as a day of reckoning—a day for settling accounts.

* *soothsayer* person who can predict the future

The Soothsayer's warning is one of several omens that foreshadow Caesar's downfall. Others include a terrible storm and a nightmare that disturbs his wife, Calpurnia. Because Caesar is unharmed as he enters the senate on the morning of March 15, he dismisses the Soothsayer's warning by noting that the ides has already come. The Soothsayer responds "Ay, Caesar, but not gone" (III.i.2). Shortly after this exchange, BRUTUS and his fellow conspirators stab Caesar to death.

Shakespeare used PLUTARCH'S LIVES as his source for this story. In the Roman historian's account, however, the Soothsayer delivers his warning well before Caesar's death. Because Shakespeare's Soothsayer utters the prediction so close to the time of the stabbing, the dramatic force of his words is increased. (*See also* **History in Shakespeare's Plays: Ancient Greece and Rome; Shakespeare's Sources.**)

IMAGERY

One of Shakespeare's greatest strengths as a writer is the effectiveness of his imagery, his use of descriptions and figures of speech that appeal to the senses. His early imagery tends to focus on stock metaphors, such as the "coral lips" of Bianca in *The Taming of the Shrew,* or on clever wordplay that has little connection to the action of a scene and may even interrupt it. Over time, however, Shakespeare refined his technique to produce more complex and meaningful images that help reinforce his plots, characters, and themes.

On a bare stage, without even a curtain to signal a change of scene, playwrights had to use words in place of scenery. Through language Shakespeare provides the audience with significant clues about the setting, as in Romeo's description of the sunrise that forces him to leave Juliet after their wedding night: "Look, love, what envious streaks / Do lace the severing clouds in yonder east" (*Romeo and Juliet*, III.v.7–8). He also uses imagery to depict events, such as the arrival of the queen's luxurious barge in *Antony and Cleopatra* or Ophelia's drowning death in *Hamlet,* that would have been impossible to present on stage. Through his characters Shakespeare provides vivid descriptions of these occurrences that enable the audience to visualize them.

Imagery may reveal aspects of a speaker's character, especially in stressful moments. For example, when Othello compares his planned revenge to a violent ocean current, the audience is given an insight into both his passionate nature and the intensity of his anger and pain. Similarly, FALSTAFF's frequent lies and humorous puns indicate his frivolous disposition. Images also intensify the emotional impact of a speech or an event. When Leontes in *The Winter's Tale* describes betrayal as a spider hiding in a cup and says it poisons the drinker only if he sees it, the ugly metaphor expresses his feelings more powerfully than any straightforward explanation.

One particularly complex type of imagery in Shakespeare's works is his use of mixed metaphors and image "clusters" to develop his themes. Hamlet's wish to "take arms against a sea of troubles" (III.i.58) is an illogical

image because a body of water cannot be brought under control with weapons, but it functions perfectly as a way to suggest not only the impossibility of winning but the hopelessness of even trying to fight. Image clusters are groups of related images that are used repeatedly to convey ideas and develop a dominant mood. Repeated images of sight and blindness, for example, illustrate the lack of moral vision in *King Lear.* In *Richard II,* references to land and gardening keep the audience aware of the king's poor care of England, his "garden." Eventually, Shakespeare had advanced so far beyond the conventional* love imagery of his early plays that he even made fun of such images, as in Sonnet 130: "My mistress' eyes are nothing like the sun." (*See also* **Dramatic Techniques; Language; Poetic Techniques; Prose Technique.**)

* ***conventional*** following established practice

INFLUENTIAL EDITIONS

See *Shakespeare's Works, Influential Editions.*

INHERITANCE

* ***legitimate*** born to parents who are married to each other

* ***dowry*** money given to a woman's husband at their marriage

The rules governing inheritance in Elizabethan England differed according to the type of property involved. Cash and other valuables, known as movable property, could be distributed in any manner. Land, however, was always passed down to the oldest legitimate* son. If the landowner was a nobleman, his eldest son also inherited his title. This practice, known as primogeniture, was very important during an age in which land was the most secure form of wealth. Passing all of a family's real property to one individual ensured that the estate would remain whole rather than being broken into many small units. There were only a few exceptions to the rule of primogeniture. One was that in a family with no sons, the estate could be distributed among the daughters.

The head of a family was under no obligation to leave any part of his estate to children other than his firstborn son. If an estate was substantial, however, he might provide for his daughters and younger sons in several ways. For example, a father could set aside dowries* for his daughters, which his heir was obliged to pay, to enable them to attract good husbands. He could also provide for younger sons to be educated to enter one of the professions, such as law, medicine, or the church. If an estate was modest, however, the other children usually were forced to depend on the generosity of the eldest son or to make their own way. Meanwhile, even wealthy landowners might not be able to provide for their children if the estate was entailed, meaning that a previous owner's will had placed legal restrictions on how the property could be used.

As Shakespeare and other writers of the day indicate, this system of inheritance often strained family relations. For example, *As You Like It* opens with Orlando complaining that his older brother, Oliver, has refused to provide him with the education stipulated in their father's will. In *King*

illegitimate born to parents who are not married to each other

Lear, the earl of Gloucester's illegitimate* son, Edmund, believes that he deserves to inherit his father's land and then plots to undermine the claims of his brother, Edgar. (*See also* **Law; Marriage and Family.**)

INN YARDS

* *Tudor* referring to the dynasty that ruled England from 1485 to 1603
* *interlude* short dramatic presentation

* *trestle* framework supported by braces of diagonally placed timbers or other structural material

* *Puritan* English Protestant who advocated strict moral discipline and a simplification of the ceremonies and beliefs of the Anglican Church

During the Tudor* period, inns were typically built around a central courtyard with several gateways, enabling the public to enter from different streets. These central yards frequently served as performance spaces for plays and interludes*. Inn yards were often large enough to accommodate a stage and a sizable crowd, yet they could be enclosed and private, making it possible to charge admission. Innkeepers benefited because the performances attracted customers. Shakespeare's company, the Chamberlain's Men, regularly performed at the Cross Keys Inn during the winter months.

For performances, a simple platform supported by trestles* or scaffolding was built at one end of the yard to serve as a stage. Such simple stages used no scenery and few props. Most of the audience members stood in the yard before the stage. Those who were better off financially could sit or stand on the balconies that surrounded the courtyard. The actors sometimes used the balcony directly above the stage if they needed an upper level to represent a castle wall or an upstairs window. Actors entered and exited through the gates behind the stage and used the rooms behind the stage as dressing rooms.

Beginning in 1559, Puritans* opposed to the theater passed various laws to limit or prohibit public performances at inns. As a result, the large suburban playhouses constructed in the 1570s became the primary venues for staging plays. Nonetheless, some companies continued to perform in inn yards until the mid-1590s. (*See also* **Acting Companies, Elizabethan; Interludes; King's Men.**)

INTERLUDES

* *allegory* literary device in which characters, events, and settings represent abstract qualities and in which the author intends a different meaning to be read beneath the surface

The term *interlude* was used in England in the late 1400s and early 1500s to describe a short dramatic presentation. A typical interlude was a brief, humorous episode requiring only a small group of actors. Scholars disagree, however, about whether interludes were performed as breaks in a longer production or were presented on their own.

Before the rise of interludes, English drama was dominated by the morality play, a form dating from the Middle Ages. Morality plays, such as *The Summoning of Everyman*, were allegories*, usually presenting the progress of an ordinary person from sin to salvation. Interludes offered a wider range of characters, themes, and settings, and they featured more specific details and individual traits. They became especially popular during the reign of Henry VII in the late 1400s. The king even sponsored a royal company to perform them. The first known drama that scholars

consider an interlude is *Fulgens and Lucres,* written by Henry Medwall around 1496. A later interlude, John Bale's *Kynge Johan,* was the first play to take English history as its subject.

By Shakespeare's time longer dramas were preferred over interludes. The longer plays enabled authors to develop their characters, themes, and plots more fully. Interludes nevertheless proved important in the history of English drama as a transition from the abstract form of the morality plays to the human variety found in the more complex dramas of the Renaissance.

Shakespeare applied his talents to long dramatic works, but he included interludes in two plays. The introduction to *The Taming of the Shrew* resembles an interlude and may have been the first in a series of interludes that were dropped from later editions of the play. In *A Midsummer Night's Dream,* a company of actors stages a play that is referred to as an interlude. Shakespeare drew on the tradition of interludes even as he helped develop the longer forms for which he earned such fame. (*See also* **Medievalism.**)

INTERPRETATION OF SHAKESPEARE

See *Feminist Interpretations; Marxist Interpretations; Psychology; Shakespeare's Reputation; Shakespeare's Works, Changing Views.*

IRVING, HENRY

1838–1905
Actor and producer

Henry Irving, born John Henry Brodribb, was considered the greatest actor and producer of Shakespeare's plays during the late 1800s. As an actor, Irving was noted both for the oddly slow and deliberate delivery of his lines and for his intellectual grasp of each character's nature.

Irving was born and educated in Somerset, England. After working as a clerk in his teenage years, he began acting at the age of 18. In his youth he rarely performed Shakespeare, but in 1874 he scored a great success in the role of Hamlet. He portrayed Hamlet as Shakespearean critics of the time viewed him: an indecisive man who worried, fretted, and delayed in fulfilling the revenge of his father's murder. Irving followed this success with productions of *Macbeth, Othello,* and *Richard III,* starring in the title role of each play.

In 1878 Irving purchased the Lyceum Theatre in London, where his company presented Shakespeare's plays for 24 years. He usually played the leading male roles, while Ellen Terry played the female leads. Irving also directed the productions and was notorious for his iron-fisted control over his actors. His business manager, Bram Stoker, may have used Irving as the model for the central character of his novel *Dracula.* Irving's company also gained fame—and criticism—for its lavish costumes, scenery, and props.

Irving dominated the world of Shakespearean theater in Britain, and in 1895 he became the first actor to be knighted. Later in life he endured illness and financial troubles, and in 1902 he lost his lease on the Lyceum Theatre. He took his productions on tour and died shortly after a performance in 1905. (*See also* **Actors, Shakespearean.**)

ITALY IN SHAKESPEARE'S PLAYS

The bustling cities of Renaissance Italy served as settings for several of Shakespeare's plays. Although the Italian peninsula had not yet been unified into a single nation, its major city-states—Venice, Florence, Mantua, Padua, Milan, Messina, Naples, Verona—shared many cultural features. Shakespeare refers to these Italian cities in ways that have charmed some audiences and caused others to find fault.

PORTRAYALS OF ITALY IN THE PLAYS. An early example of Shakespeare's Italian plays is *The Two Gentlemen of Verona*, which contains several peculiar inconsistencies. Although the main characters have Italian names, their servants are English. The play appears to take place in Verona and Milan, but at times the dialogue seems to reverse the two names and even adds a third, Padua. It is possible that Shakespeare had not firmly settled on a location before completing his script. The resulting confusion suggests that the particular metropolis was not as important to Shakespeare as were such factors as atmosphere, plot, and theme.

In *Romeo and Juliet*, which is also set in Verona, Shakespeare seems to have paid closer attention to the local setting than he had in the earlier play. His knowledge of Italian plays and poetry enabled him to create compelling portraits of the Italian people, especially the two lovers.

Perhaps his closest attention to the details of an Italian city is to be found in *The Merchant of Venice*. Shakespeare makes accurate references to the ferry that connected Venice with the Italian mainland and to other aspects of local geography. He also notes a clause in the Venetian constitution and reproduces the slang spoken among sailors in the city's busy seaport.

Other plays set, at least in part, in Renaissance Italy are *The Taming of the Shrew*, in Padua, and *Othello*, which begins in Venice. *Much Ado About Nothing* is set in Messina, *All's Well That Ends Well* in Florence, and *The Winter's Tale* on the island of Sicily.

SHAKESPEARE'S KNOWLEDGE OF ITALY. Shakespeare was skilled at using small details to convey a sense of place, whether it was England or some foreign land. This quality in Shakespeare's Italian plays has led some scholars to wonder whether he had actually visited Italy. No evidence of such a trip exists, but several sources of information about Italy did exist when Shakespeare was writing his plays.

Italian literature of the 1300s, 1400s, and 1500s was readily available in the bookshops of London, and Shakespeare clearly used many works from the continent of Europe as sources for his plots and characters. For

THE IMAGE OF ITALY

A country of violent passions and criminal behavior, of prideful men and women who threw morals and God aside while chasing their own desires: this was the popular image of Italy among Elizabethans. English conservatives railed against the culture of the Italian Renaissance, which emphasized commerce and personal achievement and was inspired by the pagan civilizations of ancient Greece and Rome. Although some English playwrights presented a dark vision of Italy, Shakespeare's portrayal of the region is far more moderate and personable, perhaps because it is usually a thin disguise for an English setting.

more firsthand accounts of Italy, he may have spoken with some of the many Italian merchants who came through London. He probably also knew John Florio, a Venetian citizen living in the household of Shakespeare's patron*, the earl of Southampton. Florio was so helpful to Ben Jonson that the playwright thanked him generously in the introduction to *Volpone*, a play of Jonson's that is set in Venice. It seems likely that Florio helped Shakespeare as well.

Evidence suggests that Shakespeare never visited Italy himself. He identified several "Italian" cities as located on a river that flows to the sea, much like London's River Thames. Similarly, many of the places mentioned in those cities closely resemble sites in London. Although Shakespeare created the illusion of Italian settings, it seems that his inspirations lay closer to home. (*See also* **Shakespeare's Sources.**)

* *patron* supporter or financial sponsor of an artist or writer

JAMES I

1566–1625
King of England and Scotland

* *patron* supporter or financial sponsor of an artist or writer
* *Tudor* referring to the dynasty that ruled England from 1485 to 1603
* *regent* person appointed to govern when the rightful monarch is too young or unable to rule

James I was king of England from 1603 to 1625, having already ruled Scotland (as James VI) since 1567. He presided over an unstable period in English history, and his reign was marred by controversy. In his private life James was a distinguished author, and he served as the patron* of Shakespeare's theater company, the KING'S MEN.

LIFE AND REIGN. James was descended from King Henry VII of England's Tudor* dynasty. His mother, Mary Stuart (commonly referred to as Mary, Queen of Scots), was forced to give up her throne in 1567, and the infant James was named king. He never knew his mother, for she fled to England, where she was imprisoned for years and was eventually executed. A series of regents* ruled in James's name during his childhood. Although his mother was Catholic, the young monarch-to-be was raised as a Protestant. In 1598 James married Princess Anne of Denmark, and the couple produced three children who lived beyond infancy. The king's marriage, however, was apparently one of convenience, because he preferred the company of men.

Few issues disrupted James's rule of Scotland until the dying Queen ELIZABETH I named him heir to the throne. Although his new subjects welcomed him at first, troubles soon arose. James handled finances poorly, and he lacked Elizabeth's personal charm. Although he was a learned man, his arrogant tendency to lecture those around him earned him such nicknames as "schoolmaster of the realm" and "the wisest fool in Christendom." Many were also offended by his obvious HOMOSEXUALITY and by his policy of awarding exclusive rights to profitable businesses to gentlemen he favored. Harsh anti-Catholic measures enacted early in his reign sparked the GUNPOWDER PLOT, an unsuccessful attempt to assassinate the king and the members of Parliament. Yet James also favored a highly unpopular alliance with Spain, a Catholic country whose fleet had attempted to invade England in 1588. These and other tensions weakened the relationship between Parliament and the monarchy and eventually led to a civil war during the reign of James's son Charles I.

PATRONAGE OF THE ARTS. James began to enjoy theater under the influence of his wife Anne. Both in Scotland and in England, he and his queen invited acting companies to perform at court. During his first year as the English sovereign, James became the patron of Shakespeare's company, which changed its name from the Chamberlain's Men to the King's Men. Four other leading companies enjoyed the patronage of the queen and her three children, and the tastes of the royal family greatly influenced Jacobean* drama. At times, however, James imposed strict CENSORSHIP on writers and artists to protect his weak political position.

Shakespeare made references to James in two plays. In *Macbeth* a vision shows a series of eight future kings descended from the character of Banquo, supposedly an ancestor to James. Shakespeare thus implies that James's heirs will rule for many generations. In the final act of *Henry VIII*, an archbishop praises the infant Elizabeth and predicts that her successor will rise to equal greatness. James probably appreciated these flatteries, and the playwright Ben JONSON noted that both Elizabeth and James esteemed Shakespeare's work.

James himself wrote at length. He published several works about religion, two books arguing his belief in the divine right of kings, and a short text called *A Counterblaste to Tobacco*, which criticized the new practice of smoking tobacco, which had recently been imported from North America. In addition he wrote and translated poetry in English, Latin, and Scots. He also sponsored a new translation of the BIBLE, now known as the King James Version. (*See also* **Government and Politics; Spanish Armada.**)

* *Jacobean* referring to the reign of James I, king of England from 1603 to 1625

JEWS

Jews in Shakespeare's England lived a shadowed life, hidden from view and frequently in danger. England had expelled its Jewish population in 1290, and Jews were still forbidden to live in the country during Shakespeare's lifetime. The law was not strictly enforced, however, and a small community of Jews lived in London, knowing that at any time they could be evicted and their property seized.

England had been an isolated nation with little outside contact for centuries, and the English were greatly suspicious of all foreigners. In addition to this general lack of tolerance, Jews suffered from the English Christians' long-held belief that Jews were responsible for the crucifixion of Jesus. Above all, Jews were resented for their common occupations as bankers and moneylenders. The practice of usury, or the charging of interest on loans—which made the profession feasible—was frowned on by religious and political authorities.

The one prominent Jewish figure in Elizabethan England—Roderigo López, court physician to Queen Elizabeth—was accused of plotting to poison the queen. His notoriety contributed to the English stereotype of Jews as greedy, scheming villains who, according to the most extreme rumors, kidnapped Christian children and murdered them in secret rituals. Yet few English Christians ever saw or met a Jew in their lifetimes.

Shakespeare was rooted in this culture when he created the character of SHYLOCK, the Jewish moneylender in *The Merchant of Venice.* He exploited his audience's fascination with the foreign and exotic Jew, portraying Shylock as a bloodthirsty villain who despises all Christians. Yet Shakespeare avoided the crude scorn and violence that had been heaped upon Jewish characters in other English dramas. Instead he made Shylock a complex human character, a victim of injustice, encouraging the audience to feel some sympathy for him. In a famous passage Shylock asks Salerio

> "Hath not a Jew hands, organs, dimensions, affections, passions; fed with the same food, hurt with the same weapons . . . as a Christian is? If you prick us, do we not bleed?"
>
> (III.i.59–64)

See color plate 6, vol. 2.

The status of England's Jews improved somewhat in 1571, when Parliament legalized usury. But it was not until King Charles I was overthrown in 1649 and the government was taken over by the Puritan* Oliver Cromwell, that Jews were legally permitted to live in England. In due course, these changes helped England establish its prominence in the fields of international finance and commerce. (*See also* **Banking and Commerce.**)

* Puritan English Protestant who advocated strict moral discipline and simplification of the ceremonies and beliefs of the Anglican Church

JIG

Today the word *jig* usually refers to a type of dance, associated mostly with Ireland, that involves quick intricate steps performed with the upper body held stiffly. This sort of jig was known in Elizabethan England, where it was usually referred to as a "Scottish" or "Northern" dance. More commonly, however, Elizabethans used the word *jig* to refer to a more elaborate type of entertainment, a skit containing music and dancing. This type of jig may have been the ancestor of modern comic opera.

In the theater of Shakespeare's time, a jig was often performed after the conclusion of the main play. The dialogue was in verse, with each section sung to a different tune and accompanied by dancing. Jigs were bawdy* and humorous, their principal subject being illicit* love affairs. Much of the humor in the jig was ridicule directed at the frailties of women. Both Shakespeare and Christopher MARLOWE viewed the jig with contempt, but two of the most famous clowns of their day—Will Kempe and Richard Tarlton—were noted for their performances in jigs.

In London, jigs were performed only at the less reputable theaters, such as the Curtain, the Red Bull, and the Fortune. They were also staged before private audiences in other locales. Jigs were banned in the London area in 1612 on the ground that they were indecent and led to riots and disturbances of the peace. Few texts of these short pieces have survived. (*See also* **Actors, Shakespearean; Elizabethan Theaters; Fools, Clowns, and Jesters; Interludes.**)

* bawdy indecent; obscene
* illicit forbidden; unlawful

JONSON, BEN

1572–1637
Playwright and poet

* *satire* literary work ridiculing human wickedness and foolishness

* *anecdote* brief account of an interesting or amusing event in a person's life

* *foreword* introduction or preface to a book, usually written by someone other than the author

Ben Jonson was a playwright, poet, critic, and contemporary of William Shakespeare. Many critics consider Jonson's work second only to Shakespeare's in the literature and drama of their era, and the two men shared both friendship and rivalry.

After attending the Westminster School as a scholarship student, Jonson served in the British army for a short time. The first of his plays to be performed was *Every Man in His Humour*, produced in 1598 by Shakespeare's company, the Chamberlain's Men. Shakespeare himself was one of the actors and may have influenced the company's decision to present the play. Jonson described the work as a "comical satire*," and during the next three years he created several more works of this type. Two other playwrights adopted Jonson's new form, and the three of them engaged in an exchange of plays known as the WAR OF THE THEATERS. In 1603 Shakespeare's company, renamed the KING'S MEN, produced Jonson's tragedy *Sejanus*. Jonson also wrote many MASQUES, costumed entertainments for which the royal architect Inigo Jones designed elaborate sets. Jonson's poems, essays, and literary criticism commanded respect as well.

Despite their friendship, Shakespeare did not escape Jonson's criticism. Jonson disliked the fanciful qualities of Shakespeare's late romances, and he also remarked on minor flaws in other works. Jonson may have been sensitive to their rivalry as leading dramatists and to the differences in their styles and methods. Even so, many legends and anecdotes* testify to their friendship, and Jonson spared no compliments when he composed a poetic preface to the FIRST FOLIO of Shakespeare's plays. In this foreword* Jonson called Shakespeare the "Soule of the Age," praising him as Britain's equal to the great authors of classical Greece and Rome and declaring that Shakespeare would never die "while [his] Booke doth live, / And we have wits to read, and praise to give." (*See also* **Plays: The Romances; Playwrights and Poets.**)

JULIET

See *Romeo and Juliet.*

JULIUS CAESAR

* *regicide* murder of a monarch

Shakespeare's tragedy *Julius Caesar* was written at the midpoint of the playwright's career. After his heroic celebration of England in *Henry V*, Shakespeare turned to the most famous crisis of Roman history: the assassination of Julius Caesar, the ruler of Rome, in 44 B.C. Closer to conventional tragic form than any of the English history plays that preceded it, *Julius Caesar* examines the theme of regicide* without actually having a king as part of the drama. Shakespeare accomplished this by adapting his Roman setting to the patterns of ideas he had been exploring in his English history plays, which in turn reflected the social realities of his own era.

TEXT AND SOURCES. Several clues enable scholars to state with confidence that *Julius Caesar* was first performed in 1599. The clearest evidence for this date is an entry in the travel diary of Thomas Platter, a Swiss physician who visited England that year. Platter notes that he saw a tragedy at the GLOBE THEATER on September 21, 1599, and his description of the play matches the plot of *Julius Caesar*. This production, which according to Platter concluded with an elaborate JIG, may have been the first performance of a drama at the newly built Globe.

Shakespeare's text is closely based on Sir Thomas North's 1579 translation of PLUTARCH'S LIVES, a series of biographies in which ancient historical figures are paired for purposes of comparison. Shakespeare drew details for his plot primarily from the biographies of Marcus Brutus, Marcus Antonius, and Caesar himself. With its vivid characterization and lively narrative, North's *Plutarch* was an attractive source for dramatists, and in places Shakespeare's play follows North's wording fairly closely. The circumstances of Julius Caesar's assassination were very well known in Shakespeare's time, so just about any book about Rome that was published during this period would have probably contained references to these events.

PLOT SYNOPSIS. The history on which *Julius Caesar* is based covers a period of about three years, from October 45 B.C. to October 42 B.C. Shakespeare's play compresses and rearranges these events, giving the impression that they all occur within a few crucial days. The play opens with Caesar's triumphant return to Rome after he has defeated the rebellious Pompey, his former friend and ally. This event is combined with the Feast of Lupercal, when Mark Antony (Caesar's lieutenant) offers the general a crown. Caesar refuses it, to the delight of the watching crowd, but some observers believe he does so reluctantly. Caesar's growing power is disturbing to his friend Brutus and even more so to Brutus's

See
color plate 7,
vol. 2.

In a dramatic scene from the 1988 Royal Shakespeare Company production of *Julius Caesar,* Marcus Brutus (played by Linus Roache) falls to his knees after he and a group of fellow conspirators assassinate Caesar.

brother-in-law Cassius, who begins forming a secret plan to assassinate Rome's new leader.

The action from the end of Act I to the end of Act III is presented as a continuous flow of events in 44 B.C., from the evening of March 14 through the following day. Cassius, who has learned that the Roman Senate plans to crown Caesar, persuades Brutus to join with him and a group of other conspirators* in a plot to murder Caesar before he can assume total power. Caesar receives several warnings that he is in danger—from a soothsayer*; from his wife, Calpurnia (who tells him about her nightmare); and finally from a teacher named Artemidorus (who has learned of the conspiracy). But he disregards them all, insisting that it would be shameful for him to stay home out of fear. The conspirators meet Caesar in the Senate, stab him to death, and then bathe their hands in his blood, remarking that their heroic deed will surely be reenacted by actors for centuries to come.

After news of the assassination has spread, Antony meets with the conspirators and gains their permission to speak at Caesar's funeral. Brutus speaks first, explaining to his fellow citizens that the conspirators acted against Caesar to prevent him from becoming a tyrant. The crowd is completely convinced and shouts its approval. Then Antony delivers an even more moving oration in which he praises Caesar, denies that he was ever ambitious for the crown, and rouses the people to a frenzy by displaying Caesar's torn and bloody robe. Finally Antony reveals that Caesar, in his will, has left 75 silver pieces to every citizen of Rome and bequeathed his gardens to the city for all to enjoy. Antony's stirring remarks turn the crowd into an angry mob that tears through the streets of Rome, seeking to kill the conspirators. The enraged citizens even murder a poet named Cinna simply because he has the same name as one of Caesar's slayers. Not surprisingly, Brutus and Cassius are forced to flee the city.

The complicated developments of Acts IV and V are condensed into a few fast-paced but significant scenes. Antony has joined forces with Caesar's nephew Octavius and with the soldier Lepidus, forming a triumvirate* to rule Rome. They make a list of their enemies, including close relatives of both Antony and Lepidus, who must not be allowed to live. Meanwhile Brutus and Cassius have gathered their own forces to fight the triumvirate. At the city of Sardis, Brutus meets with Cassius and quarrels with him about a friend who has been accused of taking bribes. He also complains that Cassius has denied his requests for money to pay his soldiers. Hurt by Brutus's accusations, Cassius offers Brutus a dagger to stab him with, but Brutus calms down and forgives him. He then discloses that he is not entirely in control of his emotions because he has just learned that his wife, Portia, has killed herself. Cassius is astonished at how calmly Brutus bears this sorrow. After he leaves, Brutus sees a vision of Caesar's ghost, which tells him that they will meet at Philippi.

Historically, two battles were fought at Philippi, but Shakespeare compressed them into a single encounter that makes up the final act of the play. Bidding each other an "everlasting farewell," Brutus and Cassius join the fight against the armies of Antony and Octavius. In the confusion that ensues Cassius receives a mistaken report that his troops are overcome and that his best friend, Titinius, has been killed by the enemy.

* **conspirator** person who plots with others to commit a crime
* **soothsayer** person who can predict the future

* **triumvirate** form of rule in which authority is shared by three people

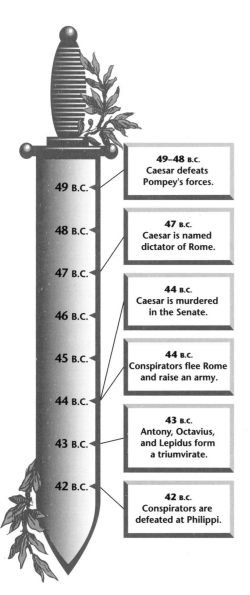

49 B.C.

49–48 B.C.
Caesar defeats Pompey's forces.

48 B.C.

47 B.C.
Caesar is named dictator of Rome.

47 B.C.

46 B.C.

44 B.C.
Caesar is murdered in the Senate.

45 B.C.

44 B.C.
Conspirators flee Rome and raise an army.

44 B.C.

43 B.C.

43 B.C.
Antony, Octavius, and Lepidus form a triumvirate.

42 B.C.

42 B.C.
Conspirators are defeated at Philippi.

Despairing, he orders his slave to kill him. When Titinius returns and sees Cassius dead, he immediately kills himself as well. The tide of battle turns, and Brutus's forces are beaten down. Knowing that his cause is lost, Brutus persuades a soldier named Strato to hold his sword while he runs upon it. His dying words are "Caesar, now be still; / I killed thee not with half so good a will" (V.v.50–51). When Antony and Octavius find Brutus's body, the latter announces that he will pardon everyone who served Brutus and that Brutus himself will be buried with honor. Antony declares that Brutus, who acted for what he believed was the common good, was "the noblest Roman of them all" (V.v.68).

ANALYSIS. Just as Shakespeare's history plays are distinctly English, providing a clear glimpse of his nation's past, *Julius Caesar* is a distinctly Roman play, not only in its setting but also in its style and themes. It explores the idea of what it means to be "an antique Roman," which Shakespeare defined as a person who is sober, dutiful, and honorable, who places greater emphasis on public service than on private life. The play's language is also characteristically Roman: simple and straightforward, with a limited vocabulary and few figurative* devices. An example is Brutus's grave and deliberate speech to his devoted Portia: "You are my true and honorable wife, / As dear to me as are the ruddy drops / That visit my sad heart" (II.1.288–90). This passage, so free of flourishes, represents the Roman style at its most direct and unadorned. The plot of *Julius Caesar* is also fairly straightforward, making it a favorite in the high school curriculum.

If the action in *Julius Caesar* seems easy to follow, but it is far from easy to interpret. The political issues that Shakespeare explores—the proper basis of government and the question of whether a noble goal can ever justify a bloody deed—are never clearly decided one way or the other. It is equally easy to see the playwright as supporting Caesar, who represents political stability and legitimacy, or as favoring the conspirators who murder him to avoid tyranny. Caesar is shown to be a much-loved ruler, yet he also has several serious flaws. Physically, he is deaf in one ear, he has "the falling sickness" (epilepsy), and there are hints that he is sterile*. His moral deficiencies are more subtle. There are many indications of his hubris—the overwhelming pride that is the fatal flaw of many tragic heroes—particularly in his public addresses, which use the grand, impersonal style of a dictator. Cassius also describes him as unable to bear pain, revealing that after a swimming match in which he nearly drowned, Caesar shook and cried out "as a sick girl" (I.ii.128).

On the other side, the conspirators' political attitudes are attractive; after murdering Caesar, Cassius urges his companions to proclaim "liberty, freedom, and enfranchisement*" to all of Rome (III.1.81). At the same time the very fact that they are plotting against a popular leader links them with other conspirators in the English history plays, who are portrayed primarily as villains. Equally unclear is the meaning of the play's many omens and disturbances in nature. The night before Caesar's assassination, a violent storm occurs, which Cassius interprets as a warning of Caesar's tyranny. But the storm can also be construed as an indication of the growing evils of

* *figurative* characterized by metaphors, similes, and other figures of speech

* *sterile* unable to reproduce

* *enfranchisement* rights of citizenship, especially the right to vote

THE HERO OF THE PLAY

Some critics have wondered why Shakespeare called his tragedy *Julius Caesar* when the character of Caesar dies before the play is half over. Writer and critic Leigh Hunt commented that Brutus was "clearly the hero of the story, and . . . should have given his name to the piece." Scholar Bernhard ten Brink disagreed, noting that the "idea that was projected into the world by Caesar" proves more powerful than any individual character in the play. This idea—the concept of authority—can be seen as the true center of the play, and unlike the character of Caesar himself, it not only survives but triumphs in the end.

* *soliloquy* monologue in which a character reveals his or her private thoughts

* *protagonist* central character in a literary work

conspiracy. Similarly, Caesar's murder can be seen either as the bloodletting required to cure a diseased society or as a wound inflicted on that society, which must be avenged by more bloodshed.

If the friends and the enemies of Caesar represent two opposing philosophies, the common people seem to lack any philosophy at all. The Roman mob is indistinguishable from the English mobs of the earlier history plays: loud, filthy, violent, and unstable. Above all, the mob is easily moved by any strong emotional appeal. The crowd's violent response to Antony's funeral oration and the senseless murder of Cinna (the poet) clearly show that the people have little interest in the political promises of the conspirators, or indeed in any political ideas at all. Instead, the mob is swayed by spectacle, grandeur, heroic effects, bold gestures, and strong emotions. Since considerable power rests in their hands, however, the presence of the Roman mob is a reminder of the public conflict at the heart of the play.

In Brutus, Shakespeare seems to be experimenting with a new kind of tragic hero, a character "with himself at war" (I.2.46). Brutus believes that Caesar's death is necessary, yet he remains sincerely disturbed by the murder. He attempts to reconcile his opposing desires, telling himself that the conspirators can be "sacrificers, but not butchers" (II.i.166), but his wish to kill Caesar without the personal stain of murder is unrealistic and ultimately irresponsible. The act of killing Caesar turns the conspirators into the "butchers" Brutus feared they would become, and Antony says as much when he pleads with Caesar's corpse: "O, pardon me, thou bleeding piece of earth, / That I am meek and gentle with these butchers" (III.i.254–55).

Unlike the practical Cassius, Brutus is an idealist, and all the political decisions he makes—to spare Antony's life, to allow him to speak at Caesar's funeral, and to fight at Philippi—prove unwise. His tragedy lies in the conflict between his personal wishes and his political beliefs. After Cassius has urged him to join the conspiracy against Caesar, Brutus remarks in a soliloquy*, "I know no personal cause to spurn at him, / But for the general. He would be crown'd" (II.i.11–12). This conflict between the "personal" and the "general" forms the basis of Brutus's tragic choice. Ultimately, he chooses to abandon his personal morals in favor of a more general, political goal. But what ensues suggests that this sacrifice of the private self to the public good has disastrous consequences.

Brutus views his suicide as an act of nobility and courage. From a Christian standpoint, however, it is difficult to interpret this gesture as virtuous, since Christian belief generally classifies suicide as a mortal sin. Roman virtue may be distinct from Christian virtue. Personal honor is at its core, along with a conviction that it is nobler to die with honor than to live in disgrace. When Brutus asserts that he "bears too great a mind" (V.i.112) to allow himself to go to Rome bound as a military captive, he chooses to die on his own terms rather than submit to the will of others. It is not at all certain that Shakespeare expected his Elizabethan audience to accept the protagonist* at his own estimate. If Brutus remains his own master to the end and his honor is untouched by any physical weakness in the face of death, he may nevertheless come across to a Renaissance Christian as the unsuspecting victim of a defective Roman philosophy.

* *Restoration* referring to the period in English history, beginning in 1660, when Charles II was restored to the throne
* *classical* in the tradition of ancient Greece and Rome

PERFORMANCE HISTORY. On the stage, *Julius Caesar* has been one of Shakespeare's most popular plays. From the time of the Restoration* to about the last quarter of the 1700s, it was produced at least once in almost every year. Its restrained, classical* style undoubtedly suited the temper of this era. Unlike many other Shakespearean plays *Julius Caesar* was never altered and rewritten to make it more palatable to the refined audiences of a later period.

For various reasons, perhaps chiefly political, *Julius Caesar* was more popular in America than it was in England during the 1800s. It appeared in New York in 51 different years of the 1800s, and during the period of 1835 to 1855 it was revived 15 times in Philadelphia. One memorable performance was a benefit staged at New York's Winter Garden Theater on November 25, 1864, to raise money for a statue of Shakespeare in Central Park. Three members of the legendary Booth family—Junius Brutus Booth, Jr., and his two brothers, Edwin and John Wilkes—assumed the roles of Cassius, Brutus, and Mark Antony. John Wilkes Booth later became better known as the real-life "Roman" who shot Abraham Lincoln on April 14, 1865.

In 1898 Herbert Beerbohm Tree staged a successful revival of *Julius Caesar* at His Majesty's Theatre in London, presenting the play to enthusiastic audiences for a hundred nights. Tree himself played Antony, and he arranged the play into three acts so that each act ended with a tableau* of Antony by himself, making it appear that his was the leading role. The stage designer, a painter named Sir Lawrence Alma-Tadema, attempted to recreate the architectural magnificence of ancient Rome. This splendid production was revived in 1899, and between 1905 and 1913 it appeared eight times at His Majesty's annual Shakespeare festival.

* *tableau* scene in which all performers stand silent and motionless

Julius Caesar has been frequently revived in the last century. One of the most notable productions was the collaboration of John Houseman and Orson Welles at New York's Mercury Theater in 1937. The 22-year-old Welles played Brutus in a bold, modern-dress version of the play that evoked fascist* parallels, with Caesar specifically made up to look like the Italian dictator Benito Mussolini. Houseman also produced a remarkable film version of *Julius Caesar* for MGM in 1953. The movie was done in the film noir style popular in the 1940s and was characterized by a very dark look and mood. Its outstanding cast included Marlon Brando as Antony, James Mason as Brutus, Louis Calhern as Caesar, John Gielgud as Cassius, and Edmond O'Brien, who usually played detectives or crooked lawyers, as Casca. (*See also* **Actors, Shakespearean; Shakespeare Festivals; Shakespeare on Screen; Shakespeare's Works, Adaptations of.**)

* *fascist* referring to a political system characterized by absolute rule and a suppression of individual rights, such as the Italian government from 1922 to 1943

KATHARINA

Katharina is the central character of Shakespeare's early comedy *The Taming of the Shrew*. The play dramatizes her progress from a bad-tempered daughter to a loving wife, a transformation that presents a problem for many modern readers.

Katharina is first introduced as the attractive but disagreeable older sister of the beautiful and sweet-natured Bianca. While many suitors seek Bianca's hand, her father has forbidden anyone to marry her until Katharina has also found a husband. The audience observes Katharina's unpleasant behavior as she snaps at her father and at Bianca's suitors and even ties up her sister and strikes her. It is clear that Katharina resents the unflattering comparisons with her favored sister, and it is likely that her ill temper is a defense against the rejection of others. When one suitor (a stranger named PETRUCHIO, who is interested primarily in her dowry*) finally expresses an interest in her, she treats him with energetic disdain. In response he promptly rises to the challenge of making her his wife and "taming" her ill nature.

Petruchio uses physical force and psychological manipulation to alter Katharina's behavior. While courting her, he praises her sweetness and good nature even in the midst of her tantrums. After their marriage he deprives her of food, clothing, and sleep, all the while declaring his love for her. At the same time he behaves rudely and irrationally toward everyone else, showing Katharina the unattractiveness of her own behavior. Eventually Katharina submits to Petruchio's will, and in the play's final scene she shows herself to be the most dutiful wife at her sister's wedding. She then gives a speech about the virtues of obedience and places her hand beneath Petruchio's foot in a formal gesture of submission.

Critics disagree about how to interpret Katharina's "taming." Many see her as a headstrong, independent woman who is mistreated by her husband and forced to yield to male authority. By altering her behavior Petruchio is left with a pale shadow of Katharina's former self. To others, her transformation is positive: she begins the play as an unhappy and unloved daughter and becomes a fulfilled and well-loved wife by learning to accept her place in society. To an Elizabethan audience the play's progress would certainly have appeared entirely natural and positive. Shakespeare probably believed that a cooperative spirit was proper for a wife, and the play reflects the importance of social order, a theme that appears often in his works. Nonetheless, what makes Katharina an interesting character is not her obedience at the end of the play but the quick wit and strong spirit she shows throughout. In this respect she may be seen as a model for the strong heroines who appear in later works, among them Beatrice in *Much Ado About Nothing*. Katharina also has many qualities in common with the DARK LADY of Shakespeare's SONNETS, which led some critics to speculate that both characters were based on a real woman in Shakespeare's life. (*See also* **Feminist Interpretations**.)

TOPSY-TURVY

An audience in Australia in 1972 was treated to a very untraditional interpretation of Katharina's final submission. In that production Kate offers her hand in friendship but suddenly has a change of heart. Instead of gently placing her hand beneath Petruchio's foot, she twists his foot and sends him crashing to the ground, showing that her words have all been in jest, that they are equals, and that he had best remember it.

* *dowry* money given to a woman's husband at their marriage

KING JOHN

Probably written in the 1590s, *The Life and Death of King John* is one of Shakespeare's history plays. It deals with the struggle of John, king of England from 1199 to 1216, to assert and defend the legitimacy of his reign.

King John

This engraving from an illustrated edition of *King John* shows young Arthur pleading with Hubert de Burgh. In the play Hubert is instructed by the king to kill the boy but is unable to bring himself to do so.

See color plate 11, vol. 2.

* *illegitimate* born to parents who are not married to each other

The historical King John is remembered as the English ruler whose nobles forced him to grant Magna Carta, or Great Charter, a list of rights belonging to the nobility. In Shakespeare's day, however, this was not seen as a major historical event, and Shakespeare includes no mention of it in the play. Instead, he focuses on what seem to have been viewed as the major crises of John's reign. Dramatizing these events in five acts forced Shakespeare to take considerable liberties with the historical time line, however, and *King John* is sometimes described as the least accurate of Shakespeare's histories.

In Shakespeare's condensed plot line, John simultaneously faces challenges from the pope and from the Catholic rulers of France and Austria, who demand that his nephew Arthur be placed on the throne. Aided by Philip the Bastard—the illegitimate* son of the previous king, Richard I—King John responds by attacking France. Arthur is captured in the battle, and John orders his murder, arousing outrage among the English lords. They rebel and join an invasion that is being led by the French prince Lewis, who seeks the English throne. Desperate to secure his crown, John yields to the pope's demands, but the church is unable to stop the French invasion. The king retreats, troubled and sick, and Philip steps forward to rally the English cause. When the rebellious lords learn that Lewis intends to kill them after gaining the throne, they return to the English side, defeating the French. The king dies, poisoned by a monk, and Philip the Bastard leads the nobles in accepting John's son, Prince Henry, as the legitimate heir to the throne. The Bastard concludes with a speech declaring that England has never been conquered unless "it first did help to wound itself" (V.vii.114).

Though often viewed as a somewhat minor work, *King John* explores the same theme as Shakespeare's other histories: the definition of rightful kingship. Ironically, in a play concerned with the legitimacy of the monarchy, it is the illegitimate Philip who proves more loyal and noble than all the English noblemen. In many ways the events in the play reflect the political problems of Elizabethan England. Queen Elizabeth herself was conceived out of wedlock, and she faced many challenges to her throne. In particular, the supporters of Mary, Queen of Scots (mother of King JAMES I), compared Mary's claim to that of Duke Arthur. The ongoing rivalries with France and the Catholic Church were also familiar to Elizabethan audiences.

King John is probably based on a 1591 play that was called *The Troublesome Raigne of John, King of England*. Some scholars, however, have suggested that this play came after Shakespeare's and was influenced by it. Of the two plays, Shakespeare's is much less violent in its attacks on the Catholic Church. Undisputed sources for *King John* include HOLINSHED'S CHRONICLES and a number of historical and popular accounts. Published in the FIRST FOLIO, *King John* was popular in the early 1600s and enjoyed a revival in London in 1737. Since then it has remained familiar to the British, especially during wars and other times of crisis. The play has received little attention in the United States or elsewhere. (*See also* **History in Shakespeare's Plays: England; Plays: The Histories.**)

KING LEAR

Many critics, particularly in recent decades, consider *King Lear* Shakespeare's masterpiece. Compared with *Hamlet*, a fascinating tragedy that was viewed for many years to be the greatest of Shakespeare's plays, *King Lear* is a more completely realized, artistic whole. Its two plots, paralleling and contrasting with each other, brilliantly develop the dramatist's themes as they carry the action forward. The characters are vividly portrayed, and when the play is performed competently, it transmits the majesty and vigor of Shakespeare's art at the height of his career.

PLOT SUMMARY. At the outset of the play, King Lear has decided to divide his kingdom among his three daughters, Goneril, Regan, and CORDELIA. He sets up a contest to find out which of them loves him most. Goneril and Regan declare in exaggerated terms how deeply they adore the old man, but Cordelia—the youngest daughter and the king's clear favorite—refuses to play the game. In response to her honesty and sincerity, the outraged Lear banishes Cordelia from his kingdom and gives her share of his lands to Goneril and Regan and their husbands, the dukes of Albany and Cornwall. At this point the king of France, recognizing the true worth of Cordelia, declares that he will marry her and take her back to his kingdom. The earl of Kent, meanwhile, recognizes that Lear's behavior is irrational and tries to intervene. For his efforts he, too, is banished, despite his long and loyal service to Lear.

After the cruel treatment by his daughters Goneril and Regan, King Lear loses his mind. American actor Edwin Forrest is shown here wearing a crown of weeds and flowers when he played the tragic figure in the late 1800s.

Soon after Lear divides his kingdom, the earl of Gloucester falls prey to the scheming of his illegitimate son, Edmund. Aiming to inherit his father's estate, Edmund plots to have his father disinherit his older half brother, Edgar, by convincing Gloucester that Edgar wants to kill him. His treachery succeeds, and the innocent Edgar flees for his life. To avoid imprisonment, Edgar takes refuge in disguise as a mad beggar, Tom o' Bedlam. Ironically, in a play where appearances so often deceive the major characters, Edgar's basic disguise is to strip himself practically naked.

Lear, who has arranged to spend one month alternately with Goneril and Regan, is next seen at Goneril's palace, accompanied by 100 knights. Besides his title, these knights are all the possessions he has kept for himself. With him also is his nameless Fool, who repeatedly mocks Lear for rashly giving up his lands. They encounter the banished earl of Kent, who has returned in disguise, calling himself Caius, to continue serving his master. Kent stands by the old man throughout the terrible ordeal that Lear subsequently endures at the hands of Goneril and Regan.

The king's troubles begin almost at once, as Goneril finds the behavior of her father and his knights intolerable. She insists on reducing his train of knights to 50. Meanwhile, she has her servants treat Lear with such disrespect that he leaves in outrage for Regan's palace. Unknown to Lear, Goneril and Regan have formed a conspiracy against him. Informed by her sister that Lear is coming, Regan and her husband leave their palace and go to Gloucester's instead. The audience is asked to imagine Lear and his men riding through the dark night trying to find Regan; eventually, they too end up at Gloucester's palace. A terrible confrontation occurs, and when Goneril arrives the two daughters strip their father of his entire band of knights, a severe blow to the old king's dignity and self-image. "I gave you all" (II.iv.249), he cries in response to their ingratitude.

Realizing how unwise he has been in dividing his kingdom and banishing Cordelia, Lear rightly fears that he is losing his mind. He runs out into a storm, which has been growing in intensity as these events have occurred. Defying the elements, he cries, "Pour on, I will endure" (III.iv.18). As he tries to outface the wind and the rain, Lear has only the Fool and Kent with him, each trying to bring him to shelter and sanity. Lear's gathering madness becomes evident when he meets Edgar in disguise as Tom o' Bedlam. All attempts by the Fool and Kent to restore Lear to his right mind fail, and seeing Edgar as a madman pushes Lear over the edge to insanity.

Observing events, Gloucester takes pity on the king and secretly tries to aid him. Edmund, in whom Gloucester has confided, reveals his plans to Goneril, Regan, and Cornwall. Cornwall gives Edmund his father's title, then punishes Gloucester by putting out his eyes and turning him out of his own castle. Gloucester next meets Edgar, who maintains his disguise while leading his father to Dover. Gloucester is overcome with bitter despair as he realizes how wrong he has been to trust Edmund instead of Edgar. Though physically blind, the old duke has gained new insight, understanding his situation far more clearly than ever before. Without hope, he seeks to end his life, but Edgar thwarts his father's melancholy by tricking him into believing that he has thrown himself from a cliff and miraculously landed unharmed.

Thanks to Gloucester's help, Lear has managed to escape his daughters' plot against his life and is brought to Dover, where Cordelia has arrived with an army to help restore him to his throne. Unfortunately, by this time the old king has lost his wits entirely, and the next time he appears, on Dover Beach, he is a raving lunatic. Ironically, in his madness Lear seems to make more sense than when he was supposedly in his right mind—when he impulsively divided his kingdom and banished those closest and dearest to him. A gentleman sent by Cordelia to seek the king finds him and leads him to her camp. One of the most moving scenes in the play follows as Lear and Cordelia are finally reconciled (IV.vii). Lear now knows that he has been "a foolish fond old man" and begs his daughter's forgiveness for the injustice he has done her. Cordelia's reply contrasts her truly generous and compassionate nature with the cruel heartlessness of her older sisters: "No cause, no cause," she insists when Lear says she has reason to hate him.

The play might have ended here, with Lear and Cordelia at last reunited in love, but more terrible events follow. (The play has several such false endings, which tend to heighten the tragic impact of its final moments.) Goneril, Regan, and Albany (Cornwall has been killed by one of his servants in a protest against Gloucester's blinding) have formed an army led by Edmund, who is now being wooed by both Goneril and Regan. In the battle between the English and French forces, Cordelia's army is defeated, and she and her father are taken to prison, where Edmund orders their execution.

Fortunately, Edgar has intercepted a message to Edmund from Goneril declaring her love for him and urging him to murder her husband, Albany. Now in a new disguise, Edgar gives this letter to Albany, who confronts his wife and Edmund with it after the battle. Edmund declares that he is resolved to fight a duel with anyone who calls him a traitor. Edgar, still in disguise, takes up this challenge and fatally wounds his brother. Seeing Edmund dying, Goneril kills herself, first confessing that she has poisoned her rival Regan.

Edgar identifies himself to his brother and reveals that their father died after learning Edgar's identity. (Unable to withstand the conflicting emotions of joy and grief he experienced at Edgar's revelation, the old duke's heart "burst smilingly.") Dying, Edmund attempts to undo some of the harm he has caused by canceling his order to have Lear and Cordelia hanged, but his effort comes too late. Lear enters with Cordelia, apparently dead, in his arms. After attempting in vain to revive her, he too dies, overcome by grief and exhaustion.

SOURCES. Shakespeare drew his story and characters from the legend of King Lear, which had been told and retold countless times, beginning with Geoffrey of Monmouth's *History of the Kings of Britain*, written around 1135. It had also appeared in a number of sources from Shakespeare's time, including HOLINSHED'S CHRONICLES, Edmund Spenser's *The Faerie Queene*, and John Higgins's addition to *The Mirror for Magistrates*.

THE FOOL WILL STAY

Perhaps the highest tribute to Lear's former greatness is the steadfast devotion with which he is served by the earl of Kent and by his Fool, who enters in Act I but disappears by the end of Act III—perhaps dead from exhaustion and exposure. The Fool's poem in Act II, Scene iv, lines 79–86, expresses the idea of true service:

That sir which serves and
  seeks for gain,
And follows but for form,
Will pack when it begins to
  rain,
And leave thee in the storm,
But I will tarry; the fool will
  stay,
And let the wise man fly:
The knave turns fool that
  runs away;
The Fool no knave, [by God].

King Lear

* *filial* of a son, or more generally, of a child
to a parent

Shakespeare's primary source was probably the anonymously written play *The Chronicle History of King Leir*, published in 1605 but performed a decade earlier. In all these versions, however, the story ends happily with Lear's youngest daughter winning the fight against her two wicked sisters and restoring her aged father to his throne. Shakespeare's decision to alter the ending and make the play a tragedy was no doubt surprising and perhaps even shocking to his audience.

For the Gloucester plot, Shakespeare borrowed from "The Tale of the Blind King of Paphlagonia," as recounted in *Arcadia* by Sir Philip SIDNEY. The story of the blind king and his two sons may have struck the playwright as an interesting parallel to the story of King Lear and his three daughters. By including it, Shakespeare expanded on the theme of filial* devotion and also contrasted the different reactions of the two old men to the schemes of their ungrateful or disloyal offspring. Some of the language used by Edgar in his disguise as Tom o' Bedlam was drawn from Samuel Harsnett's *A Declaration of Egregious Popish Impostures* (1603), which dealt with examples of demonic possession.

COMMENTARY. Samuel Johnson, one of the great 18th-century editors of Shakespeare, confessed that he could not bear to reread the ending of *King Lear*, it so violated his sense of morality and so overwhelmingly tore at his heartstrings. In 1681 Nahum Tate had gone so far as to rewrite the play and restore the happy ending found in Shakespeare's sources. It was this version, or adaptations of it, that held the stage until William Charles Macready restored Shakespeare's version in 1838. Tate's ending would surely be laughable to a modern audience. In an age that has witnessed the horrors of two World Wars, the tragic justice of Shakespeare's original *Lear*—in which the young and innocent suffer along with the guilty—seems all too real.

Poetic justice, which punishes the wicked and rewards the virtuous, is a subtle but unmistakable force in *King Lear*. Gloucester's moral lapse in conceiving the illegitimate Edmund—yielding to the temptation to visit a "dark and vicious place," as Edgar calls it in the final scene—costs him his eyes and eventually leads to the deaths of both Edmund and Gloucester. As Edmund says, "The wheel is come full circle" (V.iii.175). Moral significance may also be found in the sufferings of Lear and Gloucester. Lear responds at first with what some critics have called titanism, a superhuman anger that stands in direct contrast to Gloucester's despair. As the king becomes increasingly battered, however, he also begins to recognize his own faults, and for the first time he shows more concern for others than for himself. Lashed by the wind and rain, Lear insists that the poor shivering Fool take shelter before him. He then prays on behalf of all the "poor naked wretches" for whom he has formerly taken too little care. Similarly, after being blinded Gloucester recognizes not only his own faults but also those of a society that has permitted a large gap to exist between the rich (the "lust-dieted man") and the wretched poor who serve them, symbolized by Tom o' Bedlam.

Part of the play's tremendous power derives from these insights, earned at terrible expense. The lessons the principal characters learn are

A FOOLISH FOND OLD MAN

The plot of *King Lear* may have been influenced in part by the story of Sir Brian Annesley, a gentleman of Queen Elizabeth's court who became insane. His two married daughters sought to have their aged father confined to a madhouse and his wealth turned over to them. But his youngest daughter, Cordell (a variation of Cordelia), pleaded successfully with the royal minister to spare her father. Cordell inherited her father's estate and married William Hervey, the stepfather of Shakespeare's supporter the earl of Southampton. It is likely that Shakespeare heard the story from Southampton's family.

all the more terrible because these men are quite old (Lear is over 80) and should have acquired wisdom long ago. Gloucester, in seeking suicide, must be taught by Edgar that "Men must endure / Their going hence even as their coming hither, / Ripeness is all" (V.ii.9–11). In this play, which is full of ironies and paradoxes*, it is the young who instruct the old. Like Gloucester, the king learns from his dutiful child the meaning and value of love. The image of Lear with the dead Cordelia in his arms, described by some critics as a kind of inverted pietà* (father and daughter rather than mother and son), is deeply moving, as are the king's last words: "Look her lips, / Look there, look there!" (V.iii.311–12). The play begins with Lear demanding that all eyes focus on him, as his daughters proclaim their love for him. It ends with his attention directed to Cordelia, away from himself, even as he himself falls dead.

The play's final scene poses a puzzle to critics. One source of confusion is Lear's remark, "And my poor fool is hang'd!" (V.iii.306). It is not clear whether he refers to Cordelia—calling her *fool*, a common term of endearment in Shakespeare's time—or to the unnamed Fool, who has mysteriously disappeared from the action at the end of Act III. One possibility is that the boy actor who first played the part of Cordelia also performed as the Fool. The doubling of roles was commonplace in Shakespeare's theater, and Cordelia and the Fool never appear together on stage. However, some directors prefer to keep the Fool on stage at the end, as Grigori Kozintsev did in his great Russian film version, letting him play on his pipe as the litter bearers carry off the dead bodies.

Critics have also argued for many years over the play's ambiguous ending. Lear claims after he carries Cordelia onto the stage that she is "dead as earth," yet he tries to revive her. The text leaves open the possibility that he succeeds, or at least believes he does, and some critics maintain that Lear dies happy in the belief that he has succeeded in restoring Cordelia to life. This may be the reason that Shakespeare revised the concluding lines from the quarto version published in 1608—most likely from his original manuscript—to the text that appears in the FIRST FOLIO, published after his death. The First Folio ending assigns to Kent the line "Break, heart, I prithee*, break!" (V.iii.312), which originally was spoken by Lear. This ending is less harsh than that in the quarto, where Lear cries for his heart to break so that he may die with Cordelia. The later text also contains many other revisions that some scholars believe were made by Shakespeare himself or by another member of his acting company, the King's Men, or perhaps by both, working in collaboration.

PERFORMANCE HISTORY. The 19th-century essayist and critic Charles Lamb felt that *King Lear* was too great a play to be staged, because it could be fully rendered only in the theater of the imagination, and some critics today would agree with him. *King Lear* has recently been staged very powerfully, however. More and more often it has been performed with great success on screen as well as in the theater. The ROYAL SHAKESPEARE COMPANY (RSC) in STRATFORD-UPON-AVON staged the play three times between 1982 and 1999, and the National Theatre in London has also produced it several times. An excellent small-scale production in the National's studio

---

* *paradox* apparent contradiction

* *pietà* image of the Virgin Mary holding the lifeless body of Christ

* *prithee* pray you; please

theater, the Cottesloe, starring Ian Holm as Lear (1997), is currently available on videotape.

Earlier films and videotapes include the 1970 Kozintsev film already mentioned and a film directed by Peter Brook, also in 1970, based on the Royal Shakespeare Company's 1962 stage production with Paul Scofield as Lear. These films contrast strikingly. Scofield portrays Lear as a very strong king, whereas Yuri Jarvet in Kozintsev's film interprets Lear as a weak old man, already senile*. Brook heavily cut the text and filmed in Jutland, Denmark, using a barren landscape and primitive sets to suggest the prehistory setting of the play; Kozintsev updated the scenario, using Christian symbols and a Marxist* slant toward pity for the masses of "poor wretches" that fill the central storm scenes. In addition the Japanese film *Ran* (1985), by the celebrated director Akira Kurosawa, is also an adaptation of *King Lear*.

In 1990 three different renderings of the play were produced simultaneously in England. Two of these productions were noteworthy in that they cast a woman in the role of the Fool, a casting choice first used in Macready's 1838 production. In the RSC production directed by Nicholas Hytner, Linda Kerr Scott's performance captured the essence of the Fool's relationship to Lear (played by John Wood), especially his vulnerability. In the Renaissance Theatre's version, directed by Kenneth Branagh with Richard Briers as Lear, Emma Thompson offered a more stylized interpretation of the role. The third production, directed by Deborah Warner at the National Theatre with Brian Cox as Lear, presented David Bradley as an older Fool, Lear's contemporary. The Fool is often portrayed in this manner, despite the fact that Lear sometimes refers to Fool as "boy." The frequency with which *King Lear* is revived today testifies to its enduring appeal and special significance for our time. (*See also* **Acting Companies, Modern; Quartos and Folios; Shakespeare on Screen; Shakespearean Theater: 20th Century; Shakespeare's Works, Adaptations of.**)

* *senile* mentally impaired due to extreme age

* *Marxist* based on the ideas of communist reformer Karl Marx

See *Royalty and Nobility.*

T he King's Men was the acting company to which Shakespeare belonged during most of his career. Originally called the Chamberlain's Men, it was the most respected and financially successful company of its day. Under the patronage* of King JAMES I, the company had a major influence on the development of Jacobean* drama.

The Chamberlain's Men was organized early in 1594 by a group of actors from another troupe, Strange's Men, which disbanded after the death of its patron Henry Stanley, known as Lord Strange. The original partners of the new company included George Bryan, Richard Cowley, John

* *patronage* support or financial sponsorship
* *Jacobean* referring the reign of James I, king of England from 1603 to 1625

See
color plate 12,
vol. 3.

HEMINGES, Will Kempe, Augustin Phillips, and Thomas Pope. Richard Burbage and William Shakespeare joined soon after. They obtained the patronage of Lord Hunsdon, Queen Elizabeth's lord chamberlain, which gave them the right to stage public performances. As some of the organization's partners retired, others took their places. Bryan was replaced by William Sly, for example, and Pope by Henry Condell—who, together with Heminges, compiled the FIRST FOLIO edition of Shakespeare's plays. Burbage was the principal star of the Chamberlain's Men, performing such roles as Hamlet and Othello. Another noteworthy performer was Kempe, who played clowns and other comic roles until he left the company in 1599 and was replaced by Robert Armin.

The Chamberlain's Men performed at James Burbage's playhouse, the Theater, during the summer and at the Cross Keys Inn during the winter until the inn was closed in 1596. For the next three years, the company appeared at the Swan and Curtain playhouses and toured the countryside. It also earned many invitations to perform at court, appearing 32 times before Queen ELIZABETH I. The Chamberlain's Men built its own theater, the GLOBE, in 1599, giving the company a permanent home and greater control over its productions. It specialized in the plays of Shakespeare but also performed the work of many other playwrights, among them Ben JONSON.

In 1603 the company came under the protection of King James I and became known as His Majesty's Servants or the King's Men. It was called to perform at court with increasing frequency. After 1608 the company began to appear in the winter at the BLACKFRIARS, a small indoor theater, while continuing to perform at the Globe in the summer. During this period Shakespeare's plays and those of the company's other playwrights, principally Francis Beaumont and John Fletcher, increasingly reflected the tastes of the wealthier, more educated Blackfriars audience.

The King's Men prospered through the early 1600s, except for periods when plague* halted performances. After the death of James I, King Charles I extended his patronage to the company. Its successful 48-year run ended in 1642, when a Puritan*-controlled Parliament shut down London's theaters completely. (*See also* **Acting Companies, Elizabethan; Actors, Shakespearean; Fools, Clowns, and Jesters; Inn Yards; Playwrights and Poets.**)

* *plague* highly contagious and often fatal disease; also called the Black Death
* *Puritan* English Protestant who advocated strict moral discipline and a simplification of the ceremonies and beliefs of the Anglican Church

KYD, THOMAS

See *Playwrights and Poets.*

LADY MACBETH

See *Macbeth, Lady.*

Lamb, Charles and Mary

LAMB, CHARLES AND MARY

CHARLES
1775–1834
Essayist and literary critic

MARY
1764–1847
Writer

* *pseudonym* false name, especially a pen
name

Charles Lamb was an English essayist and literary critic whose best known works were the essays he published under the pseudonym* Elia and the *Tales from Shakespeare* he wrote with his sister, Mary.

Lamb left school at the age of 15 to become a clerk with the East India Company, the most prominent English trading house of the time. His passion for literature brought him in contact with some of the most celebrated literary figures of the day. His home became a gathering place for Samuel Taylor COLERIDGE, William Wordsworth, and other literary giants.

Lamb's life was touched by personal tragedy. His sister, who had inherited a tendency toward insanity, had killed their mother during a fit of madness. Unwilling to place his sister in an asylum, Lamb remained a bachelor in order to care for her at home. Together they wrote *Tales from Shakespeare,* published in 1807. Intended for children, this popular work features prose synopses of Shakespeare's comedies and tragedies.

The following year Lamb wrote his influential *Specimens of English Dramatic Poets Who Lived About the Time of Shakespeare.* This work played a significant role in reviving interest in Elizabethan drama. In a famous 1811 essay titled "On the Tragedies of Shakespeare," Lamb argued that these works were not well suited for presentation on the stage. He maintained that Shakespeare's poetry was cheapened by an actor's use of "low tricks upon the eye and ear." He also discussed the technical difficulties of staging certain scenes, such as the tumultuous storm scene in *King Lear* (III.ii). In the same essay, however, he championed the use of Shakespeare's original texts instead of the adaptations that were then popular. (*See also* **Shakespeare's Works, Adaptations of; Shakespeare's Works, Changing Views.**)

LANGUAGE

Shakespeare's writing is unique not for its subject matter, but for its use of language. Most of his plays and longer poems are based on well-known sources, and his sonnets draw on popular literary themes of his day, such as passion, ambition, and loss. What sets him apart is the way he uses words to transform these familiar materials. The vivid rhythms, ideas, emotions, and personalities conveyed by his language are what make Shakespeare "Shakespearean."

ELIZABETHAN ENGLISH

Although Shakespeare's language may be the source of his enduring power, it is often difficult for modern readers to understand. Languages change over time, and many words still in use today had different or additional meanings in the 1500s and 1600s. The word *fond,* for example, was a synonym for "foolish" or "infatuated," *nice* meant "finicky," and *sad* described a "sober" or "serious" person. Contractions, now limited in standard English to constructions such as *don't* and *it's,* were far more frequent and varied; *'em* for "them," *wi'* for "with," *ha'* for "have," and *o'* for "of" or "on" were some of the most common. Most importantly, Elizabethan

English was less rigid than modern English. Shakespeare and his fellow writers were remarkably free to make up words as they went along.

THE DEVELOPMENT OF ENGLISH. The English language takes its name from the Angles, one of several Germanic tribes that settled the islands of present-day Great Britain. The Angles were the first of these tribes to set down their dialect in writing, creating the earliest known version of English, called Old English or Anglo-Saxon. After the French invasion of England in 1066, known as the Norman Conquest, the influence of the French and Latin languages produced a blend known as Middle English, the language in which the poet Geoffrey Chaucer wrote his famous *Canterbury Tales.*

Around 1500 the English language went through another significant series of changes. These developments were partly due to increased political stability. In 1485 King Henry VII was crowned, ending a prolonged period of conflict known as the WARS OF THE ROSES. Technology also played a role. Printed books, as opposed to manuscripts copied by hand, became increasingly available in England beginning in the 1480s. Together these developments enabled the language to become more standardized. Literacy also increased: roughly 50 percent of the population could read English by the time Shakespeare was born in 1564.

THE INFLUENCE OF LATIN. For many Elizabethan writers Latin remained the language of choice. In the 1400s and 1500s, leading scholars throughout Europe had promoted the study of classical* texts, and the grammar schools of Elizabethan England (including the one Shakespeare probably attended) continued to stress this curriculum. Three subjects—grammar, logic, and rhetoric*—formed the core of a classical education. Students studied ancient Roman texts, including the speeches of Cicero and the poetry of Ovid and Virgil, translating them from Latin into English and then back into Latin. The study of classical rhetoric fed an appetite for ornate, highly patterned sentences and a keen appreciation for the way words sounded.

The study of Latin influenced English grammar as well. In Latin a word's function in a sentence is indicated by a particular ending, not by its position in the sentence. Present-day English, by comparison, relies heavily on the placement of words. Most clauses and sentences follow the subject-verb-object formula, as in "He opened the door." Elizabethan authors, however, often arranged sentences in ways that reflected the grammatical flexibility of Latin. Reordering words in this way can be an effective rhetorical technique, stressing key ideas and images through their unexpected or unusual placement. For example, the final speech of *Romeo and Juliet* begins: "A glooming peace this morning with it brings" (V.iii.305). This clause, structured object-subject-verb, gives special prominence to the image of "glooming peace" by putting it first instead of last ("The morning brings a glooming peace").

THE ELIZABETHAN STYLE. Several figures in England's literary world influenced the development of Elizabethan English. In the early 1500s,

* *classical* in the tradition of ancient Greece and Rome

* *rhetoric* art of speaking or writing effectively

39

driven partly by a growing sense of national pride, some talented poets (including Sir Thomas Wyatt and Henry Howard, earl of Surrey) began adapting popular European techniques of rhetoric and poetry into English. Queen ELIZABETH I, who came to the throne in 1558, was an accomplished poet and translator who encouraged and inspired an outpouring of prose and verse. London's thriving theatrical scene had already produced important stylists, among them John Lyly and Christopher MARLOWE, by the time Shakespeare began writing. Shakespeare thus inherited a language whose literary potential had been recognized but not thoroughly explored and whose component parts, including vocabulary, were open to experimentation.

SHAKESPEARE'S TECHNIQUES

The pairing of sound and sense is another crucial aspect of Shakespeare's language. In the above example from *Romeo and Juliet*, Shakespeare's choice not only stresses the adjective *glooming* (a variant of *gloomy*), with all its associations of darkness and dreariness, but also creates an effective sound pattern. The long vowel sound of the *oo* in *glooming* enables an actor to speak in a weighty, purposeful tone without artificially slowing down the pace of the lines.

VERSE AND PROSE. Parts of Shakespeare's plays are written in verse; other parts are in prose. The main distinction between the two is not rhyme—much Elizabethan verse was unrhymed—but meter (the patterns of accented and unaccented syllables in each line). A line of verse can be broken down into several metrical units, called feet. In English the most common poetic foot is the iamb, a short (unaccented) syllable followed by a long (accented) one, as in the word *defeat.* Most poetry and theatrical verse in Shakespeare's day was written in iambic pentameter, lines composed of five iambs.

Shakespeare often varies the meter of his lines to create a particular effect, as in this passage from *Henry V* describing the night before a decisive battle: "Now entertain conjecture of a time / When creeping murmur and the poring dark / Fills the wide vessel of the universe" (IV.Prologue.1–3). In the third line, the words *fills* and *wide,* both in normally weak positions in the line, are accented. This metrical irregularity slows the pace of the words, allowing the images of the previous line (*creeping murmur* and *poring dark*) to linger in the listener's ear and increase the tense mood of the passage.

Shakespeare also uses meter as a motor for dialogue between actors. In *King John* the title character persuades his follower, Hubert, to murder a rival in an exchange that begins when the king says, "Death."

> *Hubert.*   My lord?
> *King John.*   A grave.
> *Hubert.*   He shall not live.
> *King John.*   Enough.
>   (III.iii.65–66)

WORDS, WORDS, WORDS

Shakespeare often retold well-known stories in his own words—literally. According to responsible estimates he introduced approximately 1,500 words into the English language, including such common words as *addiction, kissing, skim milk, advertising,* and *luggage.* He created some new words, such as *bedroom,* by joining existing words. He also used verbs as nouns, as in *design,* or nouns as verbs, as in *champion.* Still other Shakespearean inventions, such as *puke,* have no known source. It is worth remembering that many Shakespearean words that sound familiar to modern readers were strange and new to Shakespeare's audiences, who must have enjoyed his adventurous approach to language.

See color plate 4, vol. 1.

These four brief utterances form one line of iambic pentameter. To hold the meter together, both actors must speak without pausing, emphasizing the casual ease with which horrific acts of violence are carried out in this play. Modern actors, however, unfamiliar with the pacing implied by Shakespeare's use of meter, may insert pauses between lines such as these to convey the progress of a character's thoughts. Such pauses alter the sound and impact of the lines.

It is often said that most of Shakespeare's characters speak in verse, with prose reserved for comic characters and those of low social status. In fact characters of all social classes have some prose lines. Humorous passages are often written in prose, from the crude jokes of Falstaff in *Henry IV, Parts 1* and *2,* to the sophisticated wit-play of Rosalind's flirtations in *As You Like It.* Prose is also used to deliver detailed information (Hamlet's instructions to the players), explain a course of action (Brutus's funeral speech in *Julius Caesar*), and express intense emotion (the mad scenes in *King Lear*).

Switching from verse to prose, or vice versa, changes the rhythm and pace of the lines. This difference is often so subtle, however, that listeners may not notice where one ends and the other begins. These organized sound patterns help give distinct, individual voices to Shakespeare's characters. While prose passages lack the metric structure of verse, they nonetheless contain highly developed patterns of sound, often through repeated words or phrases. An example is one of the speeches of Dogberry, the bumbling constable in *Much Ado About Nothing:*

> I am a wise fellow, and which is more, an officer, and which is more, a householder, and which is more, as pretty a piece of flesh as any is in Messina, and one that knows the law, go to, and a rich fellow enough, go to, and a fellow that hath had losses, and one that hath two gowns, and every thing handsome about him.

(IV.ii.80–86)

DRAMATIC EFFECT. Language in Shakespeare's plays—whether in prose or verse, in regular or irregular meter—is designed to be heard rather than read. The plays were written for performance; only later were they published, studied, and analyzed by scholars. In Elizabethan England the spoken word was the primary source of information and entertainment, and people were experts at listening to and remembering language.

Shakespeare wrote most of his plays for theaters that had little or no scenery and no control over lighting. The GLOBE, for example, was built with an open roof, and performances took place early in the afternoon to take advantage of available daylight. Costumes, music, and sounds such as rain and thunder were the only special effects available. Language had to provide the missing information about the setting. The first 20 lines of *Hamlet* reveal that it is midnight, "bitter cold," and at least one character is "sick at heart" with anxiety. These early lines not only *tell* the audience this information but also give the characters a way to *show* their fear and confusion. As the play opens, several guards call out each other's names as they attempt to locate one another. An audience watching the play would have had no trouble seeing all the actors, but the lines establish that the characters they are playing cannot see one another and that the scene is therefore taking place in a dark and dangerous setting.

Shakespeare's language does more, of course, than set a scene or provide a blueprint for stage movement. His use of figurative* language creates a web of associations that help communicate the speaker's circumstances and emotions. For example, in Sonnet 73, the first stanza works with a basic idea: that old age is like the bleak season of late autumn. The poet builds on this idea when he describes the leafless branches as "bare ruined choirs, where late the sweet birds sang." Shakespeare compares soaring trees with cathedral architecture and, by association, chirping birds with choral music. The resulting cluster of images conveys the poet's physical and emotional state by contrasting the pleasures of midsummer with the stark, silent emptiness of approaching winter.

Shakespeare also generates new levels of meaning through wordplay. Straightforward puns do some of this work. In *Twelfth Night* when Curio asks the lovesick Orsino if he will hunt the *hart* (deer), the duke's answer hinges on the identical sound of *heart,* the symbol of love. The use of words with multiple meanings can also create more complex associations between a specific moment and a larger theme. For example, when Hamlet first considers the idea of suicide, he rejects it because God has "fixed his canon 'gainst self-slaughter" (I.ii.131–32). The obvious meaning of the word *canon* in this context is a law concerning religious beliefs, and fixing a canon, in that sense, would mean making and enforcing a particular law. The word *canon,* however, sounds the same as *cannon,* a weapon of destruction. To fix this type of cannon means to point it in a particular direction. Thus Hamlet's reference to a law against suicide ironically creates the image of a gun taking aim. This bit of wordplay may register with a listener for only the briefest of moments if at all, but it is nonetheless appropriate for a character torn between incompatible desires who ends the play by becoming both murderer and murdered in the space of a few lines.

OVERALL EFFECT

These various aspects of Shakespeare's language are seldom encountered in isolation. Shakespeare's real achievement is his consistent ability to combine all the elements of his verbal artistry and make them work together to create a particular effect. The final scene of *Othello,* for example, opens with a soliloquy*, as the title character debates whether to murder his sleeping wife, Desdemona:

> Put out the light, and then put out the light:
> If I quench thee, thou flaming minister,
> I can again thy former light restore,
> Should I repent me; but once put out thy light,
> Thou cunning'st pattern of excelling nature,
> I know not where is that Promethean heat
> That can thy light relume.
>
> (V.ii.7–13)

* *figurative* characterized by metaphors, similes, and other figures of speech

* *soliloquy* monologue in which a character reveals his or her private thoughts

The language in these lines generates complex patterns of images, most of them centering around light and darkness and, by association, good and bad, white and black. These patterns help develop the racial and sexual themes that run through the play. To achieve their full effect, however, the lines must be reinforced by a theatrical embodiment of these images—a black man carrying a lighted torch or candle.

The passage uses the word *light* frequently: five times in seven lines. This repetition is not awkward, however, or even especially noticeable, because of inverted word order. If written in the normal subject-verb-object sequence, four of these lines would end with *light*. Instead, the verbs *restore* and *relume* (a Shakespearean invention meaning "relight") are in stressed positions. These lines also contain two complex, thematically appropriate metaphors for light: "flaming minister" and "Promethean heat." In Shakespeare's day a minister might be an agent or servant of another (like the flame that serves Othello's need to see his victim), a functionary in a court of law (Othello kills Desdemona out of a need for justice), or a clergyman (he wants to think of her murder as a sacrifice). The word *minister* is also part of a chain of religious imagery, connected most obviously to *repent* and to the idea of light as a metaphor for the human soul.

The phrase "Promethean heat" is also another spiritual reference. Prometheus, according to Greek mythology, stole fire from the gods and gave it to humankind. In one version of the story, the gods punished Prometheus by chaining him to a rock while an eagle ate his liver. Thus, the phrase "Promethean heat" can suggest a divine spark of life on the one hand and, on the other, images of trickery, guilt, and agonizing revenge, all of which are appropriate to Othello's view of his wife's situation. In another version of the Promethean myth, the king of the gods also punished mankind for accepting Prometheus's aid—by creating women. Othello's sexual jealousy is perfectly aligned with this kind of sexist fantasy, which is reinforced by his use of the word *cunning*. This word—which could mean intelligent, skillfully made, or deceitful—was also a pun on a crude word for female genitals.

It is impossible to say how much Shakespeare expected his actors or his audiences to understand of the rich web of meanings spun by his choice of words. It is also unclear whether Shakespeare himself was fully aware of all these meanings. It is clear, however, that Shakespeare's complex, energetic, and inventive language was meant to please and not to intimidate. In an age fascinated by words, Shakespeare was uniquely capable of using language to represent human experience. (*See also* **Imagery; Playwrights and Poets; Poetic Techniques; Prose Technique.**)

LAW

The English legal system in Shakespeare's time was a complex tangle of imprecise laws and procedures that had developed over several centuries. Yet most members of society, from lords to peasants, had some familiarity and experience with the system. Legal activity boomed during the growing prosperity of the late 1500s and early 1600s, and its

part in everyday life is reflected in the many legal terms, references, and jokes that appear in Shakespeare's plays and poems.

HEART OF THE LEGAL SYSTEM. The central royal courts at Westminster Hall in London formed the core of England's legal system. These were complemented by an array of courts run by the military, the church, individual estates, and other authorities, along with a network of local courts.

All the central courts had been established by different branches of the government for varying purposes. By Shakespeare's time each court had developed its own procedures and preferences, frequently conflicting or overlapping with those of the others. The Court of Common Pleas had been set up to handle the majority of ordinary cases. The Court of King's Bench was supposedly an audience before the king or queen on matters directly affecting the crown, but in fact it functioned as a second court of common pleas. These two benches were the busiest, hearing tens of thousands of lawsuits each year. The High Court of Chancery was originally established to deal with extraordinary cases that could not be addressed by the other courts. By the mid-1500s, however, it had become a regular court with its own procedures and principles—though indeed it heard fewer suits. The most elite of the central courts, the Star Chamber, was made up of high government officials. It heard a small number of cases on offenses that interfered with the justice system itself, such as perjury and forgery.

For centuries English society had accepted that the monarch held authority over the courts. In 1616 Sir Edward Coke, chief justice of the King's Bench, was removed from the bench for questioning this assumption, claiming that the king was subject to the law. However, the principles he developed—equality before the law and protection from unlawful government actions—became two of the cornerstones of modern democracy.

THE LEGAL PROFESSION. The highest legal official in England was the lord chancellor, keeper of the great seal of England. Below him were the judges of the Chancery and the other central courts, followed by a select group of high-ranking judges and lawyers known as serjeants-at-law. A case was typically heard by more than one judge. A scene in *King Lear*, in which the mad king calls his three followers to sit as judges in a mock trial of his two ungrateful daughters, reflects this practice. (The fact that two of these followers are his Fool and a nobleman disguised as a mad beggar may be a veiled attack on the abilities of Elizabethan judges.)

The common lawyers who presented counsel at court were known as barristers. Beneath them were attorneys, who managed lawsuits and advised plaintiffs, or those bringing lawsuits, and defendants. Lowly solicitors, who had no formal legal education, helped clients steer suits through the courts, hiring attorneys and barristers if necessary. In addition hundreds of clerks and other officials managed and recorded legal proceedings. Law enforcement was carried out by various constables, church officials, and local sheriffs, but no standing police force existed.

Law schools were vital parts of the profession and of London society. The 12 Inns of Chancery were lower institutions that trained and housed attorneys and court officials. The more distinguished and selective Inns of

Court numbered four: the Inner Temple, the Middle Temple, Lincoln's Inn, and Gray's Inn. Many young gentlemen enrolled at Inns of Court to gain necessary knowledge of the law, but few went on to practice it. Their classes included such arts as music and dancing, and their holiday parties were famously wild. These revels often featured dramatic entertainment, including Shakespeare's *Comedy of Errors* and *Twelfth Night.* Scholars believe that Shakespeare included several legal references in *Twelfth Night* to amuse his audience of law students. For example, in one scene the cowardly knight Sir Andrew Aguecheek writes a letter challenging a rival to a duel, but he is careful to word it in such a way that he will not be legally to blame for attacking the other man.

CIVIL LAW. Common law, as practiced in the Court of Common Pleas, the Court of King's Bench, and the local courts, required the defendant to be present for all trials except those involving loss of land. The defendant could be summoned by a writ, an order issued by a court to a law enforcement officer. A defendant could be arrested for ignoring a series of writs, but this process could take up to two years in the Court of Common Pleas. The King's Bench invented several tricks to speed the process, such as falsely charging defendants with an offense for which they could be arrested immediately. Once a defendant appeared in court, the false charge would be dropped and the true one presented. Defendants who were not located could be declared outlaws, but this status was no great handicap. Queen ELIZABETH I is said to have complained at one time about the number of outlaws serving in Parliament.

Once in court the plaintiff and defendant exchanged declarations called pleadings until the court could determine the nature of the disagreement between them. If it was a question of law, the judges gave a ruling. More often the two parties disagreed as to the facts of the case, and a jury of 12 men was called to settle the dispute. Trials typically lasted less than an hour, with few witnesses and little questioning by lawyers. The jury's verdict could not be appealed, although legal maneuvering could delay a judgment.

The High Court of Chancery placed its own body of rules, known as equity, above common law. The principle of equity stated that the laws could not cover every situation, and so the court had the right to make exceptions to the enforcement of the laws in special circumstances. The examination of the facts in a case was therefore more detailed than in a common-law case. The court collected evidence in writing, including statements from witnesses. The Star Chamber had similar procedures, but it had additional powers to issue fines and physical penalties.

Lawsuits relating to debts dominated the courts of common law, accounting for two-thirds of their cases after 1600. If a court judged that a debt was owed, it could issue a writ seizing the debtor's goods or land. If the debtor lacked enough property to raise the required sum, the court could arrest him in an attempt to persuade a third party (such as a friend or family member) to assume his debt. Special legal arrangements were developed during this period to protect tradesmen from being arrested for debt, laying the foundations for modern bankruptcy laws.

A NATIONAL PASTIME

By the early 1600s some observers felt that the English had made a national pastime of suing each other in court. Business boomed for lawyers, making them an easy target for resentful citizens. In Shakespeare's *Henry VI, Part 2*, a character exclaims, "The first thing we do, let's kill all the lawyers" (IV.ii.76–77). Yet one commentator chose to blame the people who hired the lawyers, writing that when the nation "begins to flourish, and to grow rich and mighty: the people grow proud withall."

The most complex laws were those relating to land. According to the outdated customs of the Middle Ages, land could be entailed, restricting possession to the owner's heirs. In Shakespeare's time it was possible to *bar entail* by bringing a fictional lawsuit against the owner of the land, allowing the property to be transferred to others. Another Elizabethan change to feudal* land laws was the status of farmers who held their lands in copyhold, meaning that they were tenants of the lord who owned the land. The protection of common law was extended to copyholders, allowing them to pass their lands down to their heirs.

* **feudal** referring to the medieval system of government and landowning based on rank and loyalty

CRIMINAL LAW. Most Elizabethans believed that crime rates were rising, like the increase in lawsuits, because of the nation's increasing wealth. The most serious crimes were treason, murder, and felonies such as rape, arson, manslaughter, theft, and buggery (unlawful sex acts). Most felonies were tried by six regional courts called assizes, whose semiannual sessions were headed by pairs of officials from the central courts. Felony accusations were reviewed by a grand jury. If a charge was reasonable, it would then be heard by a petty jury of 12 men. All felonies required a death sentence, but prisoners could avoid this fate if they were granted a pardon by the crown. Pardons were generally given to prisoners who had killed someone by accident or in self-defense. They might also be granted to those who begged for mercy or who were favored by the monarch, and in some cases a pardon could actually be bought.

A wide variety of other courts tried the lesser crimes known as misdemeanors. Their methods of trial varied: sometimes a jury heard the case, sometimes a judge alone heard it, and in some cases conviction was automatic. Typical punishments for misdemeanors were fines or whippings; criminals were rarely jailed because of the expense. Church courts dealt mostly with sexual misconduct and such offenses as drunkenness, golfing on Sunday, or failure to attend church. Sentences involved penance* or, in extreme cases, excommunication*. (*See also* **Agriculture; Crime and Punishment.**)

* **penance** act performed to show sorrow or repentance for sin
* **excommunication** formal exclusion from the church and its rituals

LEAR, KING

See *King Lear.*

LETTER WRITING

In Elizabethan England, letter writing was a common method of keeping in touch with friends and relatives, conducting business, and issuing official government orders. This means of communication was available to only part of the population, however, because it required that both the sender and the receiver be literate, or at least know a person willing to read or write on their behalf. At most only about half of England's population was literate during Shakespeare's lifetime.

LETTER WRITING STYLE. Letter writers often used a highly decorative style meant to convey their humility and social grace. The salutation, or greeting, that began the letter did not have a standard form, such as the "Dear . . ." that begins most modern letters written in English. Instead, Elizabethans developed a variety of phrases, such as "To a very noble mother," "My humble duty remembered," and "After my very hearty commendations." Closing lines, like salutations, were often long and formal: "And so humbly craving your ladyship's daily blessing to us both, we most humbly take our leave," "Your honour's most dutiful bound obedient servant," and "Thus I commit you to God's good protection."

The main texts of letters outdid the rest. The message was often to be found only within a maze of introductions, qualifications, and repetitions. Commas were plentiful. Typical messages included invitations, questions, reminders, purchase orders, and official commands.

DELIVERY OF LETTERS. Letters were sent over various distances. Large cities bustled with messengers carrying notes among the houses, shops, and neighborhoods. Other letters might be destined for nearby towns or the countryside many miles away.

In the 1500s King Henry VIII developed a postal system that served the royal government by delivering his official dispatches. Messengers, called postboys, were employed to carry official correspondences between resting places called stages, where the letters would be handed off to other postboys who continued the journey.

The postal system also accommodated the needs of private citizens. If a messenger's letter pouch had enough room, he could carry private correspondence as well as royal communications. The fees for these services helped the postal system run efficiently and make a profit. (*See also* **Education and Literacy; Language.**)

LIFE OF SHAKESPEARE

See *Shakespeare, Life and Career.*

LITERATURE AND DRAMA

English literature and drama reached new heights of creativity and originality during Shakespeare's lifetime. The playwright himself made some of the most extraordinary and lasting contributions to the artistic flurry known as the Renaissance, a period when the arts and sciences flourished in Europe.

ENGLAND'S REBIRTH

Elizabeth's ascension to the throne in 1558 followed many tense and unstable years that began with England's break from the Catholic Church in the 1530s. Inheriting a kingdom weakened by foreign and domestic

wars, the queen worked hard to rebuild her country's pride and international standing. The English developed more contacts with other European nations and as a result enjoyed increased trade and exposure to new ideas.

During Elizabeth's reign a growing class of wealthy patrons supported the arts, including literature and drama. English writers made bold advances in poetry, drama, and prose. The language expanded as writers borrowed and adapted new words from other tongues. Printed works sold briskly to England's literate citizens, whose numbers had greatly increased. Elizabethans' bookshelves held many religious texts, but they also contained poems, plays, fictional works, histories, translations of ancient Greek and Roman works, pamphlets on the issues of the day, and even popular songs and riddles.

POETRY

Rhymed verse was found everywhere in Elizabethan England, especially in the popular art of song. It was particularly important in upper-class society. Though some poems were printed in books, many circulated only as handwritten copies among the social and literary elite. Most of the day's prominent poets dedicated their works to aristocratic patrons*.

* *patron* supporter or financial sponsor of an artist or writer

POPULAR POETRY. The English had a long and proud history of folk songs, many of which were ballads—songs that narrate a story. Ballads were commonly arranged as rhyming quatrains, or stanzas of four lines, and were intended to be sung, often accompanied by music. Minstrels performed popular songs in the streets, markets, and town fairs. Audiences could purchase the words on printed sheets known as broadsides. Love, desire, patriotism, crime, and retribution were among the typical themes of ballads, which featured titles such as "The Lamentation of a Damned Soul" and "God Send Me a Wife That Will Do as I Say." Song collections included *The Court of Venus,* whose lusty contents earned the clergy's disapproval.

INSPIRED BY THE ANCIENTS. For well-educated Elizabethans, the Renaissance brought the discovery of ancient Greek and Roman literature. Elizabethan poets tried to emulate their classical predecessors because they were believed to have come from the greatest civilizations the world had known. English readers also admired later poets from continental Europe, where the Renaissance had begun earlier than in England.

England was already experiencing the impact of the Renaissance during the reign of Henry VIII (1509–1547). The king was learned in the arts, and his court supported such men as Sir Thomas Wyatt and Henry Howard, the earl of Surrey. Wyatt translated the *Canzoniere,* or *Songbook,* written by Petrarch, an Italian Renaissance poet who wrote in the 1300s. Many of these lyric poems* were 14-line sonnets, and Wyatt's translations inspired English poets to adopt the sonnet as their preferred form. At about the same time, the earl of Surrey translated a section of the *Aeneid,* an epic poem about the origins of Rome that Vergil had written around

* *lyric poetry* verse that expresses feelings and thoughts rather than telling a story

* *iambic pentameter* line of poetry consisting of ten syllables, or five metric feet, with emphasis placed on every other syllable

* *classical* in the tradition of ancient Greece and Rome
* *genre* literary form

See color plate 9, vol. 3.

* *morality play* religious dramatic work that teaches a moral lesson through the use of symbolic characters

* *medieval* referring to the Middle Ages, a period roughly between A.D. 500 and 1500

* *secular* nonreligious; connected with everyday life

20 B.C. Surrey's translation was the first English-language work to use blank verse, poetry written in unrhymed iambic pentameter*.

ELIZABETHAN POETS. Writers such as Shakespeare and Sir Philip Sidney demonstrated that sonnets could be used to compose works of extraordinary power and beauty. Shakespeare's *Sonnets* and Sidney's *Astrophel and Stella* are among the finest works of the era. Elizabethan poets also composed epics that championed England. Edmund Spenser's *The Faerie Queene* is both an extended discussion of moral virtues and a tribute to the English nation under Queen Elizabeth I.

Elizabethan poets imitated various classical* genres*. Several writers were inspired by pastorals, works that contrasted the innocence of rural life with the corruption of city life. Among the most successful Elizabethan pastorals in verse was Spenser's *The Shepheardes Calender.*

Satire was another genre that Elizabethan playwrights borrowed from ancient Greece and Rome. The Roman satirists Horace and Juvenal used either gentle wit or scathing mockery to expose the vices and follies of the Roman people. The first true English satire was *The Steele Glass,* produced by the Elizabethan poet George Gascoigne. He was soon joined by Ben Jonson and other social critics.

DRAMA

While excelling in poetry, Christopher Marlowe, Ben Jonson, and William Shakespeare all produced their greatest works in the extended form of verse drama written for the stage. Interest in drama boomed during Elizabeth's reign, and companies were in demand at crowded city theaters, rowdy university auditoriums, the great halls of manor homes, and INN YARDS.

Elizabethan dramatists broke away from classical models, abandoning formal restrictions and conventions. They complicated their plays by including rapid shifts of time and place and multiple plots and subplots. At the same time, they absorbed many other forms—both old and new—into their dramas, including medieval morality plays*, popular songs, prose works of legend and history, and the courtly entertainments known as MASQUES and INTERLUDES.

ROOTS OF ELIZABETHAN DRAMA. Before the Renaissance, English dramas, like most art forms, were dominated by religious themes. English medieval* theater featured a few key genres. Mystery plays dramatized scenes depicted in the Bible, in particular the birth, life, death, and resurrection of Jesus Christ. Miracle plays recounted the lives of saints and the miracles they had performed. Morality plays typically focused on a character who represented humankind in a journey from temptation to sin, repentance, and salvation. Although mystery and miracle plays lost favor in the mid-1500s during the Protestant Reformation, morality plays exerted a powerful influence over Elizabethan drama.

The Italian Renaissance introduced a new spirit of humanism that emphasized secular* life and individual achievements. Actors performing

END OF AN ERA

English literature, which had flourished under Elizabeth, began a downward trend midway through the reign of James I. The triumphant confidence of late 16th-century England faltered under James as political and religious dissatisfaction increased. Jacobean literature featured the hybrid form known as tragicomedy and tended toward bitter humor, complicated intrigues, and dark violence. These dramatic trends were condemned by Puritans, who came to power in 1642 and closed down the theaters of London.

in academies and aristocratic courts began staging Latin plays by such Roman authors as Plautus and Seneca. Soon the players had new material produced in Italian and based on the classical modes known as learned comedies. Torquato Tasso's pastoral play *Aminta*, for example, exerted great influence in Italy and abroad.

After 1550 the Italians also developed a new type of drama called commedia dell'arte, which was based on a small set of stock characters: types such as boastful soldiers, young lovers, clowns, and servants. These characters also appear throughout Elizabethan comedies. The commedia dell'arte engaged in slapstick and other kinds of broad humor, and it drew in part on the earthy language and behavior of common people. A related folk tradition asserted itself on English stages in the 1500s with rough and rowdy farces such as the anonymous *Gammer Gurton's Needle*.

NEW PLAYWRIGHTS, NEW PLAYS. As English theater troupes began to depart from the medieval forms and present fresher, more varied entertainments, opportunities arose for a new generation of playwrights to emerge in the 1570s and 1580s. Among the new dramatists was a group of well-educated worldly young Englishmen who became known as the University Wits. To the coarse comedies that preceded them, they added sophisticated themes, eloquent language, and plenty of clever humor. Their familiarity with classical literature enhanced their skills, but they also created a new array of characters, including thieves, rogues, and other figures from English street life. This informal group included Robert Greene, Thomas Lodge, Thomas Nash, and George Peele.

The University Wits led the way with their new comedies, and Greene in particular had success with romantic comedy. In this genre he was joined and contrasted by the fashionable playwright John Lyly, who defended the refined, courtly traditions of elegant comedy. Lyly often took classical myths and legends for his subjects. His successful plays and ornamental style were the accepted standard when the young Shakespeare wrote his own first romantic comedies, *The Two Gentlemen of Verona* and *The Taming of the Shrew*. Lyly's popularity faded in the 1590s, however, and Shakespeare included parodies of him in his later works.

In the genre of historical drama, playwrights sometimes found material outside classical Roman history. Marlowe set an impressive early example around 1590 with his two-part drama *Tamburlaine the Great*, based on the life of the Mongol conqueror Timur. English history took its place alongside accounts of Rome's past with such works as Shakespeare's three-part *Henry VI*.

Tragedy had a long and revered tradition among ancient Greek and Roman writers and, eventually, among Elizabethans. The first English tragedy in blank verse, *Gorboduc*, appeared in 1561. Thomas Kyd achieved immense success in the late 1580s with *The Spanish Tragedy*, in which bloody revenge was accompanied by powerful rhetoric inspired by the Roman playwright Seneca. Marlowe's *Doctor Faustus*, in which a man sells his soul to the devil in exchange for unlimited knowledge, comments on the brash and exaggerated ambitions of some Elizabethans. Shakespeare's early contributions to tragedy were *Titus Andronicus* and *Romeo and Juliet*.

THE GREATEST HITS. English dramatists produced some of the greatest masterpieces in the English language between the 1590s and the early years of King James's reign (1603–1625). In comedy Ben Jonson based good-natured satire on the traditional notion that people's personalities were determined by imbalances in the four bodily fluids called humours. *Every Man in His Humour* debuted in 1598, but Jonson's greatest comedy was *Volpone*, which he completed around 1606. Shakespeare's popular wit was on display throughout the period in such masterpieces as *Love's Labor's Lost, Much Ado About Nothing,* and *All's Well That Ends Well.*

Historical drama flourished in Marlowe's *Edward II* and in Shakespeare's two-part *Henry IV,* along with his *Henry V* and *Henry VIII.* In the great histories, events from England's past were recast in new versions with questionable historical accuracy but undeniable dramatic appeal. Playwrights often emphasized themes that related to current issues in English politics, so that many of the history plays had as much to say about the present as about the past. They offered serious consideration of such topics as morality, leadership, kingship, duty, and nationhood.

Perhaps because of their somber subjects and severe conclusions, tragedies are considered by many to be the masterpieces of Elizabethan and Jacobean* literature. The tragedies usually focus on a main character whose greatness, or potential greatness, is undermined by a personal flaw such as pride or jealousy. Marlowe, Jonson, and Cyril Tourneur, who wrote *The Revenger's Tragedy,* all produced impressive tragedies, but none reached the summits Shakespeare achieved in *Hamlet, Othello, King Lear,* and *Macbeth,* plays that placed his reputation above those of all his contemporaries.

PROSE

Although dramas often included some passages in prose, most prose literature was found elsewhere. Prose works covered a range of topics and purposes as varied as those of their writers. Fictional works included romances, fables, and early forms of the novel. Pamphlets and essays addressed issues that ranged from religion to literature to politics. Writers also produced extended texts on spiritual and philosophical subjects, as well as descriptive and expository works of history, geography, biography, and science.

FICTION BEST-SELLERS. Prose fiction developed from the medieval romance, a tale written in a romance language, such as Italian, French, or Spanish. Typical subjects of romances included honor, love, magic, battle, and adventure, themes that writers continued to pursue during the Elizabethan period. Versions of the legends of King Arthur and Robin Hood were highly popular with Elizabethan readers, as were collections of tales such as *Palace of Pleasure* and the *Gesta Romanorum.*

Translations of prose romances from the continental* Renaissance also sold well. English originals included the first prose comedy in English, George Gascoigne's *Jocasta,* and the prose pastoral romances

* ***Jacobean*** referring to the reign of James I, king of England from 1603 to 1625

* ***continental*** referring to the European continent

51

Arcadia, by Sir Philip Sidney, and *Rosalynde,* by Thomas Lodge. Other novelists included John Lyly and Thomas Nash, who wrote *The Unfortunate Traveller.* Readers could also find lighter prose compositions, such as the jokes collected in *The Hundred Merry Tales* and the word puzzles in *The Book of Riddles.*

OPINIONS AND CONTROVERSY. Access to printing presses made possible not only books but innumerable short texts in pamphlet form, often without bound covers. Their authors, known as pamphleteers, developed witty and combative styles of argument in which they debated the issues of the day. The University Wits—Lodge, Nash, Peele, and Robert Greene—were known for their pamphlets on political, social, and literary matters. Among the most vocal pamphleteers were groups of Catholics and Puritans who used hidden, illegal presses to publish their competing religious views.

The pamphlets were a step in the development of more reflective essays. Sidney's *An Apologie for Poetrie,* also known as *The Defence of Poesie,* was the first essay of literary criticism in English. George Gascoigne and Thomas Campion also produced early essays about the forms and values of literature. Ben Jonson was among the most prolific writers of opinionated criticism, but the period's weightiest essays came from the scholar Sir Francis Bacon, who collected and published his influential *Essays, Civil and Moral.*

PHILOSOPHY AND RELIGION. Extensive treatments of philosophy and religion were among the era's most impressive intellectual achievements. Bacon produced the ambitious *New Organon,* a work about logic that sought to replace the classical Greek *Organon* of Aristotle. Thomas More's *Utopia* criticized contemporary Europe and described a fictional ideal society. Clergyman Richard Hooker composed an eight-volume discussion of the theology of the Church of England that was noted for its clear style and evenhanded judgment. Other religious works of the era included the King James translation of the Bible and the writings of Martin Luther, who began the Protestant Reformation.

HISTORY AND SCHOLARSHIP. An important and revered work of religious history was John Foxe's *Acts and Monuments,* popularly referred to as his *Book of Martyrs,* which memorialized the Protestants who suffered and died during the Reformation. Other histories included Raphael Holinshed's *Chronicles,* a key source for Shakespeare's plays, and Richard Hakluyt's travel books, which summarized the geographical knowledge of the time. Other authors produced valuable contemporary accounts, such as William Harrison's *The Description of England,* which explored England's social class structure, and John Stow's *Survey of London.* Francis Bacon undertook to describe and classify the sciences, and other works of natural science included John Maplet's *A Green Forest, or A Natural History.* (*See also* **Acting Companies, Elizabethan; Acting Profession; Dramatic Techniques; Playwrights and Poets; Poetic Technique; Printing and Publishing; Prose Technique; Shakespeare's Sources.**)

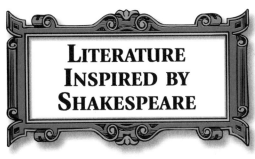

LITERATURE INSPIRED BY SHAKESPEARE

* *canon* authentic works of a writer

* *soliloquy* monologue in which a character reveals his or her private thoughts

* *Romantic* referring to a school of thought, prominent in the 1800s, that emphasized the importance of emotion in art

* *Victorian* referring to the reign of Victoria, queen of England from 1837 to 1901

If, as the old saying goes, imitation is the sincerest form of flattery, then probably no writer has ever been more abundantly flattered than William Shakespeare. No other author appears to have had more influence on those who succeeded him. Over the last four centuries, writers throughout the world have embraced Shakespeare as a source of inspiration. Themes, characters, and even entire plots have been drawn from the Shakespearean canon* to create new works of poetry, drama, and fiction.

POETS AND SHAKESPEARE. One of the first great writers to recognize a debt to Shakespeare was the English poet John Milton, whose earliest published work (in the 1632 Second Folio edition of Shakespeare's works) was a poem in praise of the playwright's skill. Milton's later masterpiece *Paradise Lost* has strong parallels with Shakespeare's *Othello*. In Milton's epic Satan's rebellion against God and his plan to destroy Adam and Eve recall the villainous IAGO's plot against Othello, his superior officer. Satan's later speech of remorse for his deeds, at the beginning of Book IV of *Paradise Lost,* echoes a soliloquy* by Claudius, the king who has murdered his brother, in *Hamlet* (III.iii.36–71).

The Romantic* poets of the 1800s took Shakespeare as their model. English poet John Keats believed that Shakespeare's spirit watched over him and guided his own creativity. He carried a well-worn copy of the playwright's works, in which he made extensive notations. Based on evidence in his poem "Endymion," scholars have suggested that Keats owed much to *A Midsummer Night's Dream* and *The Tempest*. He also wrote a sonnet inspired by *King Lear.*

NOVELISTS AND SHAKESPEARE. Many novelists have used Shakespearean references to illustrate the personalities of their own characters. For example, in *Tom Jones* author Henry Fielding shows how unsophisticated his character Partridge is through his reaction to a performance of *Hamlet* in which the great actor David Garrick plays the title role. He is surprised that so many people find Garrick an exceptional actor:

> Why I could act as well as he myself. I am sure if I had seen a Ghost I should have looked in the very same manner, and done just as he did. And then to be sure, in that Scene, as you call it, between him and his Mother, where you told me he acted so fine, why lord help me, any Man, that is any good Man, that had such a Mother, would have done exactly the same. I know you are only joking with me.

Partridge considers the actor playing the king far superior, because he "speaks all his words distinctly, half as loud again as the other. [Anybody] may see he is an Actor." Fielding indirectly pays tribute to the authenticity of Garrick's performance by having the foolish Partridge disapprove of it.

Victorian* novelist Charles Dickens, in *Great Expectations,* also features a scene set at a performance of *Hamlet.* The narrator, Pip, observes:

Literature Inspired by Shakespeare

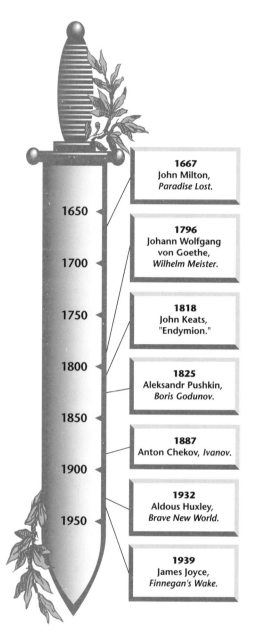

1650

1700

1750

1800

1850

1900

1950

1667
John Milton,
Paradise Lost.

1796
Johann Wolfgang
von Goethe,
Wilhelm Meister.

1818
John Keats,
"Endymion."

1825
Aleksandr Pushkin,
Boris Godunov.

1887
Anton Chekov, *Ivanov.*

1932
Aldous Huxley,
Brave New World.

1939
James Joyce,
Finnegan's Wake.

Whenever that undecided Prince had to ask a question or state a doubt, the public helped him out with it. As for example; on the question whether 'twas nobler in the mind to suffer, some roared yes, and some no, and some inclining to both opinions said "toss up for it"; and quite a Debating Society arose.

This passage not only reveals the rudeness of the London citizens attending the play, but also contrasts them with Pip, who finds their behavior strange.

Johann Wolfgang von Goethe, a German author of the Romantic period, used *Hamlet* to characterize the hero of his novel *Wilhelm Meister.* When Wilhelm takes the part of the prince in a performance of the play with his friends, he attempts to "become one person with my hero," assuming Hamlet's "load of deep melancholy" and entering his "strange labyrinth of so many moods and peculiarities." He works his way through the play, explaining the various scenes to his fellow actors, and concludes with what is now a famous metaphor for Hamlet's situation: "Here is an oak tree planted in a costly vase which should only have borne pleasing flowers in its bosom, but the roots expand and the vase is shattered."

In the United States, Shakespeare's influence may be seen in the works of major 19th-century poets (such as Walt Whitman, Ralph Waldo Emerson, and Emily Dickinson) and fiction writers (such as Washington Irving, Nathaniel Hawthorne, and Herman Melville). At the age of 29, Melville lamented over what a "dolt and ass" he had been not to have become familiar with Shakespeare's works sooner. He declared, "I fancy that this moment Shakespeare in heaven ranks with [the angels] Gabriel, Raphael and Michael. And if another Messiah ever comes 'twill be in Shakespeare's Person." At the same time, Melville was confident that the United States would someday produce a writer of comparable genius: "Believe me, my friends, that men not very much inferior to Shakespeare, are this day being born on the banks of the Ohio." Melville later made Shakespeare's King Lear the model for the vengefully obsessed Captain Ahab in his novel *Moby-Dick.*

SHAKESPEARE IN RUSSIA. Shakespeare has earned a special place in Russian literature. Russian writers have more often incorporated Shakespeare into their poems, plays, and novels than authors in any other country. In 1825 Aleksandr Pushkin, who is as highly honored among Russian writers as Shakespeare is among English ones, presented his historical tragedy *Boris Godunov,* "arranged . . . according to the system of our Father Shakespeare." Several of the scenes are based on extracts from Shakespeare's plays.

In 1849 Ivan Turgenev wrote a short story called "The Hamlet of Shchigri District," in which the Hamlet figure is not a prince but a petty, self-centered man doomed to failure. Turgenev wrote, "Hamlets discover nothing, invent nothing, and leave nothing behind them except their own personalities." He elaborated on this idea in an 1860 lecture titled

* *protagonist* central character in a literary
work

"Hamlet and Don Quixote—the Two Eternal Human Types." A similar sentiment is expressed in Anton Chekhov's play *Ivanov* (1887), when the protagonist* describes himself as "a Hamlet, a superfluous man!" The character of Hamlet had come to be seen as a symbol of the ineffectiveness of Russian government and society—a kind of paralyzing disease that was called Hamletism. In Turgenev's novel *Virgin Soil* the hero exclaims, "O Hamlet, Hamlet, Prince of Denmark, how can one escape from the shadow of your spirit?"

Fyodor Dostoevsky, author of the great Russian novels *Crime and Punishment* and *The Brothers Karamazov,* also used Hamlet as a symbol. He included Othello and Falstaff in his novels as well, seeing these three characters as representing three reactions to the chaos of life. Hamlet embodied the tragic nature of life, Othello its innocence and purity, and Falstaff its vileness—"the slimy breed" who feed on others. Dostoevsky described Shakespeare as "a prophet sent by God to reveal to us the mystery of man, of the human soul." The playwright's influence on Russian writers continued well into the 1900s. Boris Pasternak, the author of *Doctor Zhivago,* translated several of Shakespeare's plays and claimed that "no man has attained such accuracy in his knowledge about man" as Shakespeare.

SHAKESPEARE IN THE MODERN ERA. In 1901 Volney Streamer, an admirer of Shakespeare, published with his friends a small volume called *Book Titles from Shakespeare.* In it he listed 132 books whose titles came from Shakespeare. In a second edition (published in 1911), he had found 400 books with Shakespearean titles. Today a computer search would turn up thousands, among them William Faulkner's *The Sound and the Fury,* Anthony Burgess's *Nothing Like the Sun,* and countless mystery novels with either a Shakespearean title or plot drawn from the poet's life and work.

Most of the 20th-century works influenced by Shakespeare can be thought of as "spin-offs." Writers have taken his plays as starting points for creating their own works. In T. S. Eliot's poem "The Love Song of J. Alfred Prufrock," for example, the narrator declares, "No! I am not Prince Hamlet, nor was meant to be." He sees himself less as the hero of his own life than as an "attendant lord," whom he describes in terms that recall the character of POLONIUS: "politic, cautious, and meticulous; / Full of high sentence, but a bit obtuse; / At times, indeed, almost ridiculous; / Almost, at times, the Fool."

Aldous Huxley's novel *Brave New World,* published in 1932, is sprinkled with Shakespearean references throughout. Its title is taken from a line in *The Tempest,* in which the heroine MIRANDA exclaims, "O brave new world, that has such people in't" (V.i.183–84). Huxley's novel is set in an emotionless, technology-driven society of the future. The only remaining wild place is a so-called Savage Reservation, which corresponds to the magical island where the main characters are shipwrecked in Shakespeare's play. Just as PROSPERO, the protagonist of *The Tempest,* uses magic to control events on his island, the scientists in *Brave New World* use special powers to manipulate their environment. Huxley re-creates

SHAKESPEARE'S CRITICS

Shakespeare's praise has not been entirely universal. One particularly notable critic of his work was the French writer Voltaire, who in 1748 described Hamlet as "a piece gross and barbarous," resembling "the fruit of the imagination of a drunken savage." Leo Tolstoy, the world-famous Russian novelist, was even more sweeping in his attacks. He claimed that when he first encountered Shakespeare's works as a young man, he found them tedious and repulsive. Rereading them years later, at the age of 75, he had the same reaction, only "felt with even greater force." He concluded that "Shakespeare cannot be recognized either as a great genius, or even as an average author."

Prospero's servant CALIBAN in the character of John, a "savage" inhabitant of the reservation who educates himself by reading the plays of Shakespeare.

Perhaps no modern writer has been more indebted to Shakespeare than the Irish novelist James Joyce. In his novel *Ulysses,* first published in 1922, Joyce used fictional characters to explore the relationship between Shakespeare's life and his work. For example, he describes a scene from *Hamlet* in which "a player comes on under the shadow. . . . It is the ghost, the king, a king and no king, and the player is Shakespeare who has studied Hamlet all the years of his life which were not vanity in order to play the part of the spectre." This passage refers to the popular belief that Shakespeare himself played the part of the Ghost in the first production of *Hamlet.* In another section of *Ulysses,* one of the main characters examines the names Shakespeare used in several plays and argues that they reveal that the playwright's wife, Anne HATHAWAY, committed adultery with Shakespeare's brother Richard.

Joyce explored Shakespeare's work in even greater detail in his experimental novel *Finnegans Wake,* which links Shakespeare's personal life and characters to Joyce's own. The protagonist, Stephen, debates whether he is more like Hamlet or the innocent victim, Hamlet's father. According to literary critic Adaline Glasheen, the hero actually represents Shakespeare himself. She points to the fact that the wife in the novel is named Ann and that the couple, like the Shakespeares, have three children, two of whom are twins. Altogether, *Finnegans Wake* contains more than a thousand references to Shakespeare.

Tom Stoppard's 1967 play *Rosencrantz and Guildenstern Are Dead* reenacts *Hamlet* from the point of view of ROSENCRANTZ AND GUILDENSTERN, two minor characters who take Hamlet to England to be killed but end up being murdered themselves. The Stoppard play focuses on the two doomed men, who have little understanding of the setting into which they have been thrust. Stoppard also cowrote the script for the Oscar-winning film *Shakespeare in Love,* a fictional account of the writing of *Romeo and Juliet.* Another modern theatrical work influenced by Shakespeare is *Who's There?,* written by the noted Shakespearean director Peter Brook. The book presents *Hamlet* through the eyes of several prominent dramatic theorists of the 1900s.

Shakespeare's irresistible appeal continues today. John Updike, one of America's most popular writers, published *Gertrude and Claudius,* a novel based on *Hamlet,* in February 2000. Updike's narrative explores the illicit affair between Hamlet's mother and her husband's brother, which brings about the events of Shakespeare's tragedy. Richard Eder, in a *New York Times* review, described the novel as a "skitter of fireworks" that "illuminates questions about Shakespeare, about what a classic means and also the unexplored hills and forests that lie on either side of the path art pushes through." Nearly 400 years after his death, Shakespeare continues to inspire contemporary writers, and they in turn illuminate the playwright and his works. (*See also* **Actors, Shakespearean; Art Inspired by Shakespeare; Characters in Shakespeare's Plays; Music Inspired by Shakespeare; Shakespeare's Reputation.**)

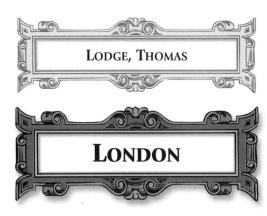

LODGE, THOMAS

See *Playwrights and Poets.*

In Shakespeare's time London was England's only city. No other community could compare with it in terms of size or population. The city covered a relatively small area, bounded on three sides by the walls the ancient Romans had built to defend the city and on the fourth by the River THAMES. What constituted the City of London in the 1400s and 1500s is largely limited to the financial district today.

LONDON'S NEIGHBORHOODS. Access to the city was through six main gates and several "postern gates," small openings that would admit a pedestrian. Although the walls and gates have all but disappeared, the names of the main gates—Newgate, Bishopsgate, Cripplegate, and others—are still used to identify the neighborhoods adjacent to them. The gates were closed at nine o'clock at night, and access to the city was denied until the following morning. Historians disagree about how vigorously the curfew was actually enforced.

The city's neighborhoods were often characterized by the specific goods or services available for purchase there. For example, goldsmiths gathered in Cheapside and cobblers* on Shoe Lane. Fresh fish could be purchased on Bridge Street, close to the docks where boats were unloaded. London Bridge, the only structural span between the city and the south bank of the Thames, was a neighborhood unto itself. The bridge was a huge structure built on 19 arches; only small boats could pass beneath it. Both sides of the bridge were lined with buildings, and the center served as a thoroughfare to and from the city. London Bridge provided a means for farmers from south of the city to bring their produce into town. A gate and tower guarded the southern end of the bridge. The decapitated heads of traitors were displayed on pikes here as a warning to others.

London Bridge connected the city with the lively but notorious district of Bankside. This neighborhood, in the borough of Southwark, was one of several suburbs that were referred to as "liberties" because they were outside the jurisdiction of city officials. As such they became havens for thieves, lepers*, drifters, prostitutes, vagabonds, and other lowlifes. Bankside was home to several Elizabethan playhouses and to other entertainment venues, such as the bearbaiting, bullbaiting, and cockfighting arenas.

Other London neighborhoods that would have been familiar to Shakespeare were those that contained the four Inns of Court at the legal center of the city. Lawyers had their offices and libraries here. Young gentlemen studied here, many using the inns' student dormitories and dining halls. Students also availed themselves of the common rooms that provided ample space for socializing and for the staging of plays and other entertainments.

* **cobbler** maker and repairer of shoes and other leather goods

* **leper** person who has leprosy, a chronic infectious disease that affects the skin and nerves, leading to deformity and paralysis

St. Paul's Cathedral was London's social center. Because the interior of the church was bustling with secular activities, worshipers were forced to gather outside the cathedral to listen to a sermon.

* Tudor referring to the dynasty that ruled England from 1485 to 1603

* buttress stone or wood structure that supports the outer wall of a building

West of the City of London was Westminster, site of the monarch's principal residence, the court, and Parliament. Aristocratic families built impressive mansions along the Thames between the city and Westminster. On the northern bank of the river, these gracious homes were set back from the water and surrounded by trees and gardens for maximum privacy.

North of London was an area called Moorfields, a planted open space that was used as a park for archery, hunting, and other outdoor sports. Beyond Moorfields was an area called Shoreditch, the home of two Elizabethan theaters.

CITY STREETS AND THOROUGHFARES. Most of London's streets were crowded, narrow lanes. Although they were designed for foot traffic, people also took horses, farm animals, and carts along these roadways. Many streets had an open channel cut through the center into which people emptied their household wastes. The city also had a few broad thoroughfares, generally leading to public buildings or out to the countryside, but these roads were mainly for coach travel.

The streets of London tended to be dark, because the upper stories of houses were built to overhang them. Overhangs gave homeowners more square footage than they had paid for but also prevented sunlight from reaching the streets below. Street lighting at night had to be provided by householders, who were required by law to keep a lantern hanging outside their doors. The results were mixed because people could not be made to maintain a *lighted* candle in the lantern all night.

The easiest way to avoid London's crowded streets and get from place to place was by boat on the Thames. The monarch and other aristocrats had barges to transport them. Ordinary citizens relied on boatmen to carry them—for a fee—upstream, downstream, or across the river. The boatmen prided themselves on effectively managing the tidal currents of the Thames and announced which way they were headed by shouting, "Westward ho!" (upstream) or "Eastward ho!" (downstream).

LIVING IN LONDON. London houses were generally two or three stories high, although they could be as tall as five or six stories. Merchants had their shops on the ground floor and lived with their families, apprentices, and servants behind and above the shops. Some families, if they had the room, took in boarders. The houses were built of wood with plastered walls and small hand-blown-glass windowpanes. The beams were painted black and the plaster white, creating the style of architecture now regarded as characteristic of the Tudor* period.

By the late 1500s the population of London was approximately 200,000. The city became so crowded that people started building shaky structures in any available space, even between the buttresses* of St. Paul's Cathedral. Existing buildings were divided into increasingly smaller living units to accommodate the growing population.

SOCIAL CENTER. St. Paul's Cathedral, which dates from the Middle Ages, was more than a house of worship. It was also the social center of

the city. People came there to meet friends, hear the latest gossip, make deals, find employment, leave messages, or just be seen. While still serving the needs of worshipers (services were held in the choir or outdoors), most of the church had been given over to secular pursuits. The cathedral yard and surrounding streets were filled with booksellers and buyers. Most of the plays Shakespeare published in his lifetime were issued from St. Paul's.

Merchants and lawyers regularly chose the great central aisle (known as Paul's Walk) as the place to meet clients and conduct business. On a pillar in another part of the cathedral, unemployed men listed their qualifications and the type of work they sought. Fashionable people went to St. Paul's to see and be seen. Social climbers came (sometimes with their tailors) to copy the latest styles or to gain an invitation to dinner. Prostitutes came to look for customers; thieves and con men walked the central aisle, picking pockets or engaging in other mischief. City authorities made several attempts to end or curtail these activities but generally were unsuccessful.

POWER AND POLITICS. Although Londoners paid allegiance to the monarch, the city itself was self-governing. Aldermen were elected for life to represent each of the 26 wards, or districts, of the city. The aldermen appointed various officials to administer the wards' everyday affairs but made all financial decisions themselves. Elected by the citizens of London, aldermen were established businessmen, and were generally prominent members of the guilds*. Along with 200 other citizens, who served for a period of one year, aldermen sat on the Court of Common Council. This body made the laws for London, regulations that ranged from how apprentices should be treated to how streets should be repaired and maintained.

Elected by the aldermen, the lord mayor served for a year. He was the ceremonial representative of the city, outranking everyone but the monarch.

Because London was the financial heart of England, it received special attention from the crown. Local bankers and businessmen lent money to the monarch in return for having their interests protected by the crown. For example, although Catholic rules about meatless days would not have been binding on Protestants, they were enforced by the crown in order to protect fishermen, fishmongers, shipbuilders, and others involved in the fishing industry.

SHAKESPEARE'S LONDON. Shakespeare knew London well, having spent most of his professional life there. He is said to have enjoyed the company of friends and colleagues in the inns and taverns for which the city is still famous. He most likely visited the Boar's Head, the tavern featured so prominently in the plays about Henry IV. The inns and taverns were ideal places for meeting foreign tradesmen, sailors, soldiers, and other travelers, so Shakespeare probably had no need to leave England to create the Scottish setting for *Macbeth* or the Italian setting for *The Taming of the Shrew*. All he needed was to be a good listener, which apparently he

See color plate 12, vol. 1.

* *guild* association of craft and trade workers that set standards for and represented the interests of its members

CITY WATER

Because the Thames is a tidal river, and therefore salty, and because human waste flowed into the river, Londoners imported their drinking water from springs and wells outside the city. Large pipes made from lead or hollowed logs carried water to central parts of the city. From these locations water carriers filled large wooden vessels and delivered the precious liquid to their customers.

In the early 1600s the New River Company constructed a 40-mile channel that delivered water to a series of reservoirs north of the city. From there water was carried through pipes to the city. A few lucky households along the pipeline to the city were hooked directly into this supply.

was. (*See also* **Geography; Mermaid Tavern; Sanitation; Transportation and Travel.**)

LOST PLAYS

The so-called lost plays are works rumored to have been written by Shakespeare. They are not included in lists of Shakespeare's plays because their texts are no longer available. Other works that may have been written by Shakespeare but are not usually included among his works are known as *apocrypha*, a word that refers to texts of uncertain authorship.

TWO LOST PLAYS. The names of two lost plays are known to most scholars through references and versions in other sources. The first is *Cardenio*, which was performed by the KING'S MEN in 1613. Forty years later the publisher Humphrey Moseley entered a copyright in the Stationers' Register for *The History of Cardenio*, written jointly by William Shakespeare and John Fletcher. Moseley's manuscript has not survived, but in 1727 the Shakespearean editor Lewis Theobald staged a play called *Double Falsehood*, which he claimed was based on a manuscript of *Cardenio*. Both the lost play and Theobald's version were based on an episode in Miguel de Cervantes' novel *Don Quixote*, a Spanish work that was translated into English in 1612.

Shakespeare and Fletcher collaborated on *The Two Noble Kinsmen* and perhaps on *Henry VIII*, so they may well have worked together on *Cardenio. Double Falsehood*, however, resembles Fletcher's plays more than Shakespeare's. When John HEMINGES and Henry Condell (two members of the King's Men) compiled the FIRST FOLIO of Shakespeare's plays, they omitted *Cardenio*, perhaps because they knew Shakespeare had little part in it.

Another "lost" play, *Love's Labor's Won*, may never have existed at all. In 1598 the title was included in a publication by Francis Meres (a literary critic) that listed several of Shakespeare's comedies. Most scholars believed that the title referred to *The Taming of the Shrew*, the only known early comedy that Meres omitted, until the recent discovery of another document (from 1603) that lists both plays. *Love's Labor's Won* may be a lost Shakespearean comedy that was written by 1598. It seems more likely, however, that it may have been an alternate title for an early version of *All's Well That Ends Well.*

TWO APOCRYPHAL TEXTS. Nearly 50 plays, in addition to the 38 generally accepted as Shakespearean, have been proposed as works wholly or partially written by Shakespeare. Most scholars, however, consider very few, if any, of these claims legitimate*. Some of the so-called apocrypha are manuscripts that were mistakenly or deceitfully attributed to Shakespeare by editors and booksellers. Only two texts are commonly accepted as possible Shakespearean works: *Edward III* and *Sir Thomas More*. A few scholars also classify *The Two Noble Kinsman* with the apocrypha, even

* legitimate valid or acceptable

though it was published as a work by William Shakespeare and John Fletcher.

Scholars have long struggled to identify the author of *The Raigne of Edward III*. Humphrey Moseley attributed the play to Shakespeare in 1656, but the modern scholar Kenneth Muir has argued persuasively that only small portions of the text resemble Shakespeare's other work. The play contains some IMAGERY typical of Shakespeare and includes a line that also ends Shakespeare's Sonnet 94. Muir suggests that Shakespeare made revisions to an existing play but left most of the original as it was.

Sir Thomas More has posed one of the most complex problems for scholars. Its subject is a Catholic statesman who accepted death rather than agree to Henry VIII's decision to sever the Church of England from the papacy. The play was apparently written by Anthony Munday but rejected by the MASTER OF THE REVELS. Revisions were made by at least four other playwrights. Many scholars believe that three pages of those revisions are in Shakespeare's handwriting. This identification is difficult because the only other samples of Shakespeare's writing are six copies of his signature. Studies have shown, however, that the passage in question includes spellings, images, and ideas that appear elsewhere in Shakespeare's works. (*See also* **Poets and Playwrights; Sonnets, The.**)

LOVE

Throughout his career Shakespeare appears to have been preoccupied with the meaning and value of human love. His characters seek, find, and lose love in various ways and forms, and his dramatic situations frequently revolve around the search for the blessings love can bring. His SONNETS also examine different ideas and manifestations of love, describing two powerful relationships in the poet's life: a passionate affair with a beautiful but cruel woman and an intimate friendship with a handsome young man. Taken as a whole, Shakespeare's works do not seem to point to a single view of love. Rather they suggest an immense variety of possibilities.

ROMANTIC LOVE IN THE PLAYS

The Bodleian Library's copy of Shakespeare's FIRST FOLIO, which was available to Oxford undergraduates during the 1600s, shows visible darkening on the outside edges of the pages that contain the text of *Romeo and Juliet,* indicating that this was a work to which readers frequently turned. Oxford students were among the first readers to be fascinated by this story, which has become one of the best-known romances in all of literature. Most of Shakespeare's plays, however, do not present romantic love in so lyrical and all-encompassing a manner. Young love in particular is treated with far more skepticism in his comedies.

COMEDIES. The youthful lovers in Shakespeare's early comedies—such as *The Two Gentlemen of Verona, Love's Labor's Lost,* and *A Midsummer Night's*

THE FOOD OF LOVE

In the opening line of *Twelfth Night,* music is described as "the food of love," and indeed many of the songs in Shakespeare's plays are about love. The variety of these songs reflects the many views of love found in the plays. *Love's Labor's Lost* ends with a comical song about how married men fear having unfaithful wives. The somewhat sarcastic humor of this song contrasts with the deep melancholy of Desdemona's "Willow" song in *Othello,* about an unhappy woman who has been betrayed by her lover. Ophelia's famous "mad scene" in *Hamlet* combines comic and tragic love songs, following a mournful ballad about a dead lover with a bawdy tune about a maiden being seduced.

Dream—can be seen as counterbalances to the tragic glory of Romeo or Juliet. The men in particular seem very immature—fickle, shallow, hasty in making promises of love and equally hasty in breaking them. *The Taming of the Shrew* provides an even more cynical look at courtship and marriage. The resolution that emerges from a tempestuous couple's lengthy battle for dominance is not a love of equals but the apparent submission of a wife to a husband, far from an ideal relationship from a modern standpoint. Although the outcomes of these love stories can be interpreted as happy, they are far from perfect, and they leave the impression that the couples involved will find true happiness only when their affections are more settled, more realistic, and more seasoned.

The middle romantic comedies allow young lovers to test their feelings before making final commitments. The intelligent and appealing heroines of these plays approach their own loves and lovers with suitable caution. Portia in *The Merchant of Venice* and Rosalind in *As You Like It* use DISGUISE to test the strength of their partners' affection. Assuming the appearance of men, they can interact with the men they love in ways that were unavailable to them as women. In similar fashion Viola in *Twelfth Night* is protected by a page's disguise. Because her employer, Orsino, sees her as a boy, he comes to care for her as a person rather than treating her as he does the beautiful Olivia—madly declaring his love when he barely knows her.

The men in these middle plays are also more mature than the young lovers of the early comedies and thus better candidates for marriage. The lovers Beatrice and Benedick in *Much Ado About Nothing* are both mistrustful of the opposite sex and determined not to marry. Because of this they interact with each other as individuals—opponents in "a kind of merry war"—before they first begin to admit that they see each other as potential romantic partners. Their love, when it bursts into the open, is therefore founded on a true knowledge of and fondness for each other. Lovers in the middle comedies experience love as a process—a condition they grow into, not a prize that comes to them automatically because they are young and attractive. These comedies celebrate youthful love without idealizing it or taking it for granted.

After these plays, with their realistic but generally positive views of love and marriage, Shakespeare's later comedies—*Measure for Measure, All's Well That Ends Well*, and especially *Troilus and Cressida*—grow increasingly cynical on the subject of love. The heroines of these dramas are no longer able to take effective control of their lives and loves, and the men they pair up with are not particularly suitable as life partners. The standard comic ending, in which all the characters pair neatly off and marry, is either nonexistent or tends to be presented ironically. The heroes and heroines of these plays may have admirable qualities, but those qualities tend to exist outside of or even at the expense of romantic couplings.

TRAGEDIES. In addition to *Romeo and Juliet* there are several noteworthy portrayals of love between men and women in Shakespeare's tragedies. In most cases the romantic relationship is not so much the focus of the

tragedy but appears as one of several victims of it. Hamlet's affection for OPHELIA is destroyed by his intense disillusionment with his mother and with the Danish court in general; Othello's marriage to DESDEMONA collapses as IAGO works to expose its hidden weaknesses; and the intense partnership between Macbeth and his wife is poisoned by their ambition.

Only in *Antony and Cleopatra* did Shakespeare revisit the idea of tragic love. The lovers in this play, however, are almost opposites of the youthful Romeo and Juliet, who seem to be experiencing love for the first time. Mature, calculating, and worldly, Cleopatra and Antony sometimes seem more like political allies than lovers. When they manage to rise above the factors that make their relationship problematic, however, their passionate devotion to each other is moving to witness, even as it drives them toward their deaths. Their ability to endure as lovers without the illusions or idealism of youth makes their tragedy just as powerful as—although very different from—the absolute devotion of Romeo and Juliet.

OTHER TYPES OF LOVE

Shakespeare's exploration of love in his plays was not limited to romantic attachments between men and women. The love bonds between friends and family members often appear to be powerful forces that can both hurt and heal.

FRIENDSHIP. Elizabethans celebrated same-sex FRIENDSHIPS as pure and unselfish types of love that were not necessarily related to sexual passion. Shakespeare dramatizes this type of bond in *The Merchant of Venice*, whose title character unhesitatingly pledges all he has, even his life, for the sake of his closest friend. Close friends in Shakespeare's plays often share some form of blood relationship: Celia and Rosalind are cousins in *As You Like It*, as are Beatrice and Hero in *Much Ado About Nothing*. A friend can assume the role of a trusted confidant*, providing comfort in a time of need, as Horatio does for Hamlet. Other types of friendship, however, can be more costly. Prince Hal's merry companionship with the drunken knight Falstaff in *Henry IV Part 1* and *Part 2* partly distracts him from his duties and temporarily harms his reputation.

One type of friendship that may be strange to modern audiences is the devotion with which the earl of Kent serves King Lear. Similarities may be found in the relationship between Emilia and Desdemona. Because these characters are not equals, their relationship may not strike modern viewers as ideal examples of friendship. For Elizabethan audiences, however, the fidelity of a loyal servant was one of the highest forms of love and gratifying to see.

FAMILY LOVE. The love between parents and children appears in various ways in the plays. Perhaps because Shakespeare's female characters were all originally played by young boys, he created far fewer portrayals of mothers than of fathers. But there are a few striking examples of the love between mother and child. In *King John,* for example, Constance mourns with great sorrow over the loss of her son Arthur. A more problematic

* confidant person with whom thoughts and feelings are shared

See
color plate 15,
vol. 2.

mother-son relationship appears in *Hamlet,* as the young prince shows an almost jealous anger at his mother's remarriage, even before he learns that her second husband is also his father's murderer. Hamlet's devotion to the late king is one of Shakespeare's most striking examples of a son's love for his father. Other examples of this relationship are found in Edgar's sacrifices for Gloucester in *King Lear* and in Prince Hal's growing concern for his father in the two *Henry IV* plays.

The family connection that seems to have fascinated Shakespeare most, however, is the bond between father and daughter, which he explored in *King Lear* and in his final romances (*Cymbeline, Pericles, The Winter's Tale,* and *The Tempest*). In these plays the healing power of a daughter's love is an antidote for men who find female sexuality threatening and problematic. Because Shakespeare retired soon after writing these plays, returning to Stratford where his two daughters lived, some scholars have speculated that his thoughtful portrayal of father-daughter love had a personal basis.

LOVE IN THE SONNETS

Even more than his plays, Shakespeare's sonnets appear to reveal his personal views—and perhaps his personal experiences—of love. They tell the tale of two complicated, ongoing relationships in the narrator's life, both of which bring intense pain as well as moments of joy. One of these implied relationships is a love affair with a woman who has come to be known as the DARK LADY, a name that reflects her morals as well as her complexion. The sonnets addressed to the Dark Lady express feelings that range from sexual obsession to a certain regretful humor.

The other leading figure in the sonnets (the one to whom the majority of the poems are addressed) is a young man often referred to as the Fair Youth. Shakespeare portrays this person in idealized terms, even though the object of the poet's affection shows a certain carelessness with his friend's feelings, particularly when he becomes involved in a sexual relationship with the Dark Lady. Scholars have long speculated as to whether the characters of the Dark Lady and the Fair Youth were based on real individuals and if so who they were. Discussion of the relationship between the poet and the Fair Youth also focuses on whether or not the poet's passionate declarations of love for his friend suggest that their relationship had a sexual side.

What the poems reveal in any case is that Shakespeare could acknowledge that love, as experienced in the everyday world, was flawed, often painful, and subject to constant change. At the same time he could affirm that "love is not love / Which alters when it alteration finds, / Or bends with the remover to remove" (Sonnet 116). He could say, in other words, that love endures even when it is not returned, that the ideal of love remains valid even if a realization of it proves impossible to achieve. Whatever form love takes, this poem implies, it is good in itself. Even with all its sorrows and uncertainties, love helps give meaning and shape to human life. (*See also* **Friendship; Gender and Sexuality; Homosexuality; Katharina; Loyalty; Sonnets, The.**)

LOVER'S COMPLAINT, A

* *unrequited* not returned

* *convention* established practice

A "complaint" is a poem in which the narrator expresses unhappiness about a particular situation, usually unrequited* love or life in general. First introduced in the 1300s, complaints were written in rhyme royal, a verse pattern featuring seven-line stanzas with a rhyme scheme of *ababbcc*. Shakespeare used this pattern in his longer poem THE RAPE OF LUCRECE. Complaints were very popular in the 1590s, when *A Lover's Complaint* was probably written.

Originally published with Shakespeare's *Sonnets* in 1609, *A Lover's Complaint* is a poem of such poor quality that many critics doubt whether the playwright actually composed it. The poem begins with an elderly shepherd encountering a young woman beside a stream. She is weeping and destroying love letters. The rest of the poem is devoted to the woman's unhappy tale. She had met a man who, though attractive and well-liked, was known to be unfaithful in love. The man attempted to win her over, acknowledging his past faults but swearing that in her he had finally found true love. At first she refused him, but when he wept at this rejection, she gave in to him, only to be abandoned soon after. The woman laments that she was deceived but acknowledges that she would probably fall for his charms again.

Critics have faulted *A Lover's Complaint* as awkward and unsophisticated, even while praising some of its passages. The poem is widely viewed as a clumsy imitation of the verse of Edmund SPENSER, but its characters and setting go beyond the conventions* of the complaint form. Although *A Lover's Complaint* is a fair example of Elizabethan poetry, nearly all critics agree that its quality falls far short of most Shakespearean poems. In addition, it includes some words that Shakespeare did not use in his other works. Unless other evidence comes to light, it will probably continue to be regarded as a poem of uncertain authorship. (*See also* **Poetry of Shakespeare.**)

LOVE'S LABOR'S LOST

* *courtier* person in attendance at a royal court

One of Shakespeare's early comedies, *Love's Labor's Lost* was for many years dismissed by scholars as an imperfect early work not worthy of serious critical attention. More recently, however, critics have come to appreciate it as an elaborate parody of certain Elizabethan ideas, especially those about writing and about love. Modern audiences also relate to the universal appeal of the play's basic situation—the desires, follies, and frustrations of youthful love—and of the witty and attractive characters who play it out.

PLOT. The entire play is set at the court of King Ferdinand of Navarre (a region that is part of modern France, near the Spanish border). The king and three of his courtiers* have devised a plan to make their court into "a little academe" (I.i.13), where they will spend three years in study and contemplation. To accomplish this, they intend to refrain from all worldly pleasures, restricting their eating and sleeping and, most particularly, avoiding the company of women. Only one of them, Lord Berowne,

Love's Labor's Lost

LOVE'S LABOR'S WON

Francis Meres's list of six comedies (printed in 1598) for which Shakespeare was known included one with the intriguing title *Love's Labor's Won*, perhaps a companion piece to *Love's Labor's Lost*. A second reference in 1603 suggests that such a play was in print, but no known copy exists, and there are no other records of one. Some scholars have suggested that *Love's Labor's Won* may be an alternate title for one of the known comedies, perhaps *Much Ado About Nothing* or *All's Well That Ends Well*, but nothing is certain.

* *medieval* referring to the Middle Ages, a period roughly between A.D. 500 and 1500

is skeptical about this plan, believing that their vows will be impossible to keep. His prediction comes true almost immediately, when the princess of France arrives with her three ladies-in-waiting. The four lords are quickly overcome by their own affections, and their plan collapses completely as each pursues the lady who has captured his fancy.

The main action of the play is an elegant mating dance between the four lords and the four ladies. Much of its humor depends on the witty verbal sparring between the men and women, particularly Berowne and Lady Rosaline. Although King Ferdinand and the princess are the highest-ranking characters in the play, Berowne and Rosaline are the most fully developed. The wordplay they exchange resembles that of some other noteworthy romantic couples in Shakespeare's comedies, such as Beatrice and Benedick in *Much Ado About Nothing*. In these verbal battles the men, who showed such pride in their own intelligence and scholarship, are generally outwitted by the women, who maintain control throughout the play. Among other things, they put on masks and trick their men into wooing the wrong partners.

A broader variety of humor is provided by several minor characters. The schoolmaster Holofernes constantly shows off his knowledge by packing his speech with Latin words and phrases, for which he often supplies not one but several English translations. The soldier Armado is a similarly pompous show-off whose speech is always elaborate and flowery, while the peasant Costard pretends to be a bumbling fool who never understands anything the other characters say to him. In the play's final scene these low characters put on a pageant for the lords and ladies in which they assume the roles of the "Nine Worthies," legendary ancient heroes.

At the end of the play, just as the lords and ladies have reached a kind of understanding in their relationship, a mysterious figure named Marcade suddenly enters to announce that the princess's father has died and that she must return to France at once. The name *Marcade* may be a version of *Mercury*, referring to the messenger of the gods in ancient Roman mythology. It may also be intended to suggest "mars Arcadia," a reference to the poem *Arcadia* by Sir Philip SIDNEY, which glorifies peaceful country life. Marcade's announcement sounds a gloomy note that mars, or damages, the country setting just as it reaches its festive peak. The lords scramble to win the ladies' hands in marriage, pleading, "Now at the latest minute of the hour, / Grant us your loves" (V.ii.787–88), but the ladies refuse. Instead, each insists that her lover spend a year and a day at a particular task to prove himself worthy before she will accept him. The theme of a lover performing tasks for his lady is part of the medieval* tradition of courtly love.

The ending of *Love's Labor's Lost* is quite unusual for a comedy, which typically concludes with a marriage or, more often, several. Berowne comments that "Our wooing doth not end like an old play: / Jack hath not Gill [Jill]" (V.ii.874–75). Instead, the play concludes with a pair of songs, "Spring" and "Winter," performed by the low characters. The first of these, sung in praise of the cuckoo, puns on the similarity between the bird's name and the word *cuckold*, referring to a husband whose wife is unfaithful.

plague highly contagious and often fatal disease; also called the Black Death

quarto referring to the format of a book or page; a sheet of paper folded twice, yielding four leaves or eight pages

In *Love's Labor's Lost,* four young gentlemen fail in their attempt to shun the company of women. This photograph is from a 1978 production of the play by the Royal Shakespeare Company.

TEXT AND PERFORMANCE HISTORY. *Love's Labor's Lost* was written relatively early in Shakespeare's career, perhaps just after the London theaters reopened in 1594 after being closed for more than a year due to an outbreak of plague* in London. The play was first printed in a quarto* edition in 1598. The title page of this text said that the play had been performed for Queen Elizabeth I "last Christmas," which could mean the Christmas of either 1597 or 1598, or possibly even 1596. The play received another royal performance before Queen Anne, wife of King James I, during the Christmas season of 1604–1605.

In the same year that *Love's Labor's Lost* first appeared in print, writer Francis Meres listed the play in his *Palladis Tamia (Wit's Treasury)* as one of six noteworthy comedies by Shakespeare. In 1599 and 1600 some of the poems written by the play's characters were taken out of the play and published or quoted in poetry collections. The play appeared in the FIRST FOLIO in 1623. Another quarto edition, published in 1631, reported on its title page that *Love's Labor's Lost* had been performed by Shakespeare's acting company, the KING'S MEN, at both the GLOBE THEATER and BLACKFRIARS. This evidence, along with other references from the period, suggests that *Love's Labor's Lost* was a relatively well-known and popular play in its time. This may surprise modern readers, who often find the play's language difficult or unclear. But part of the confusion is due to the fact that the play contains many TOPICAL REFERENCES that modern readers do not understand.

The play apparently fell into disfavor in the late 1600s and in the 1700s. According to scholar Miriam Gilbert, *Love's Labor's Lost* is the only one of Shakespeare's plays that was not performed at all in 18th-century England. It began to be performed again in the 20th century, however, with important productions by such directors as Peter Brook, John Barton, and Robin Phillips. These stagings have shown just how successfully theatrical the play can be—comical, absurd, touching, provocative, and sometimes even chilling in its references to death. Kenneth Branagh's film version, a musical released in 2000, was designed to contribute even more to the popularity of the comedy.

COMMENTARY. For many years, scholars dismissed *Love's Labor's Lost* as an "apprentice work," one that Shakespeare produced before he was fully in command of his skills as a writer. It fell into disfavor in England during the 1700s in part because its plot, with a lack of dramatic action and a heavy dependence on elaborate wordplay, came to be seen as artificial. Some writers even found it vulgar, with puns that seemed to associate it with the lowest forms of humor.

Beginning in the 1950s *Love's Labor's Lost* began to attract more positive critical attention. As modern scholars improved their understanding of Elizabethan theories of language, they were able to place the play in the context of Renaissance audiences and their expectations. At the same time, the comedy began to enjoy more success in the theater, leading critics to reconsider their earlier dismissals of its supposed theatrical flaws. Modern scholars now see the play's more elaborate and flowery passages as parodies of, rather than examples of, the extravagant Elizabethan writing style at its worst.

Loyalty

The plot of *Love's Labor's Lost,* unlike that of most of Shakespeare's works, has no identifiable source, but the play certainly reflects and draws on a rich historical and cultural background. One of its elements is the idea of an "academe" or academy, a concept of education dating back to the ancient Greek philosopher Plato. During the 1600s French and Italian humanists revived Plato's approach to learning. In the new humanist tradition the academy came to be viewed as a forum that enabled human beings to reach a higher plane of existence by improving themselves on earth. Another classical* theme is to be found in the play's repeated references to the heroic deeds of Greek and Roman legend. King Ferdinand praises his companions' efforts to be "brave conquerors—for so you are / That war against your own affections / And the huge army of the world's desires" (I.i.8–10). This concept of heroism is later parodied in the pageant of the Nine Worthies.

Some critics believe that the "little academe" at the court of Navarre pokes fun at a society formed by Sir Walter Raleigh, a courtier of Queen Elizabeth, to study mathematics and ASTRONOMY. A line in Act IV, Scene iii, refers to the "school of night," a phrase some scholars considered a misprint for many years but now see as a reference to Raleigh's group. Critics have also suggested that the pompous Don Armado is based on Raleigh. Other characters, including Holofernes and the witty page Moth, have also been seen as caricatures of Elizabethan contemporaries. The low characters resemble stock figures found in the commedia dell'arte (popular Italian comedy of the Middle Ages), including the bookish schoolmaster (Holofernes), the arrogant soldier (Armado), and the clever and foolish servants (Moth and Costard).

The main theme of the play is the triumph of love and worldly joy over cold intellectualism. The king and his three companions pride themselves on the purity of their scholarly goals, seeking "to know which else we should not know" (I.i.56). Ironically, it turns out that they do not even know themselves. The "army of the world's desires," as represented by the four beautiful, witty women who appear on their doorstep, proves to be more of a brave "conqueror" than do the scholars who attempt to resist it. In the end all four of the men reject the idea that isolated study is a higher pursuit than love and pleasure. Instead, Berowne affirms, they have learned that in ladies' eyes they may find "the books, the arts, the academes, / That show, contain, and nourish all the world" (IV.iii.349–50). (*See also* **Directors and Shakespeare; Friends and Contemporaries; Medievalism; Pastoralism.**)

* *classical* in the tradition of ancient Greece and Rome

LOYALTY

Elizabethans believed that all things in the universe, from God to the dirt underfoot, had a proper place in a vast hierarchy* known as the great chain of being. It was considered natural and proper for those positioned lower on this cosmic ladder to show respect and loyalty toward their superiors. Subjects were expected to be loyal to their monarch, children to their parents, wives to their husbands, and servants to

* *hierarchy* ordered structure based on rank

their masters. Disruptions in this universal order, either on a large scale (the overthrow of a king by his subjects) or on a small one (the disobedience of a child toward his or her parents), resulted in related disturbances elsewhere as a consequence.

Hamlet expresses this sense of universal disruption when he remarks, "The time is out of joint" (I.v.188). He refers to the fact that his uncle, Claudius, has murdered his father and usurped* the throne, violating not only the loyalty a younger brother owed an older one but also the loyalty a subject owed his king. Other plays also show the dramatic consequences of a subject's disloyalty to the reigning monarch. Most of the history plays touch on this subject in one way or another. In *Richard II*, for example, a legitimate (if weak) king is overthrown, and the three plays that follow—*Henry IV, Parts 1* and *2*, and *Henry V*—all deal in some way with the civil discord that results.

The most explicit example of the damage caused to the state by a subject's disloyalty occurs in *Macbeth*. Early in the play when Macbeth contemplates killing King Duncan, he reflects that Duncan is

> here in double trust:
> First, as I am his kinsman and his subject,
> Strong both against the deed; then, as his host,
> Who should against his murderer shut the door,
> Not bear the knife myself.
>
> (I.vii.12–16)

This murder is so unnatural that nature itself is overturned, and wild storms, earthquakes, and "strange screams of death" occur in the night. Macbeth's own nature is changed as well. A brave and noble soldier when the play begins, he gradually loses all his humanity and by the end of the play has become a monstrous tyrant.

Balanced against these examples of violent betrayal, however, are a few shining examples of true loyalty. The most striking of these appear in *King Lear*. In the first scene of the play, the king banishes his loyal follower the earl of Kent for daring to question his judgment. Kent disguises himself and returns, using a new name, to continue serving the king. When Lear is later stripped of his power and forsaken by his two ungrateful daughters, Kent remains by his side, even as the king wanders across a bare plain in a raging storm. So does Lear's nameless Fool, who declares his intention to stay by his master through bad times as well as good with these words: "The knave turns fool that runs away" (II.iv.84). Though completely devoted to the king, the Fool still mocks and criticizes him, pointing out his foolishness in allowing his daughters to take over his kingdom. Kent and the Fool show by their words and actions that a truly loyal subject does not always aim to please. Speaking honestly is part of the duty of a true friend.

This same lesson is reflected in the character of Cordelia, the king's youngest daughter. She, like Kent, is banished by the king for speaking the truth in the play's first scene. Lear has asked his three daughters to say how much they love him, promising the largest share of his kingdom to the one who loves him most. Her older sisters flatter the king shamelessly, but Cordelia declares simply that she loves him "according to my bond,

* *usurp* to seize power from a rightful ruler

nor more nor less" (I.i.92). Lear takes her words as a rejection, but in fact she makes a powerful statement. According to the Elizabethan concept of loyalty, Cordelia's "bond" to Lear is a very strong one because he is both her father and her king. By loving "according to her bond," she promises her father the duty of a subject and the devotion of a daughter, both far more valuable than the false flatteries of her sisters. (*See also* **Fools, Clowns, and Jesters; Friendship; Morality and Ethics.**)

MACBETH

* *medieval* referring to the Middle Ages, a period roughly between A.D. 500 and 1500
* *usurp* to seize power from a rightful ruler

See color plate 1, vol. 2.

One of Shakespeare's greatest tragedies, *Macbeth* tells the story of a medieval* lord who usurps* the throne of Scotland. Driven by his aggressive wife and his own ambition, Macbeth murders his king to gain the crown. Afterward he is haunted by guilt, anxiety, and ghostly visions. His life spirals downward into a nightmare of violence, and he is eventually killed by those whom he has injured. This seemingly straightforward tale is actually one of surprising power and complexity. So mysterious are the characters and the themes that scholarly criticism and stage productions of the play have shown extremely varied responses.

PLOT. *Macbeth* opens with the three "weird sisters," mysterious, chanting figures identified as "weyward" WITCHES in the FIRST FOLIO (1623). The use of the term *weyward* suggests that they are evil women who lead their victims astray. They meet with two Scottish thanes (lords), Macbeth and Banquo, returning home from a successful battle against the rebellious Macdonwald. They greet Macbeth, promising that he will become "thane of Cawdor" and later gain the kingship. To Banquo they make a puzzling prediction: that his descendants will be kings, but he will not. As soon as the witches disappear, messengers arrive from King Duncan, informing Macbeth that Duncan has in fact made him thane of Cawdor. Shocked by the witches' prophetic power, Macbeth imagines committing murder to gain the throne, but the thought fills him with horror as well as attraction.

Macbeth's wife, at home, receives a letter from her husband informing her of the witches' prophecy and learns that Duncan intends to celebrate victory at their castle. Determined to see her husband become king, she calls upon evil spirits to fill her with "direst cruelty" so that she may overcome Macbeth's "human kindness" and persuade him to commit murder. (In the original printing, *human* is spelled *humane*, the usual form of the word in Shakespeare's time. The modern sense of *humane*, associated with "kindness," is pertinent.) Later while Duncan feasts, Macbeth contemplates the possibility of assassinating the king, describing Duncan's virtues in so positive a manner that the monarch seems almost godlike. Fearing both the physical and moral consequences of the crime he comtemplates, Macbeth decides to abandon the plan. When Lady Macbeth hears this, however, she challenges his manhood and claims that in his place she would not hesitate to "[dash] the brains out" of her own child. Entranced by his wife's fiendishly masculine spirit, Macbeth renews his murderous plan.

In the deep night of the castle, Macbeth goes forth to murder the king "with Tarquin's ravishing strides" (a reference to the villain in THE RAPE OF LUCRECE). Immediately afterward he is filled with unnatural horror. He shrinks from the sight of his bloody hands, and he hears strange sounds and ghostly voices claiming that "Macbeth shall sleep no more" (II.ii.40). He seems distracted, but his senses are vividly alive. Lady Macbeth scorns his fears, insisting that "a little water clears us of this deed" (II.ii.64), but the uncanny sounds in the night suggest otherwise. When morning comes Duncan's body is discovered, and Macbeth rather unconvincingly lays the blame on the king's sleeping guards, killing them first so they cannot prove otherwise. Duncan's two sons, fearing for their own lives, flee the kingdom. As a result they are suspected of planning their father's murder, and Macbeth is therefore named king.

Having gained power, however, Macbeth is unable to contain his anxieties. He now fears Banquo, who suspects his treachery and who knows that his own children have been promised the throne. Macbeth hires killers to murder Banquo and his son, Fleance. Banquo dies, but his son escapes. That evening Macbeth sees the ghost of Banquo appear and reappear at his banquet table. No one else at the banquet can see the ghost, however, and Lady Macbeth tries to explain it as a figment of her husband's distraught imagination. Macbeth's ravings spoil the feast, despite his wife's attempts to calm him. It soon becomes clear that an emotional distance has developed between Macbeth and his wife, who knew nothing of his plan to murder Banquo or of his suspicions of Macduff, the thane of Fife, who was absent from the banquet.

Tormented by his fears, Macbeth returns to the witches to inquire about his fate. They summon a series of apparitions that answer his questions with riddles. They tell him to beware Macduff but also assure him that no one "of woman born" can harm him and that he will never be defeated "until Great Birnam wood to high Dunsinane [castle] hill / Shall come against him" (IV.i.92–93). They also reveal a magical mirror in which Macbeth sees the throne of Scotland occupied by Banquo's descendants. In a bloodthirsty rage he orders an attack on Macduff's castle in which his wife and all his children are killed. Macduff, meanwhile, has fled to England to plead with Malcolm, Duncan's son, to mount an invasion against Macbeth. Macduff succeeds in his mission but at great cost, losing the family he has foolishly left at risk.

The final act of the play reveals that Lady Macbeth has become insane. She walks and talks in her sleep and attempts to wash imaginary bloodstains from her hands. The atmosphere is heavy with a sense of doom as Macbeth's allies desert him, the invading forces press closer, and the king's emotions waver between resignation and defiance. News of his wife's death prompts Macbeth's famous "Tomorrow, and tomorrow, and tomorrow" speech (V.v.19–28), which expresses a sense of life's folly and meaninglessness. Refusing to surrender, he hurls himself into battle, where Macduff awaits him. Macbeth taunts Macduff with the prophecy that he cannot be harmed by anyone born of woman, but Macduff reveals that he was "from his mother's womb / Untimely ripp'd" (V.viii.15–16), that is, delivered by Caesarean section rather than "born"

In this illustration based on an 1866 performance of *Macbeth,* Lady Macbeth encourages her husband to carry out their plan to murder King Duncan.

in the normal way. Macduff slays Macbeth and brings his head, mounted on a pole, to the triumphant Malcolm.

TEXT AND SOURCES. The text of *Macbeth* that appeared in the First Folio in 1623 was apparently based on a theater's PROMPT BOOK. The script is unusually short for a tragedy and may have been trimmed for performance. The play also shows evidence of minor revisions by another playwright, probably Thomas Middleton.

Macbeth was probably completed in 1606, shortly after the execution of the alleged conspirators* in the GUNPOWDER PLOT, a shocking attempt by Catholic dissidents* to murder the Protestant king JAMES I. The play refers to this insurrection in a scene that occurs immediately after King Duncan's murder. The drunken porter of Macbeth's castle, pretending to be the gatekeeper of hell, admits "an equivocator," probably a reference to Father Garnet, a Jesuit priest convicted as a party to the Gunpowder Plot. Garnet had written a treatise instructing Catholics to conceal the truth from Protestant authorities by saying one thing but meaning another. *Macbeth* thus draws on political events that raised enormous fear and anxiety in Jacobean* England.

The main source for Macbeth is HOLINSHED'S CHRONICLES (1587 edition). Holinshed's story has a strong connection to King James, who claimed to be descended from Banquo. Although Banquo is a sympathetic figure and appears to be on the side of good, he is also morally compromised because he has reason to suspect Macbeth's crime but takes no action against it. Shakespeare emphasizes this aspect of Banquo's character more than Holinshed did. How James reacted to this ambiguity, if he noticed it, is unknown, but any play depicting the violent overthrow of a crowned king—Duncan, or even Macbeth—could hardly have been pleasing to Shakespeare's monarch and patron*. According to scholar David Norbrook, democracy even claims some precedence over monarchy in the play, as when certain thanes assert their right not only to overthrow their anointed ruler but also to reject the rightful heir to the throne if he does not meet their moral standards.

The character of Lady Macbeth was probably inspired in part by the legend of Medea, a sorceress who punished her unfaithful husband by murdering their children. In addition, the figures of the three witches reflect shifting attitudes in Renaissance England about the existence of witchcraft. Author Reginald Scot expressed skepticism in *The Discovery of Witchcraft* (1584), but King James was a firm believer in the power of witchcraft and often questioned accused witches personally (usually by means of torture). Because most of those accused were women, anxieties about witchcraft both influenced and were influenced by society's attitudes about the nature of women, a subject debated in books and pamphlets through much of the 1500s.

COMMENTARY. On its surface the plot of *Macbeth* seems like a straightforward moral fable about a good man who yields to the temptations of evil and suffers the appropriate punishment. But closer examination reveals a much more complex and uncertain morality. The "tragic hero" is a

* *conspirator* person who plots with others to commit a crime

* *dissident* one who disagrees with an established political or religious system

* *Jacobean* referring to the reign of James I, king of England from 1603 to 1625

* *patron* supporter or financial sponsor of an artist or writer

murderer but not a cold-blooded one. Macbeth cannot escape his guilt over his evil deeds. Meanwhile the "good" characters in the play reveal surprising flaws. Banquo harbors his own ambitions and fails to accuse Macbeth. Macduff abandons his wife and children and, in order to unseat Macbeth, is willing to accept a surprising amount of immorality in a new king. At times the characters' motives are confusing. Attention centers on the relationship between Macbeth and his wife, but the communication between them is often so indirect that it is almost hidden from the audience. Their crime appears to reflect ambition, but Macbeth never shows much pleasure or even interest in political power. It almost seems as if the protagonists* do not know what they really want or why they want it.

Many readers have speculated that Macbeth's tragedy is driven by supernatural forces (the figures of the "weird sisters," referred to as *weyward* in the earliest printing to suggest their power to lead others astray) rather than by conscious, human choice. The question of whether *Macbeth*'s characters act or are acted upon depends to some extent on whether the three witches influence the future or only predict it. To some degree the play reflects the traditional debate over whether human life is controlled by fate or free will. A related issue is whether Lady Macbeth is seen as an evil figure, a kind of fourth witch.

Macbeth and Lady Macbeth appear to have no children, but they are haunted by images of future generations, such as the descendants of Banquo who are destined to inherit the throne. The tension surrounding the issue of succession in *Macbeth* may reflect the political atmosphere of England in 1606. Queen ELIZABETH I had recently died, leaving no direct descendants, and the heir to her throne was a foreigner, unknown to most and mistrusted by some. The play's political implications, however, are unclear—like most of its other themes. Even the hopeful ending, in which the rightful heir is placed on the throne, carries a hint that the evils of Macbeth's reign may be repeated because Macduff, as the traitor's slayer, now occupies the same position that Macbeth did at the beginning of the play.

The play's structure is as unusual and complicated as its meaning. The tragedy is nightmarish and horrifying, yet it also provides a notable amount of stage spectacle, including battles, music and dance, and dramatic special effects. One viewer, Samuel Pepys, remarked in the 1660s that he found the drama remarkable for its "variety" and "divertisement" (amusement)—"a strange perfection in a tragedy." Many of these spectacles, such as Banquo's bloody ghost, can serve paradoxically to validate Macbeth's inward delusions because they are so vivid and believable. The play is also remarkable for its shortness and for the fact that it has only a single plotline, with none of the subplots found in Shakespeare's other great tragedies. But the very shortness and straightforwardness of *Macbeth*'s plot can make it more mysterious because the themes of the play and the motives of the characters are never fully developed. Some scholars have even wondered (without finding any evidence) whether an earlier version of the text might have included a conspiracy scene lost in modern adaptations.

Macbeth is notable for its psychological horror. In fact acting it can be so unsettling that the play has been accused of placing a curse on its performers. The atmosphere of horror in *Macbeth* may show the influence of

---

** **protagonist** central character in a literary work*

THE SCOTTISH PLAY

A 1928 production of *Macbeth* was plagued by all sorts of disasters, from a fire on the night of the dress rehearsal to a collapsing set. This and other ill-fated productions gave the play a reputation for being cursed. Superstitious actors consider it bad luck to pronounce the name of the play anywhere inside a theater. When they need to refer to *Macbeth,* they call it "the Scottish play." The characters of Macbeth and Lady Macbeth, similarly, are known as "the Scottish king" and "the Scottish queen."

the Roman playwright Seneca, a source Shakespeare had used often in his early plays but mostly abandoned in his later work. The struggle between good and evil for the soul of the protagonist also recalls the morality plays* popular in the mid-1500s but out of fashion by the time *Macbeth* was written. Perhaps in recalling Roman tragedy, medieval morality plays, and recent dynastic politics, Shakespeare was giving cultural and historic depth as well as currency to the problem of evil.

PERFORMANCE HISTORY. The shortest of Shakespeare's tragedies, *Macbeth* has suffered fewer cuts for performance than have other Shakespearean plays. In the 1660s William Davenant added dancing and music, simplified the language, and expanded the female roles. His adaptation was the most popular version of the play for about 60 years. In the mid-1700s David Garrick restored most of the original play to the stage, although he did not reintroduce the appearance of Macbeth's severed head at the end.

From the late 1700s through the 1800s, the most noteworthy performers to attempt the roles of Macbeth and Lady Macbeth were John Philip Kemble and his sister, Sarah Siddons. Siddons in particular could inspire terror with her dignity and passion, and she is still remembered as one of the greatest Lady Macbeths of all time. Victorian* representations of Macbeth took a variety of approaches. Some emphasized the heroism of the title character, while others focused on his disintegration. Many productions paid close attention to the witches' deception of Macbeth, but director Henry IRVING's lavish production emphasized the king's own responsibility for his evil deeds.

In the 1900s Orson Welles's famous "voodoo *Macbeth*" (1936), set in Haiti, created a dense atmosphere of doom and evil. There have also been several well-known film versions of *Macbeth,* including a graphically bloody version produced in 1971 by director Roman Polanski, probably targeted toward younger viewers. Akira Kurosawa's film adaptation, *Throne of Blood* (1957), set Shakespeare's play in Japan with the main characters as samurai* fighters. Modern productions of *Macbeth,* as scholar Bernice Kliman has observed, tend to take one of two approaches. Either they emphasize the central pair, focusing on the characters' guilt, or they emphasize the play's overall atmosphere, placing the blame on more vague, ever present forces of doom and evil. These varied approaches to performing *Macbeth* reflect the uncertainty and mystery in the play's text. (*See also* **Actors, Shakespearean; Directors and Shakespeare; Feminist Interpretations; Gender and Sexuality; Ghosts and Apparitions; Macbeth, Lady; Shakespeare's Sources; Shakespeare's Works, Adaptations of.**)

MACBETH, LADY

Lady Macbeth is the ambitious wife of Macbeth in the play by the same name. Her character embodies both demonic energy and human weakness. She persuades her husband to murder the king of Scotland and usurp* the throne, but then she collapses under the guilt she feels for her role in the crime.

Macbeth's wife is mentioned in HOLINSHED'S CHRONICLES, Shakespeare's primary source for *Macbeth,* but other sources undoubtedly contributed to her character as well. The legend of Medea, a sorceress who murdered her own sons, may have influenced Shakespeare's portrayal of Lady Macbeth. Medea was the central figure of ancient Greek and Roman plays by the playwrights Euripides and Seneca. Shakespeare may also have been inspired by certain notable women active in government and politics during his day. One example is Mary, Queen of Scots, whom Queen ELIZABETH I executed for plotting against her. Scheming, dangerous, and attractive, Shakespeare's Scottish queen shares many characteristics with Queen Mary.

Early in the play, Lady Macbeth seeks demonic power. She calls on agents of evil to "unsex" her and fill her with "direst cruelty" so that she will feel no guilt about her crime. She tempts her husband to commit murder in a scene charged with emotion—eager anticipation, sexual tension, and secrecy. In a later scene when Macbeth's determination to commit the crime is wavering, she convinces him to proceed by attacking him with insults against his manhood. She claims that in his place she would have "dash'd the brains out" of her own child (I.vii.58), a statement that requires her to appear as a mother, a ruthless killer, and a persuasive temptress all in one breath.

The complexity of Lady Macbeth's character, as shown in this scene, proves her downfall later in the play. Having succeeded in her plan to gain the crown, she can neither suppress her human sympathies nor wash the crime from her mind. While Macbeth rises to greater heights of power and brutality, his wife largely disappears from the action. Her final appearance shows her sleepwalking, babbling to herself in an insane, guilty nightmare. She dies offstage, quite possibly from a suicidal act, and her husband barely notices or comments on her death. The violent energy of Lady Macbeth's life may reflect the "masculine" power that Renaissance authors sometimes saw in women, with a mixture of admiration and fear. This fascinating character has inspired brilliant performances from actresses such as Sarah Siddons, Helena Faucit, Ellen Terry, and Judi Dench. (*See also* **Actors, Shakespearean; Macbeth.**)

MADNESS

Several of Shakespeare's plays explore the concept of insanity. Some of the playwright's characters are truly mad, while others merely assume the appearance of madness. In either case the behavior associated with madness presents a departure from, and a challenge to, society's normal expectations.

MENTAL ILLNESS IN ELIZABETHAN PSYCHOLOGY. The Elizabethan understanding of "mania," or mental illness, was based on a theory of nature that dated back to ancient Rome. This theory divided the natural world into four elements: fire, air, earth, and water. Each of these elements was associated with one of four bodily fluids. These fluids, known

Madness

In *King Lear*, Edgar disguises himself as a wandering lunatic named Poor Tom. He is shown here with wild and disheveled hair, a characteristic that Elizabethans associated with madness.

* *phlegm* thick, slimy mucus found in the respiratory tract

* *hallucination* imaginary vision brought on by madness, illness, or drugs

* *bawdy* indecent; lewd

as humors, were blood, choler (yellow bile), melancholy (black bile), and phlegm*. Too much or too little of a given humor could cause various mental and physical conditions. According to the theory of humors, an imbalance was commonly caused by a powerful emotional experience, such as a painful romance or the death of a loved one. The humors were also thought to be affected by age, seasonal changes, and the movements of the stars and planets. Madness was often considered to be outside the sufferer's control, stemming from either natural or supernatural causes. In some cases, however, sufferers could be faulted for failing to understand their emotions well enough to control them.

MELANCHOLIA. Melancholy, as its name suggests, was associated with sadness, and an excess of black bile was thought to cause it. Severe melancholia was much like what modern psychologists call depression. Sufferers, known as melancholics, were unreasonable and emotionally unstable, exaggerating and dwelling on their sorrows until they could hardly think of or do anything else. They lost interest in life and might have wild mood swings and contemplate suicide.

Shakespeare's most famous melancholic is Hamlet. The experience that triggers his melancholia is his father's death and his mother's hasty marriage to the brother of her late husband. Hamlet complains that he has "lost all [his] mirth" and "forgone all custom of exercises" (II.ii.296–97). He means that he is unhappy and is no longer interested in his favorite activities. His stepfather, the king, expresses the Elizabethan view that such intense emotions should be controlled by reason, saying that Hamlet's "unmanly grief" shows "a will most incorrect to heaven" (I.ii.95). Other characters who suffer from melancholia include Antonio in *The Merchant of Venice* and Don John in *Much Ado About Nothing*.

An extreme case of melancholia could produce dangerous symptoms. Sufferers lost all reason and restraint and might experience hallucinations*. Elizabethans believed that this state of extreme, or pathological, melancholia was typically caused by overwhelming grief. An example of pathological melancholia is Ophelia's behavior in *Hamlet* after she learns that the prince has killed her father, Polonius. A gentleman describes her symptoms with pity: "She speaks much of her father . . . and hems, and beats her heart, / Spurns enviously at straws, speaks things in doubt / That carry but half sense" (IV.v.4–7). In a famous scene Ophelia wanders about the court distributing flowers (a common Elizabethan symptom of madness) and singing snatches of bawdy* love songs. When she later dies by drowning, it is not clear whether her death is an accident resulting from her impaired judgment or a deliberate suicide, though the former seems more likely.

LOVE MADNESS. Several of Shakespeare's plays express the Elizabethan idea that people can be driven to madness by love. A troubled romance can trigger an attack of melancholia, as in *Twelfth Night*, where several characters pine for the love of others. Shakespeare pokes fun especially at Duke Orsino, who seems to enjoy the repeated rejection of Olivia because it lets him indulge in feelings of wounded love. The play's Clown

BEDLAM BEGGARS

Those who suffered from mental illness in Elizabethan England were often doomed to suffer further at the hands of public officials. The halls of London's Bethlehem Hospital were filled with insane patients, who were commonly beaten and kept in chains. Some patients were released with licenses to beg. They wandered through town and country, often driven away with whippings from local authorities. The hospital's nickname, Bedlam, also referred to any mentally ill wanderer. The association of Bedlam with insanity led to its current use as a word for confusion and chaos.

* *aside* remark made by a character onstage to the audience or to another character, unheard by other characters present in the same scene

remarks, "Now the melancholy god protect thee . . . for thy mind is a very opal" (II.iv.73–75), comparing the duke's disturbed thoughts to the swirling appearance of a cloudy gemstone.

Extreme cases of love madness could lead to violent jealousy, particularly in those who lacked the ability to recognize and control their passions. The best example in Shakespeare is Othello, whose trusted lieutenant IAGO falsely persuades him that his wife is unfaithful. Iago pricks at Othello's insecurities until his rage unravels his judgment and fractures his speech: "Pish! Noses, ears, and lips.—Is't possible?—Confess—handkerchief!—O devil!" (IV.i.42–43) he cries out before collapsing in a trance. Othello's jealousy finally drives him to murder his wife before he realizes the truth and then kills himself in disgust. This play may be Shakespeare's clearest illustration of the destructive power of madness.

VISION THROUGH MADNESS. While the power of madness can be destructive, it can also lead sufferers to insights they might never have had while sane. This idea is expressed most powerfully in *King Lear*, when the aged king rashly divides his kingdom and disowns his only loyal daughter. After being betrayed by his other children, Lear loses his wits and runs raving into a fierce storm. Stripped of all the outward appearances of normality and sanity, the king arrives at the most basic, natural state of humankind. In his mental agony he perceives things he was unable to see when he was prosperous and sane, such as his own folly in rejecting his faithful daughter, CORDELIA. But this truthful vision comes at a high price, for his kingdom is in shambles, and he himself is a physical wreck.

The idea that madness reveals truths that would otherwise be hidden is also expressed in *Hamlet*. While losing a battle of wits with the prince, POLONIUS remarks in an aside*, "Though this be madness, yet there is method in't" (II.ii.205–6). He then observes that the cleverness of Hamlet's comments is "a happiness that often madness hits on, which reason and sanity could not so prosperously be deliver'd of" (209–11). This speech is ironic, however, as Hamlet is only pretending to be insane in order to divert attention from his plan to murder the king. Hamlet has not gained insight through madness; but by pretending to be mad, he has enhanced his ability to express his radical ideas freely, without the restraints of rational thought and behavior. Hamlet's behavior shows that pretended madness can be useful, enabling characters to utter uncommon insights without the dangerous effects of real madness.

A similar type of feigned madness plays a role in *King Lear*. The Fool makes many pointed observations about the king's behavior, but he makes them in a nonsensical way, mixing in fragments of poetry. By this seemingly odd behavior, which resembles madness, he is able to get away with remarks that would be punished if they were spoken directly (as they are in the character of Kent, who is banished from Lear's kingdom for his honesty). Pretended madness also proves helpful to Edgar, a nobleman falsely accused of plotting his father's death. He escapes arrest

in the disguise of a wandering lunatic called Tom o' Bedlam (a nickname for London's Bethlehem Hospital, where the insane were confined). Edgar assumes the appearance of a "Bedlam beggar" by smearing his face with dirt, tangling his hair into knots, and speaking in a tumble of riddle and rhyme interrupted by shrill cries against the devils that supposedly plague him. This counterfeit lunacy allows Edgar, like Hamlet, to survive while he works to set right the wrongs that have been done in his homeland. Edgar's experience shows that, while true madness destroys society, pretended madness can enable characters to escape from the insanity that afflicts society and eventually to help heal. (*See also* **Astronomy and Cosmology; Disease; Fools, Clowns, and Jesters; Macbeth, Lady; Medicine; Psychology.**)

MAGIC AND FOLKLORE

Elizabethans of every social class believed in the power to predict or control earthly events through spells, charms, rituals, omens, and other methods. Most people also had faith in folklore, which told of fairies, demons, ghosts, witches, and other supernatural creatures. Although scientists were making important discoveries, such as how blood circulates through the body, they were still unable to explain many other natural occurrences, such as eclipses and storms. As a result belief in magic and folklore remained strong, even while scientific knowledge advanced.

MAGIC

During the Elizabethan era the three most commonly practiced forms of magic were astrology, alchemy, and spirit conjuring. Astrology and alchemy were considered part of natural science, which included all investigations into the working of the universe. Spirit conjuring, however, was considered evil and therefore condemned by the English government and the Anglican Church.

STARGAZING. Astrology, which sought to predict and control the future, was by far the most popular and widely practiced form of magic among Elizabethans. Faith in astrology stemmed from the belief that the earth stood at the center of the universe and was surrounded by a series of interlocking spheres. The innermost sphere contained the moon, followed by spheres holding the sun, planets, and stars. God and the angels resided in the outermost sphere, known as the primum mobile, which moved all the others. Because God controlled the movement of the stars, astrologers believed that they could discover his will by carefully observing the journey of heavenly bodies across the sky.

The most influential people of the time believed in astrology. Queen ELIZABETH I employed astrologers to cast the horoscopes of some of her suitors. She also used astrology to determine possible heirs to her throne. In addition, Elizabeth commanded John Dee, her personal astrologer, to

consult the stars and determine the luckiest possible day for her coronation.

Highly educated people, such as physicians, practiced astrology. Physicians believed that most illness resulted from an imbalance of four vital bodily fluids—blood, phlegm*, black bile, and yellow bile— known as humors. Because they also believed that the stars' movements directly affected the humors, they often considered a patient's horoscope when making a diagnosis. Patients who suffered from sudden attacks of illness were sometimes diagnosed as "planetstruck," meaning that their health had been adversely affected by the movement of a particular planet.

Not everyone accepted astrology, however. Religious leaders condemned stargazing. They said it was sacrilegious* to believe that human destiny was determined by the stars rather than by a person's free will or by God's plan. Although Shakespeare's opinion of astrology is unknown, his characters often speak about the stars. In *King Lear* the earl of Kent says "It is the stars, / The stars above us, govern our conditions." (IV.iii.32–33). In the same play Edmund, the bastard son of Gloucester, dismisses the stars' power, saying it is bad behavior that is to blame for people's misfortunes:

> This is the excellent foppery [foolishness] of the world, that when we are sick in fortune—often the surfeits [results] of our own behavior—we make guilty of our disasters the sun, the moon, and stars, as if we were villains on necessity, fools by heavenly compulsion, knaves, thieves, and treachers [traitors] by spherical predominance; drunkards, liars, and adulterers by an enforc'd obedience of planetary influence; and all that we are evil in, by a divine thrusting on.
>
> (I.ii.118–26)

LEAD INTO GOLD. The principal goal of alchemy was to turn lead and other inexpensive metals into gold and silver. Alchemists also searched for the elixir of life, a magical potion that would provide immortality. Belief in alchemy was based on the idea that all matter was composed of four elements: fire, air, earth, and water. Alchemists believed that they could change one substance into another by altering the balance of the four elements. The process they sought to master was called transmutation.

The possibility of manufacturing gold interested many Elizabethans, including the queen. She provided some alchemists with money to pursue their search for the philosopher stone, a substance that supposedly would transform any metal into gold. Other prominent Elizabethans, such as Sir Walter Raleigh, also supported research in alchemy. Although some alchemists were dedicated investigators, many others were simply frauds. In his comedy *The Alchemist,* Ben Jonson ridiculed these pseudoscientists and their gullible followers.

Shakespeare rarely mentions alchemy in his works. In *Julius Caesar,* however, he uses alchemy as a symbol for Brutus's ability to transform

---

* *phlegm* thick, slimy mucus found in the respiratory tract

* *sacrilegious* disrespectful toward something sacred

unfavorable public opinion into popular support: "O, he sits high in all the people's hearts; / And that which would appear offense in us, / His countenance, like richest alchemy, / Will change to virtue and worthiness" (I.iii.157–60).

RAISING SPIRITS. Spirit conjuring, known as necromancy or sorcery, was the most controversial form of magic. Sorcerers sought to control spirits through spells, charms, and rituals in order to compel their assistance. Faith in sorcery was partly based on the Christian belief that God and the angels intervene in people's daily lives. Several methods for contacting spirits were taken from religious works, such as the *Cabala*, a collection of Jewish mystical beliefs and practices.

Many sorcerers were devoutly religious men who sought to contact good spirits. John Dee, the era's most famous sorcerer, held seances during which he claimed to speak with the archangel Gabriel. He desired to contact benevolent spirits in order to seek answers to religious questions, such as how best to reunite the Catholic and Protestant churches. Dee also asked spirits to answer questions about scientific matters.

Despite the virtuous goals of some sorcerers, conjuring spirits was considered a dangerous and evil practice. Critics argued that God and the angels cannot be summoned by spells, and that any spirits contacted by sorcerers must be devils. Opponents of sorcery pointed out that, according to the Bible, the devil sometimes disguises himself as a benevolent

In Shakespeare's day alchemy was considered a branch of science rather than a form of magic. Alchemists attempted to convert lead and other common metals into gold and to brew potions that could help people live forever.

angel in order to ensnare people. Government authorities also strongly opposed sorcery, and in 1563 Parliament declared the conjuring of evil spirits a crime punishable by death.

In *The Tempest*, Shakespeare provides an example of both a good and a bad sorcerer. Prospero is an example of a virtuous sorcerer because he gains his magical powers through intense study of books on magic and uses his powers only for good. Sycorax, on the other hand, is an example of an evil conjurer, who gains her powers through contact with the devil. In fact her union with the devil defines her as a witch.

FOLKLORE

Elizabethan folklore included a large collection of beliefs about the supernatural. Most people believed in the existence of otherworldly creatures, omens, and magical cures.

THINGS THAT GO BUMP IN THE NIGHT. Supernatural creatures were blamed for many misfortunes, including illness, crop failures, and business failures. The average Elizabethan believed in fairies, ghosts, and demons. These beliefs were based on the pagan* notion that nature was swarming with otherworldly creatures and spirits. In addition the church taught that Satan and other devils roamed the world, constantly attempting to trap humans.

Fairies, also referred to as "little people," were believed to be among the most common supernatural creatures. Because they appeared only between midnight and dawn, however, they were rarely seen directly. Instead, people discovered "fairy rings," circles of trampled crops where the little people had danced in the moonlight.

Fairies could be even more destructive, however. They were blamed for all types of mischief, including souring milk, pinching sleeping housemaids, and leading travelers astray. It was also believed that some fairies sat atop sleepers' stomachs, causing cramps and nightmares. Even worse were those who stole beautiful, healthy children and replaced them with puny, sickly infants, known as changelings.

Fairies could also be helpful, however, and it was thought that fairy godmothers protected and assisted some children. In *A Midsummer Night's Dream*, Shakespeare depicts fairies as happy, friendly creatures who play harmless pranks on foolish humans. Shakespeare's conception of fairies was so influential that it eventually replaced traditional folklore, which taught that the little people were often cruel.

WARDING OFF MISFORTUNE. Superstitions connected with death abounded in Elizabethan England. Many people believed that death was foretold by certain events, such as a cow entering the garden. Another common belief was that those who stayed awake and fasted on Midsummer Eve (June 24) would see all the townspeople destined to die in the following 12 months. Many other superstitions told of ways to avoid calamity. After an accident at home, for example, an owner would throw three beans over the threshold to guard against further misfortune. The

* **pagan** referring to ancient religions that worshiped many gods, or more generally, to any non-Christian religion

81

act of ringing church bells was thought to scare away evil spirits, and bay leaves were used as charms to ward off danger.

Shakespeare made dramatic use of superstitions about death. In *Richard II*, for example, he alludes to the common belief that the dying can see into the future. As John of Gaunt lies on his deathbed, he predicts that King Richard's frivolous behavior will result in the monarch's downfall: "Methinks I am a prophet new inspir'd / And thus expiring [dying] do foretell of him: / His rash fierce blaze of riot cannot last, / For violent fires soon burn out themselves" (II.i.31–34).

WARNING SIGNS. It was commonly believed that omens preceded disasters. Many people claimed that the appearance of a comet in 1596 foretold a catastrophic flood that struck England later that year.

In *Macbeth*, Shakespeare summed up many of the portents that supposedly warned of tragic death. Lady Macbeth, while waiting for her husband to kill King Duncan, hears an owl's shriek, a traditional harbinger of violent death. The night of the murder is disturbed by several other warnings of approaching disaster, including a storm, ghostly screams, and an earthquake. (*See also* **Astronomy and Cosmology; Fairies; Ghosts and Apparitions; Puck; Supernatural Phenomena; Witches and Evil Spirits.**)

MALVOLIO

Malvolio is the main object of ridicule in Shakespeare's *Twelfth Night* and the focus of the play's comic subplot. He is the ill-tempered steward, or guardian, of the heroine Olivia, who is herself the object of Duke Orsino's affection. Like Orsino, Malvolio wishes to marry Olivia—not because he loves her, however, but because the marriage would make him a nobleman. In contrast to most of the other characters, many of whom are fun-loving, high-spirited members of the duke's court, Malvolio is pompous, prudish, and conceited, with no tolerance for what he regards as frivolous behavior.

In Act II, Malvolio puts an end to the raucous partying of Sir Toby Belch, Sir Andrew Aguecheek, the lady Maria, and the clown Feste and threatens to tell Olivia about their noisemaking. The revelers decide to play a trick on him, one that leads to his downfall and temporary imprisonment for insanity. Maria writes a letter that appears to come from Olivia, which she drops in his path. In this message "Olivia" asks her secret lover to approach her wearing an outlandish costume. Although the letter does not mention Malvolio by name, he persuades himself that it is meant for him, and he dresses accordingly. When he comes to Olivia, dressed so uncharacteristically, she thinks he has gone mad. After the humiliations of his folly, Malvolio appeals to Olivia. Although she pities him for the suffering he has undergone and promises him a fair hearing for his complaints, no one else takes Malvolio seriously, and as he stalks out he swears revenge on everyone who has made him look ridiculous.

Malvolio is one of Shakespeare's most interesting comedic characters and a key figure in the play. In fact, some 17th-century adaptations call the play "Malvolio," and the role has long been a favorite among Shakespearean actors. Like SHYLOCK in *The Merchant of Venice,* Malvolio becomes a somewhat sympathetic figure because the abuse he suffers seems disproportionate to his offenses. Malvolio's anger seems justified in light of the taunting he has endured, and his final exit is unsettling. Although Malvolio is not a tragic figure, such as King Lear or Macbeth, his shabby treatment and his lack of remorse are difficult to reconcile with the otherwise happy ending of the play. The tension audiences feel between the humorous and the tragic at the conclusion of *Twelfth Night* is a distinguishing feature of Shakespeare's mature comedies. It anticipates the mood found in the tragicomedies and romances that followed this play. (*See also* **Humor in Shakespeare's Plays.**)

MANNERS

* *decorum* proper behavior

In Shakespeare's society manners were more than a matter of courtesy. Elizabethans believed that there was a proper order in society, just as there was in nature, and that everyone had a role to play in that order. Nobles and peasants, masters and servants, adults and children, men and women were all held to different standards of behavior. For all groups, however, appropriate actions were believed to produce good thoughts. To behave inappropriately was a sign of inner weakness or moral corruption. With such a high value placed on decorum*, it is no surprise that children were taught manners from an early age or that adults constantly strove to perfect their own.

WELL-BEHAVED CHILDREN. One of the books most widely used for the instruction of children was *De Civilitate,* by the Dutch scholar Desiderius Erasmus. It instructed children on the correct behavior from the moment they arose in the morning until they went to bed at night.

Most of Erasmus's teachings concerned the proper treatment of others. The most important rule for children was to show respect to their elders, particularly to their parents. They were to speak only when spoken to and then to answer briefly and truthfully. When addressing their elders children were expected to speak in a quiet but unhesitating manner, looking directly at them without fidgeting or stammering. Children were also encouraged to be courteous to their classmates, to servants, and to people of lower social status.

In terms of appearance Erasmus stressed neatness and cleanliness: making one's bed soon after rising, washing and brushing teeth, and wearing clean, unwrinkled clothes. A child should not be sullen, but at the same time he or she should not smile or laugh too much. Excessive smiling was a sign of deceit, while too much laughter indicated either an evil soul or an empty head. Some of Erasmus's requirements, such as walking quietly and "with grace" when accompanied by a friend, must have been very difficult for many children to follow.

Manners

* hierarchy ordered structure based on rank

PERSONAL HABITS. Schooling in manners did not end with childhood. The rigid social hierarchy* of English society had just begun to relax slightly in Shakespeare's time, making the title of "gentleman" available to some of humble birth. Those who aspired to achieve that status needed to conduct themselves in a "gentlemanly" fashion—with ease and confidence but without arrogance or boastfulness.

Many of the habits and fashions of Italy and France were being imported into England, and adults eagerly read books that instructed them in proper behavior. Several of these so-called conduct books were aimed at women, advising them on how to interact with men in particular. According to these manuals a lady should always be modest in both dress and demeanor, looking down when speaking rather than meeting her partner's eyes. She should not draw too much attention to herself or speak too often. She should never question her husband's authority and should always accept his criticisms quietly and patiently.

Some rules of behavior applied equally to both sexes. Wearing heavy perfumes was frowned on, as was dressing in a manner inappropriate to one's age, figure, or class. It was considered poor manners to speak ill of anyone or to discuss matters that would embarrass others. Boasting, bragging, talking too much, laughing at one's own jokes, and interrupting others were all serious breeches of courtesy.

* Tudor referring to the dynasty that ruled England from 1485 to 1603

Table manners also changed significantly during the late 1500s. During Tudor* times diners were expected to eat in silence while passages from the Bible or other sacred books were read aloud. By Elizabeth's reign table conversation was encouraged but only under certain conditions. Such conversation should be pleasant, never about business or other matters that would give rise to disputes. Gentlemen should avoid discussing subjects that ladies at the table could not understand or that would force a guest to admit ignorance. Jokes and amusing stories were encouraged, as long as they were not mean-spirited and avoided mentioning bodily mutilation.

DECORUM IN SPEECH. Elizabethan notions of decorum also extended to grace in speaking and writing. Just as there was a proper action for every setting, there was also a proper word for any subject, speaker, and audience. The phrasing of a statement was as important as the idea being expressed.

One of the most important subjects in English grammar schools was rhetoric, the art of speaking or writing effectively. The three major principles of rhetoric were richness of expression, creativity in the selection of material to support one's argument, and skillful organization of ideas. This type of training produced the distinctive literary style of the period, in which sentences contained levels of meaning and symbolism. Shakespeare's works exemplify what Elizabethan writers aimed to achieve. For every successful Elizabethan writer, however, there were many more in whose hands the use of these same literary techniques produced what critic George Puttenham called a "bombasted," or overly padded, writing style. (*See also* **Clothing; Education and Literacy; Food and Feasts; Language; Personal Hygiene; Social Classes.**)

MARK ANTONY

See *Antony and Cleopatra; Julius Caesar.*

MARKETS AND FAIRS

Although the England of Shakespeare's time was not yet the great commercial nation it would one day become, it had a thriving economy. One of the mainstays of Elizabethan trade was the town market day. Local farmers brought their produce to sell, CRAFTWORKERS displayed manufactured goods, and eager housewives filled the town square to purchase the week's necessities. Far more exciting than the local market, however, was the hustle and bustle of a great fair. On such special occasions, fairgrounds were filled with food, wares, and entertainment of every possible kind, offering shoppers the chance to buy goods rarely available to anyone living outside LONDON.

MARKET DAYS. One of the features that distinguished an Elizabethan town from a mere village was its marketplace. To hold a market, a town had to receive permission from the monarch. By the late 1500s, about 600 English towns had been granted this right. These market towns served as centers for distributing both farm goods and manufactured wares. Shakespeare's hometown of STRATFORD-UPON-AVON had held its weekly market every Thursday since the early 1300s. Even an extremely small town might be granted the right to hold a market if there was no larger town nearby. The small markets found in these towns gave rise to an old English proverb: "Three women and a goose make a market."

Markets were typically held once a week, although larger towns might have them twice a week. For example, Queen Elizabeth granted the town of Winchester a license to hold market days on Wednesday and Saturday. Because competition for wares could be fierce, towns within 20 miles of each other avoided holding their markets on the same day of the week. If one town held a market on Tuesday, the nearest town might have its own on Friday, enabling farmers to bring fresh produce to both markets.

On the morning of a market day, stalls and tables were set up throughout the marketplace. Some belonged to local farmers, who were permitted to sell their butter, eggs, vegetables, and fowl only on market days. Others were set up by small-scale manufacturers who did not keep a regular shop and therefore sold their products only at markets. Buyers flooded into the town as well, significantly increasing the population of some smaller market towns and giving a boost to local businesses that dealt in food, drink, and entertainment.

Traditionally, a bell would ring to signal the official opening of the market. To ensure that all sellers had a fair chance, merchants were forbidden to sell their wares until the bell had rung. This tradition prevented sellers from forestalling, arriving early and snapping up the available customers. As soon as the bell sounded, the marketplace erupted in a frenzy of activity. Traders called out their wares to potential buyers, sometimes exaggeratedly praising the virtues of their goods, while shrewd buyers

haggled over prices. Business typically lasted for only a few hours. Buyers and sellers frequently ended their market day at the local tavern, trading stories of the day's successes and failures.

ANNUAL FAIRS. Fair days, held once a year in most areas, lifted the town market to a new level. Fairs provided a location for the sale of livestock, seed, and other agricultural commodities in addition to the everyday household goods available at local markets. Like a modern-day convention or sporting event, the annual fair was a major boost to the economy of any Elizabethan town. Not only could traders be charged for stall space, but the local inns and restaurants experienced a boom in business as they catered to the many buyers and sellers visiting the town. A license to hold a fair was therefore an even bigger prize than the right to hold a market.

An Elizabethan fair was a feast for the eyes. A pageant, including a parade of town officials, marked the start of several days of buying and selling. A large fair might last a month or longer. A city of tents covered a large open space, usually just outside the town. Merchants set up stalls filled with all kinds of wares, from basic household supplies (such as grain, wood, coal, cloth, and produce) to luxury items (such as spices, silks, and brass). Farmers from distant places, usually unwelcome at the local markets, were also allowed to sell their goods. Tables were covered with the newest fashions (usually from London) for both gentlemen and ladies. Young women examined the latest ribbons and silks, and men bought their sweethearts lace and scented gloves. A present purchased at a fair was known as a fairing.

The fair was much more than a place to buy and sell, however. Visitors would find many sideshows lining the aisles of tents and tables. Some displayed curious animals such as a goose or rooster with more than two legs or a dancing monkey. One tent might feature a singer crooning the latest ballad of the day, the next a puppet show presenting famous—and often rowdy—tales. Preachers tried to convert the fallen, and quack doctors (called mountebanks) promoted cures for every known ailment. Naturally, all manner of food and drink were available for sale. There was much drinking throughout the day, while pickpockets and prostitutes worked the assembled crowd.

The largest fair in Elizabethan England was probably Stourbridge Fair, held just outside of Cambridge. Because England's waterways were the most reliable means of transporting goods, Cambridge's closeness to the THAMES made it ideal for trading. Stourbridge Fair lasted for three weeks each year and was famed throughout England. Another noteworthy fair was Scarborough Fair, the subject of the traditional folk ballad by the same name. One of the oldest fairs in England, Scarborough received its charter from King Henry III in the mid-1200s. Like most of England's fairs it was hugely popular and drew visitors from a wide area. It lasted a month and a half, an unusually long time even for an Elizabethan fair, perhaps because it was held in an isolated part of Yorkshire where traveling was difficult. (*See also* **Banking and Commerce; Cities, Towns, and Villages; Jonson, Ben; Pageants and Morality Plays; Transportation and Travel.**)

A FAIR TO REMEMBER

One of the most popular plays of the early 1600s was *Bartholomew Fair,* written in 1614 by Shakespeare's friend Ben Jonson. The real Bartholomew Fair was a market held annually in the London suburb of Smithfield on Saint Bartholomew's Day (August 24). Jonson's boisterous, colorful comedy captures all the excitement of a typical Elizabethan fair: puppeteers, gingerbread sellers, toy makers, pickpockets, and prostitutes fill the stage with their wares and antics. Unlike any other playwright Jonson offers a glimpse into the human circus that was an Elizabethan fair.

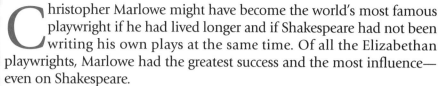

MARLOWE, CHRISTOPHER

1564–1593
Playwright

* *iambic pentameter* line of poetry consisting of ten syllables, or five metric feet, with emphasis placed on every other syllable
* *protagonist* central character in a literary work
* *atheist* person who denies the existence of God

* *plague* highly contagious and often fatal disease; also called the Black Death

See color plate 9, vol. 3.

Christopher Marlowe might have become the world's most famous playwright if he had lived longer and if Shakespeare had not been writing his own plays at the same time. Of all the Elizabethan playwrights, Marlowe had the greatest success and the most influence—even on Shakespeare.

In 1588 as Shakespeare began his career in the London theater, Marlowe was considered the finest English dramatist of his day. He had established blank verse (unrhymed iambic pentameter*) as the standard medium for drama, and his heroic protagonists* inspired others, notably Shakespeare, to create such powerful characters as Richard III, King Lear, Macbeth, and Othello.

Born a cobbler's son, Christopher Marlowe led a double life as a playwright and a spy. He was a well-educated, homosexual man who wrote poetry and translated Latin works into English. Marlowe also had a reputation as a drinker, a fighter, and an atheist*. He had become involved with Thomas Walsingham, the leader of a team of international spies. In 1593 Marlowe went with some friends to the village of Deptford to escape the plague* in London. During an argument over the payment of a bill, he stabbed a man. That man then stabbed Marlowe just above the right eye, killing him instantly. He was only 29 years old when he died. Some historians have suggested that a government agent may have killed Marlowe in order to silence him. His killer was pardoned soon after the murder.

Marlowe is best remembered for the plays he wrote between 1587, when he received his university degree from Cambridge, and 1592, a year before his untimely death. Several of these plays are about men driven by overwhelming ambition: *Tamburlaine the Great,* Parts I and II, the story of a warrior obsessed with power and destruction; *The Tragical History of Doctor Faustus,* about a man who sells his soul to the devil; and *The Jew of Malta,* about the crafty villain Barabas. The last of these plays may have been the model for Shakespeare's *The Merchant of Venice.*

While the influence Marlowe had on Shakespeare seems clear, some scholars have suggested that the flow of inspiration went both ways and that the two playwrights knew each other. Whatever their relationship, Shakespeare knew Marlowe's work well. Numerous words, scenes, and situations in his plays echo Marlowe's writings. (*See also* **Playwrights and Poets; Poetic Techniques; Prose Technique.**)

MARRIAGE AND FAMILY

Most Elizabethans expected to marry. Although the main purpose of marriage was to produce children, successful marriages were also supposed to provide material comforts and companionship. Like Elizabethan society as a whole, families were structured as hierarchies*. The husband served as the household's leader, with his wife, children, and servants under his direction.

MARRIAGE AND MONEY. Marriage in Shakespeare's day was a decision that involved members of both families. In fact economic status—the

* *hierarchy* ordered structure based on rank

See
color plate 6,
vol. 1.

HORNS OF A DILEMMA

Because marriages were often arranged without regard to love, some people looked for romance outside the home. Such marital unfaithfulness—called cuckoldry when it involved a woman cheating on her husband—was a source of many jokes in Shakespeare's plays. The mention of horns of any type, from deer antlers to musical instruments, was likely to be a cuckold joke. In *Much Ado About Nothing,* for example, Benedick suggests that if he ever marries they will have to "pluck off the bull's horns" and put them on his forehead. Frequent jokes about cuckoldry in Shakespeare's time indicate that unfaithfulness in marriage was a common, and much feared, occurrence.

amount of wealth a family possessed—played a significant role in determining who married whom. Romantic love and physical attraction were considered to be relatively unimportant.

Wealth played an even greater role in marriage decisions among the upper classes than among the lower classes. Marriage among the rich usually meant the joining of two powerful families. Marriages that would benefit the families of both spouses were enthusiastically pursued. A lesser nobleman of great wealth, for example, might marry a woman of modest means and greater nobility. In this way both families improved their social and economic positions.

Once upper-class families agreed to a marriage, several financial transactions were considered. For example, the bride's family promised to give the new married couple a dowry, a gift of money and property. The groom's family agreed to supply the couple with enough money to live on. These arrangements ensured that the new couple could live comfortably throughout their lifetimes.

Among all classes the marriage process followed a similar path. First, a betrothal was held, during which the couple announced before witnesses their intention to marry. Because betrothals were legally binding, it was deemed socially acceptable for the couple to engage in sex. In fact records show that many Elizabethan brides were pregnant when they walked down the aisle to be married.

Marriage ceremonies occurred in church, which could be at either the bride's or the groom's parish. In the weeks preceding the ceremony, the couple's plans to wed were announced at church services on three consecutive Sundays. These public announcements, known as banns, provided an opportunity to raise objections to the marriage. If a person could provide a valid reason why the couple should not marry, the wedding was forbidden. Reasons to prevent a marriage included an earlier betrothal to another person.

A WOMAN'S PLACE IN THE FAMILY. Women had few options in Elizabethan times. Most were raised to marry, rear a family, and perform domestic chores. Because men were considered to be superior to women, wives were expected to obey their husbands.

The importance placed on a wife's obedience to her husband is evident in Shakespeare's tragedies and comedies. In *Othello,* Desdemona remains loyal to her husband even though he has strangled her and left her for dead. When asked who killed her, she says with her dying words: "Nobody; I myself." In his comedies Shakespeare defies society's expectations by presenting wives who tend to dominate their husbands. This role reversal is evident in *The Merry Wives of Windsor,* where Mistress Ford outwits both her jealous husband and the fat knight, Sir John Falstaff. In *The Taming of the Shrew,* Shakespeare presents Katharina, a strong-willed woman who spends much of the play refusing to be the obedient wife.

RAISING THE CHILDREN. In wealthier families women did not nurse their own children. Instead, they turned them over to a wet nurse. It was

This portrait of a wealthy Elizabethan family illustrates the roles of men and women in marriage. As ruler of the family, the man looks confidently ahead while the children seem to gather around their mother.

* **apprentice** person bound by legal agreement to work for another for a specified period of time in return for instruction in a trade or art

common for the babies to live with the nurse's family and for the parents to visit. Only when they were weaned would the children be brought back home.

Although the wealthiest families hired live-in tutors for their children, many Elizabethans sent their sons away to be educated. Some sent their boys off to become apprentices* to craftsmen or tradesmen. Girls might also be sent off for training in domestic service in a large manor house. Many children lived with their parents for only a short time. Most children left home in their early teens.

There was little privacy in most Elizabethan homes. Houses were especially small among the poor, and many family members lived in close quarters. In Shakespeare's time it was common for entire families to sleep in the same room, with several children sleeping in the same bed. (*See also* **Education and Literacy**.)

MARXIST INTERPRETATIONS

* **capitalist** referring to an economic system in which individuals own property

Marxism is the political and economic theory developed by Karl Marx and Friedrich Engels in the mid-1800s. Its central idea is that the unequal distribution of wealth in capitalist* societies leads to a struggle between different social classes, which is the main force behind social and political change. Marx himself wrote very little about Shakespeare, except for some remarks on *The Merchant of Venice* and *Timon of Athens*. These works, with their focus on the corrupting power of money, apparently helped shape Marx's views of capitalist society. Later Marxist thinkers and literary critics analyzed Shakespeare's works in much more detail. Marxist interpretations tend to focus on how Elizabethan society, politics, and economics influenced Shakespeare's plays.

Marxist interpretations are based on the idea that Shakespeare wrote for an audience consisting mainly of the working classes. Many Marxist critics claim that the most important influences on Shakespeare's work came not from his classical* sources but from popular culture—folktales, morality plays, and interludes—aimed at a less literate audience. They also attempt to show how the plays reflect Shakespeare's views of society and class conflict. For example, according to one Marxist interpretation, the history plays show Shakespeare's enthusiasm for the rise of English nationalism during the 1500s. This feeling of national identity helped maintain the rigid class structure of Elizabethan society, which was linked to ideas of social order that were popular at the time. Shakespeare's comedies, written around the same time as the histories, are seen as a celebration of the social order. But the interests of the developing middle class, of which Shakespeare was a member, soon came into conflict with those of the aristocracy. Marxist commentators see this clash reflected in *Julius Caesar*, a play that raises questions about the sources of legitimate* political power.

Mainstream critics find much of value in the Marxist emphasis on understanding the social context in which Shakespeare wrote. It is sometimes pointed out, however, that Marxists place too little importance on the classical sources Shakespeare used. While every author's works are shaped by the author's social circumstances, they are also influenced by the author's literary background. It is not easy to separate the two, and neither factor can be ignored when evaluating a body of literature. (*See also* **Shakespeare's Sources; Social Classes.**)

* *classical* in the tradition of ancient Greece and Rome

* *legitimate* valid or acceptable

MASQUES

The masque, a form of dramatic entertainment, originated in ancient fertility rites and evolved in the 1400s from two sources. One was the Italian court amusements, or dramatic performances. The other source was the English tradition of mummery, in which ordinary people disguised themselves and serenaded their friends and neighbors on holidays, such as during the Christmas season. As masques developed in England, they became more elegant and subdued. Among the aristocracy, they frequently involved surprise visits from costumed friends bearing gifts and accompanied by musicians and other entertainers.

Formal masques were often staged on special occasions, such as the weddings or birthdays of members of the royal family. Sometimes they preceded a festive event, such as a ball. They became increasingly important during the reign of James I. The king's wife, Queen Anne, enjoyed the gaiety and opulence of these spectacles. As a result enormous sums of money were spent on scenery, costumes, and special effects, such as a castle or ship mounted on wheels. Presented on stage, these Jacobean* pageants featured fantastic disguises, music, and dancing. Inigo Jones, Queen Anne's personal architect, designed magnificent sets, while the

* *Jacobean* referring to the reign of James I, king of England from 1603 to 1625

In the second act of *Henry VIII,* a group of players performs a masque for the king and his court. This illustration by F. Lloyds shows the scene as staged by actor-manager Charles Kean in 1859.

poet and playwright Ben Jonson raised the verbal art of the masque to new heights. Jonson is also credited with inventing the "antimasque," a parody that actually reintroduced some of the original elements of the traditional masque.

* **betrothal** mutual promise to marry in the future

Shakespeare incorporated masques in several of his plays. *The Tempest* includes a masque to celebrate the betrothal* of Ferdinand and Miranda (IV.i). A royal masque is re-enacted in *Henry VIII* (I.iv). Masquelike elements also appear in *Romeo and Juliet* (I.iv), *Much Ado About Nothing* (II.i), *The Winter's Tale* (IV.iv), and *A Midsummer Night's Dream.* (*See also* **Disguises; Dreams; Festivals and Holidays; Pageants and Morality Plays; Play Within the Play; Vice, The.**)

MASTER OF THE REVELS

* **lord chamberlain** chief officer of the English monarch

* **prompt book** annotated copy of a play, which contains instructions for entrances, exits, music, and other cues

In England in the 1500s and 1600s, royal entertainments, or revels, were held between All Saints' Day (November 1) and Lent, the following spring. The master of the revels—first appointed in 1545, under King Henry VIII—arranged, supervised, and paid for all court entertainment.

The master reported to the lord chamberlain*, and by Shakespeare's time, the Revels Office had grown to include the master and four full-time employees. The duties of this office and the power of the master had also increased. In addition to hiring theater companies to perform at court, the Revels Office provided scenery and costumes for the performances. The master of the revels was in charge of selecting the plays for a given season and for overseeing their content. As unofficial censor, he had the authority to deny a license to any play if he disapproved of its content. When he granted a license, the signed and stamped copy of the approved script was immediately bound into the prompt book* for safekeeping.

The master of the revels also collected various fees: for granting licenses to provincial acting companies, for authorizing the publication and performances of plays, and for awarding players special permission to perform during Lent. The master of the revels was known to accept bribes. His official annual salary was £10, but at least one master, Edmund Tilney, was known to have made about £100 in one year.

The Revels Office fell into disuse in 1642, when the theaters were officially closed. Sir Henry Herbert attempted to revive it in 1660 but failed. (*See also* **Acting Companies, Elizabethan; Playwrights and Poets; Shakespearean Theater: 17th Century.**)

MEASURE FOR MEASURE

In the past *Measure for Measure* was viewed as a difficult and unpleasant play. The characters' motives are often unclear, and it can be difficult to evaluate their actions. In the introduction to a 1951 edition of the play, scholar Hardin Craig called it "one of Shakespeare's worst plays." Many modern readers, however, regard it as one of his finest achievements, and it has become popular with audiences as well. The play's title refers to its main theme: the idea that a crime should always be matched by an appropriate punishment. The text explores the ideas of justice, forgiveness, and moral compromise.

SOURCES AND PLOT. Shakespeare adapted the plot of *Measure for Measure* from two earlier works: *Hecatommithi*, written in 1565 by the Italian dramatist Giambattista Giraldi (better known as Cinthio), and *Promos and Cassandra* (1578) by George Whetstone. *Measure for Measure* is one of three Shakespearean works known generally as the "problem plays," a term coined by scholar F. S. Boas in 1896. (The others are *Troilus and Cressida* and *All's Well That Ends Well.*) These plays cannot easily be classified as comedy or tragedy. They have many comic elements, but their atmosphere is disturbing, especially from a moral standpoint. The characters face agonizing moral dilemmas, and the audience cannot easily determine what is right and what is wrong.

The duke of Vienna goes away on a secret mission, leaving his deputy, Angelo, in charge. Secretly, however, he returns disguised as a friar to monitor his deputy's performance. Angelo enforces old laws governing sexual behavior and sentences Claudio, a young man who has made his fiancée pregnant, to death. Claudio's sister, Isabella, who is about to enter a convent, pleads for his life. Overwhelmed by Isabella's beauty, Angelo offers to spare Claudio's life if she will "yield up [her] body to [Angelo's] will" (II.iv.164). Shocked by Angelo's proposition, Isabella declares, "More than our brother is our chastity" (II.iv.185). When she tells Claudio of the offer, however, he pleads with her to give in to Angelo's desires. Furious that Claudio would ask her to make such a sacrifice, she curses him. The disguised duke then offers a solution. He explains that Angelo was once engaged to a woman named Mariana, who is still in love with him. He suggests that Isabella pretend to keep the

A MORAL DILEMMA

Scholar A. C. Hamilton has noted that "the response of university students [to *Measure for Measure*] is usually muted and puzzled. I wondered why this should be until an enterprising student of mine canvassed an entire women's dorm to find out how her fellow students would respond to the terms of Angelo's ransom. Some 76 persons responded with a variant of the question: 'Well, what's this Angelo like?'" Hamilton's story reveals how much the audience's response to this play can depend on the choices made in a particular production.

In this scene from *Measure for Measure,* by 19th-century painter William Holman Hunt, Isabella visits her brother, Claudio, in jail. She is dismayed to learn that Claudio wants her to accept Angelo's shameful offer so that he may avoid punishment.

appointment with Angelo but send Mariana in her place. Both women agree to this plan.

The morning after his encounter with the woman he believes to be Isabella, however, Angelo orders Claudio's execution and demands that the prisoner's head be sent to him that afternoon. The duke urges the jailer to execute another prisoner, Barnardine, instead of Claudio. When Barnardine refuses to submit, the jailer proposes substituting the head of another prisoner who has died that day of a fever. The duke agrees and then tells Isabella that her brother has died and that she should expose Angelo's crime when the duke returns to the city.

In the last act the duke sheds his disguise and pretends he has just returned to the city. When Isabella comes to him with her accusation against Angelo, he at first pretends not to believe her. Angelo denies her claims, even when Mariana reveals her own part in the plot. The duke then reveals his knowledge of the scheme. He sentences Angelo to death for violating the law, but Mariana pleads for his life, and the duke agrees to spare him if he will marry Mariana. He then has Claudio brought in to show that he is still alive and promises him a similar pardon if he will marry his pregnant fiancée. In a final plot twist, the duke proposes marriage to Isabella: "I have a motion much imports your good, / Whereto if you'll a willing ear incline, / What's mine is yours, and what is yours is mine" (V.i. 535–37).

This plot may seem unrealistic, but it is only a slight exaggeration of situations that occur in modern society. It is often the case that laws concerning sex remain in effect for years without being enforced, until someone in power suddenly decides to apply them. Angelo's attempt to abuse his power for sexual ends is a familiar story to modern readers, an extreme case of sexual harassment. Barnardine's resistance to his impending execution—"I swear I will not die to-day for any man's persuasion" (IV.iii.59–60)—also strikes a modern note. In Texas in 1999 a condemned prisoner refused to leave his cell and five guards were needed to force him to the death chamber.

CHARACTERS. Isabella is the crucial figure in this plot. Her refusal to give in to Angelo's desires is the central issue. Some see her insistence on preserving her virtue even at the cost of her brother's life as selfish. For Isabella, however, the sacrifice she is being asked to make is far more than her life, because she believes her soul would "die for ever" if she yielded (II.iv.108). In the end she joins Mariana in pleading for Angelo's life, saying, "I partly think / A due sincerity governed his deeds, / Till he did look on me" (V.i.445–47). Isabella has learned to soften her unbending virtue with forgiveness.

Angelo is a striking dramatic portrait. The corrupt judge who makes the law a shield for his own sexual misdeeds is an old story and a familiar character, but Angelo is not a mere hypocrite. He is astonished to find himself tempted by Isabella's beauty and recognizes his own fault in yielding to the temptation: "What's this? What's this? Is this her fault, or mine? / The tempter, or the tempted, who sins most, ha?" (II.ii.162–63). When his crime is unmasked, he acknowledges his guilt and pleads for

"immediate sentence then, and sequent death" (V.i.373). In a society that sees sexual acts as shameful, Angelo is ashamed to be himself.

The character of the duke also provokes conflicting reactions. He claims his motives are ethically pure: he has not been strict enough in enforcing laws against sexual crimes, so he intends to leave Angelo in charge to do it for him. But as a friar points out, he could have enforced the laws himself if he had wished. Placing the responsibility on Angelo seems like a way to restore the laws without losing his popularity. While in disguise, the duke engages in repeated acts of trickery to accomplish his goals without exercising his legitimate authority. He may also be seen as needlessly cruel to Isabella in pretending that Claudio is dead. He shows mercy to Claudio and Angelo, but he insists (for a short time) that Lucio, a minor character who has criticized the duke in his presence while he was disguised, be put to death, because "slandering a prince deserves it" (V.i.524). These morally complex situations make any straightforward response to this play impossible.

INTERPRETATIONS. The history of *Measure for Measure* on stage, especially in recent decades, highlights its problems and opportunities. In December 1604 it was staged at court before King JAMES I, and many scholars think the legal arguments found in the play would have appealed to the king. The duke's remark "I love the people, / But do not like to stage me to their eyes" (I.i.67–68) may have been a direct reference to James, whose dislike of public appearances was well known. The play was revived on a regular basis throughout the Restoration* period and most of the 1900s. Sarah Siddons, the leading actress of the 1700s, continued to play Isabella until, grown bulky with age, she had to be assisted out of her kneeling position in the final scene. Somewhat neglected during the Victorian* era, *Measure for Measure* has come into its own again since World War II.

A key decision in a modern production of *Measure for Measure* is how to stage Isabella's response to the duke's proposal. For most of the play's history, critics took her acceptance for granted. Scholar John Masefield wrote that the duke "makes Isabella his Duchess," an assumption not supported by the text. The first production to challenge this traditional view was directed by John Barton for the ROYAL SHAKESPEARE COMPANY in 1970. The play ended with Isabella alone on the stage, plainly in an agony of doubt and indecision. Later productions went further, showing Isabella wordlessly rejecting the duke. Modern productions vary in their treatment of this scene. Some Isabellas accept the duke, some reject him, and still others leave the character's options open at the end, as the text suggests—coolly considering a decision that is yet to be made. These varying interpretations clearly reflect a modern, feminist-influenced society. Directors no longer perceive marriage as the automatic close to the play, and neither do their audiences.

Part of Isabella's decision has to do with the way the character of the duke is interpreted. In the past he was treated as almost godlike, the agent of God on earth, and it was assumed that Isabella would accept him as such. Since 1970 this view of the duke has been challenged. He is often played as manipulative, careless of other people's feelings, and masking

* *Restoration* referring to the period in English history, beginning in 1660, when Charles II was restored to the throne

* *Victorian* referring to the reign of Victoria, queen of England from 1837 to 1901

his own shady motives. Reviewing a production directed by Jonathan Miller 1975, Irving Wardle quoted the duke's line "hence shall we see, / If power change purpose: what our seemers be" (I.iii.53–54) and went on to remark that the duke was "the biggest seemer of the lot." It came as no surprise when Isabella rejected him.

Another issue in this scene centers around Claudio's reaction to Isabella. Alive and pardoned, a joyful Claudio usually embraces his sister, but one recent Claudio turned away from her, unable to forgive her for refusing to save his life. This moment is symbolic of the lack of a clear moral center in *Measure for Measure.* A production of the play must impose its own reading through casting and performance. Even determining which is the leading role can be a matter of interpretation. In the past powerful and well-known actors, such as John Gielgud and James Mason, were typically cast as Angelo, while lesser-known actors took the role of the duke. In recent years, however, the duke has come to be seen as a much more complex and interesting character, a hollow man of authority who conceals and perhaps does not even recognize his own private motives. Actors may now find the duke to be as challenging a role as that of Angelo.

Directors have a fair amount of freedom to change the time period of *Measure for Measure* because the text contains very few references to the clothing or weapons of the period. Many modern directors have taken advantage of the fact that Vienna, the play's setting, was also the home of Sigmund Freud, who invented the practice of psychotherapy. Setting a production in the Vienna of Freud's day—the late 1800s and early 1900s—highlights the play's atmosphere of hidden sexuality. For example, the disguised duke's comment that "I never heard the absent Duke much *detected* for women" (III.ii.121–22) is a perfect example of a Freudian slip*. Also much of the play's action takes place in a prison, a setting easily adapted to a modern time period with such special effects as grilles, fluorescent lighting, and the sound of doors slamming along corridors. Strikingly modern in its plot as well as its themes, *Measure for Measure* is now fully acknowledged as one of Shakespeare's finest creations. (*See also* **Morality and Ethics; Shakespeare on Screen.**)

* *Freudian slip* accidental remark that reveals an unconscious attitude or wish

MEDICINE

Health was a major concern in Elizabethan England. A growing population contributed to the spread of DISEASE, particularly in the crowded city of London. Poor SANITATION was the predominant cause of disease in both the towns and the countryside. Sickness was particularly common among the poor, and it could also contribute to greater poverty by making people unable to work. It is therefore not surprising that the demand for medical treatment was very high.

DEADLY DISEASES. Perhaps the most dreaded disease in Elizabethan England was the plague*, which spread rapidly, had no known cure, and was often fatal. Outbreaks of the plague were frequent in urban areas and

* *plague* highly contagious and often fatal disease; also called the Black Death

Medicine

EVERY MAN IN HIS HUMOR

Elizabethans believed that the overall balance of the four humors in a person's body determined that person's basic disposition or personality. When blood was the dominant substance, the person would be energetic and happy, like Gratiano in *The Merchant of Venice*. A person with too much melancholy would be sad and depressed, like Jaques in *As You Like It*. Someone with too much choler would be hot-tempered and argumentative, whereas a person dominated by phlegm tended to be slow and lazy.

* *phlegm* thick, slimy mucus found in the respiratory tract

claimed many lives. An outbreak in 1593 is reported to have killed 15,000 people in the London area alone. To combat the plague city leaders struggled to clean the streets, to eliminate many of the city's dunghills, and to destroy animals that might carry disease, such as stray dogs, cats, and pigs. Innkeepers were required to clean their stables regularly, and citizens were warned against dumping filth into the streets.

To ward off the plague people dosed themselves with a substance called dragon-water and used hot cloths to make themselves sweat. If they developed carbuncles, the open sores associated with the plague, they applied a chicken with its tail feathers plucked out to the sore. Households struck by the plague were quarantined, or isolated from contact with others to prevent the disease from spreading. A prayer such as "Lord, have mercy upon us," was inscribed on the door. Other families in the neighborhood attempted to protect themselves through prayer as well. The master of the household uttered the prayers, with his entire family kneeling beside him, in a room perfumed with incense or sweet-smelling herbs. Those who survived the plague were considered "safe," immune from further infection, and consequently were in high demand to nurse those who became ill.

Even deadlier than the plague, but fortunately less common, was the so-called "sweating sickness." A patient would suffer a high fever that usually proved fatal within 24 hours. Other major diseases included malaria, spread by mosquitoes; syphilis, which was sexually transmitted; and scurvy, caused by poor diet and particularly common among sailors. In the villages and countryside smallpox probably caused more deaths than any other illness. No one understood the disease, and those who survived it were often scarred for life. A common treatment was to fumigate the smallpox sufferer with cinnabar (mercury sulfide) in a large meat-pickling vat.

MEDICAL PRACTICES. Elizabethans saw their world as an orderly place in which everything—from political conditions to medical conditions—was connected. A healthy body was a reflection in miniature of a properly ordered universe. A disturbance in the stars could produce illness, and medical practice in the late 1500s reflected this view.

Most Elizabethans believed that health was governed by four basic fluids, or humors: blood, phlegm*, yellow bile, and black bile. The four humors had to be in balance to maintain health. For this reason a popular cure was bloodletting, removing "excess" blood from the patient's veins. Many doctors recommended that otherwise healthy people be bled on a regular basis to keep their humors properly balanced. Because many Elizabethans believed that the positions of the stars could also affect a person's health, doctors often considered a patient's horoscope when planning treatment. Other remedies included drugs made from HERBS, minerals, and animal parts.

Elizabethans took health matters so seriously that many spent years studying medicine just to deal with their own medical problems. They paid close attention to all physical symptoms, even trivial-seeming ones such as pimples. Many people treated themselves with herbal remedies,

which were often old family secrets passed down from previous generations. In addition to physical problems such as headaches, backaches, and toothaches, Elizabethans sought relief from mental problems such as anxiety and insomnia. Melancholy (depression) was considered a particularly "English" mental problem, which could be brought on by marital strife, financial difficulties, or the loss of a loved one.

Those who chose to see a professional for their medical problems often bargained with the doctor over the proper "cure." The physician received part of his fee at the first visit and the remainder when the cure was complete. Physicians' fees varied widely. Some were so high that the patient had to pay them off in yearly installments. Many doctors were unable to support themselves through medical practice alone and had to work at other jobs to supplement their incomes. Part-time medical professionals might also be merchants, clergymen, landowners, schoolteachers, or even literary figures such as Shakespeare's contemporaries Robert Greene and Thomas Lodge.

TYPES OF HEALERS. Physicians in Elizabethan England held medical degrees from either Oxford or Cambridge University. They studied the works of the ancient Greek physicians Hippocrates (sometimes called the father of medicine) and Galen. Like all other scholarly texts, these works were either written in or translated into Latin, the language of higher education. Even the most up-to-date medical information was written in Latin at this time. Ancient medical knowledge was still highly respected, and doctors were warned against excessive experimentation. Many medical students traveled abroad to further their scientific studies.

Because Elizabethan physicians were forbidden to shed blood, surgery was performed by medical practitioners known as barber-surgeons. This painting, created in 1581, shows an anatomy lesson being taught with the aid of a human corpse.

After completing his studies every new doctor was examined by the Royal College of Physicians before receiving a license to practice medicine.

Since the Middle Ages, when physicians were associated with the Catholic Church, they had been forbidden to shed blood. Therefore, treatments involving bloodshed, such as surgery, were the responsibility of surgeons, a group of medical practitioners that was distinct from physicians. Surgery was closely associated with barbering, which also relied on sharp-edged tools and basins. A surgeon acquired his skills by becoming an apprentice* to a practicing surgeon, much like any other craftworker. Surgeons were called on to bandage wounds, remove bullets and arrowheads, set broken bones, and pull teeth (a task that could also be performed by a barber). Surgeons rarely performed operations in which the body was opened. There was no anesthetic in Shakespeare's time, and patients were fully conscious when limbs had to be amputated. Many died soon afterward from infection or from the shock to their systems.

Elizabethan pharmacists, known as apothecaries, fell beneath both physicians and surgeons on the social ladder. Like surgeons, apothecaries had no formal medical training and learned their skills through apprenticeship. The trade was first given official recognition in 1543 and was part of the grocers' guild* until 1617, when it formed a guild of its own. Apothecaries dealt mostly in herbs and tonics, but they could make a good living by selling tobacco on the side. The extreme poverty of the apothecary in Shakespeare's *Romeo and Juliet*, who illegally sells Romeo a deadly poison, is evidently not typical of those who belonged to his profession.

In rural areas and small villages throughout Europe, medical problems were often handled by "wise women," old women who knew and practiced folk cures. Much of this folklore involved the use of herbs and other local plants as cures for every ailment from constipation to a broken heart. A few of these women had the skill to set broken bones as well. In Shakespeare's plays old wise women are frequently referred to as beldames.

SHAKESPEARE AND MEDICINE. Doctors are featured in Shakespeare's plays more often than any other professionals. One of the most famous is Dr. Butts, the king's physician in *Henry VIII*, who uncovers the plotting of the king's counselors against his new archbishop. In the centuries following the Elizabethan age, many scholars found it hard to believe that Shakespeare knew so much about medicine. Many believed that the playwright was also a physician or an apothecary. Others suggested, more convincingly, that Shakespeare may have relied on the knowledge of his son-in-law John Hall, who was a physician.

The number of medical references in Shakespeare's plays, however, does not necessarily indicate that Shakespeare knew more about medicine than his contemporaries. Most Elizabethans were very concerned with their health and were thus familiar with basic medical theories. Also, the use of doctors as comic characters had been commonplace for many years. The most notably comic physician in Shakespeare is Dr. Caius in *The Merry Wives of Windsor*. (*See also* **Astronomy and Cosmology; Death**

* *apprentice* person bound by legal agreement to work for another for a specified period of time in return for instruction in a trade or art

* *guild* association of craft and trade workers that set standards for and represented the interests of its members

and Funerals; Education and Literacy; Friends and Contemporaries; Guilds; Personal Hygiene; Psychology; Work.)

MEDIEVALISM

* **classical** in the tradition of ancient Greece and Rome
* **morality play** religious dramatic work that teaches a moral lesson through the use of symbolic characters
* **convention** established practice
* **medieval** referring to the Middle Ages, a period roughly between A.D. 500 and 1500

See color plate 9, vol. 2.

Shakespeare and other Elizabethan writers were influenced not only by classical* sources but also by the dramatic practices of the Middle Ages. The morality plays* of this period produced a set of recognizable characters, plots, and themes that Shakespeare and his contemporaries adapted in accordance with the theatrical conventions* of their own day.

STOCK CHARACTERS. Medieval* morality plays, as their name suggests, existed mostly to illustrate moral lessons for viewers. Their characters, therefore, tended to exist as symbols rather than as three-dimensional personalities with human motives and desires. The central figure represented Mankind, and the other characters who attempted to influence his behavior might have names such as Good Deeds, Charity, or Understanding.

The most famous of these standard, or "stock," characters was the VICE, who represented humanity's wicked instincts. Although this character was presented as a villain, he also had a certain appeal. His ready wit, in particular, enabled him to tempt Mankind—and added a dose of humor to plays that were essentially serious in nature. The Vice may be seen as the forerunner of an Elizabethan stock character, the Fool or jester. Many of Shakespeare's villains, including IAGO and Richard III, are descended from the Vice. They never give clear reasons for their malicious behavior—it seems to be simply part of their nature—and they succeed in their evil plans by charming or outwitting the people around them.

Sir John FALSTAFF, the drunken knight from *Henry IV, Parts 1* and *2,* can also be seen as an adaptation of the Vice, tempting Prince Hal into a rowdy life of drinking and carousing. In these plays, however, Shakespeare creates a twist on the relationship between the Vice and Mankind. While the Vice of the morality plays usually misleads and controls the hero, in these two plays it is the prince who outwits his friend. The ending of the story, however, corresponds to the traditional ending of the morality play. As Mankind escapes from a life of sin by banishing his Vice, Hal—now King Henry V—banishes Falstaff from his court. Ironically, Shakespeare may have done too good a job transforming the Vice into a human being. Falstaff's attractive qualities, his wit and good nature, are more striking than his negative traits, and audiences usually end up feeling sympathy for the banished knight, whereas medieval audiences rarely felt sorry for the Vice.

MEDIEVAL IDEAS OF LOVE. In medieval literature the body was viewed as an enemy of the soul. The ideal of romantic love was therefore wholly spiritual, distinct from the desires of the flesh. This view led to the tradition of courtly love, in which the lover idealized his beloved and pledged his life to her service. Shakespeare explored the idea of courtly love in *Love's Labor's Lost,* where a king and his three courtiers vow to renounce all earthly pleasures and devote themselves to higher learning but fail

because they fall victim to the charms of four visiting ladies. The four men end up promising to spend a year serving their ladies to prove themselves worthy of their love, after which they will be married. With this ending, Shakespeare combines the physical and spiritual sides of love.

Another medieval view of love was the concept of Christian love and forgiveness, which is central to many of Shakespeare's works, particularly *The Merchant of Venice.* In this play vengeance, represented by the character of SHYLOCK, is defeated by mercy, embodied in the character of Antonio. Shakespeare also explores the power of forgiveness in *The Two Gentlemen of Verona.* A young man tries to steal his best friend's lady, but when his friend discovers his plot, the young man apologizes and begs forgiveness. His friend not only immediately grants it but even offers to give up the lady as a gesture of reconciliation.

THE WHEEL OF FORTUNE. In medieval times people believed strongly that life on earth was unpredictable, governed by forces beyond human control. The turnings of fate were often depicted as a wheel to which human beings clung. A person who succeeded in riding Fortune's wheel to the top of its cycle might achieve wealth and status, but eventually the ever-turning wheel would descend, bringing the same person down with it. Because it was impossible to stay atop Fortune's wheel, people in the Middle Ages believed that the only good life was the one that came after death.

The turning of Fortune's wheel figures in many of Shakespeare's plays, especially *Romeo and Juliet.* Throughout the first half of the play, luck seems to be with the lovers, but immediately after they are married, their fate changes for the worse when Romeo kills Juliet's cousin Tybalt in a duel. Romeo sees this turn of events as the working of fate rather than his own doing, and he cries out, "O, I am fortune's fool!" (III.i.136).

Like most of the medieval ideas that Shakespeare used, the concept of Fortune's wheel is modified in his works. His characters may be trapped by events beyond their control, but he also makes them responsible for their own actions. This combination of fate and choice is evident in *Macbeth.* The title character knows, through the predictions of the witches, that he is destined to be king, but it is his own decision to gain the crown dishonestly, through murder, that ultimately causes his downfall. (*See also* **Characters in Shakespeare's Plays; Fate and Fortune; Fools, Clowns and Jesters; Love; Renaissance, Influence of the.**)

MERCHANT OF VENICE, THE

* *anti-Semitic* referring to prejudice against Jews

Shakespeare's most controversial play, *The Merchant of Venice* centers on SHYLOCK, a Jewish moneylender who dominates the action, even though he appears in only five scenes. Shylock often seems to be a vicious, greedy, and bloodthirsty villain, and some critics have responded to the character by attacking the play as anti-Semitic*. Argument over this issue continues to arouse strong feelings among readers, playgoers, and theater professionals, just as it has for much of the play's varied 400-year history.

Shylock, the Jewish moneylender in *The Merchant of Venice,* is one of Shakespeare's most controversial characters. He has been portrayed as a comic scoundrel, a bloodthirsty villain, and a tragic victim. This engraving shows Shylock, played by Charles Macklin, as an intensely evil figure.

PLOT SUMMARY. The play opens with Antonio, the merchant identified in the title, describing to his friends a strange sadness that has lately taken hold of him. In due course Bassanio, Antonio's dearest friend, comes to ask him for a loan to finance a trip to Belmont, where he hopes to win the hand of a wealthy heiress named Portia. Although Bassanio has failed to repay previous loans, Antonio is willing to lend him more money. Unfortunately his fortune is temporarily tied up in overseas ventures. Not wanting to disappoint Bassanio, however, Antonio tells him that he will borrow the necessary funds.

They seek out a moneylender named Shylock, who hates Antonio because he is a Christian who despises all Jews as unbelievers and because he lends money at no interest, thereby lowering the rates that Shylock and others can charge and damaging their business. Claiming that he wishes to be friends with Antonio, Shylock agrees to supply him with the sum he requests at no interest, provided that Antonio will agree to surrender a pound of his flesh if he is unable to pay the debt within three months. Bassanio is reluctant to let his friend agree to these terms, but Antonio assures him that at least some of his ships will return in time and will be carrying more than enough treasure to repay the loan.

Meanwhile, Shylock's daughter Jessica has fallen in love with a Christian named Lorenzo. With the help of Bassanio and several other friends, the two run away together, taking a portion of her father's money and jewels with them. When Shylock discovers that his daughter is gone, he is shattered both by her betrayal and by the loss of part of his fortune. Moreover, when he learns that many of Antonio's ships have perished at sea, Shylock vows that he will take revenge on the Christians and demand the penalty if Antonio's debt is not repaid on time. Shylock defends his vengefulness as something he has been taught "by Christian example." In a very moving speech, he asserts that he is a human being like everyone else and does not deserve the scorn his Venetian oppressors have heaped on him: "Hath not a Jew eyes? Hath not a Jew hands, organs, dimensions, senses, affections, passions?" (III.i.59–73).

In Belmont, Portia and her waiting-woman Nerissa discuss the various noblemen who have come to woo this famous lady. According to the terms of her father's will, every suitor must enter a "lottery" in which he is presented with three metal caskets. The one who can guess which container holds Portia's portrait will win her hand and fortune. The prince of Morocco selects a golden casket marked with the inscription "Who chooseth me shall gain what many men desire" (II.vii.5). When he opens it, he finds only a skull with a scroll inside it, advising him that "All that glisters is not gold" (II.vii.65). A second suitor, the prince of Arragon, opts for a silver casket labeled "Who chooseth me shall get as much as he deserves" (II.vii.7), but it contains only "the portrait of a blinking idiot" (II.ix.54), with a scroll reading "Seven times tried that judgment is / That did never choose amiss" (II.ix.64–65).

As Arragon departs, Bassanio arrives to take up the challenge. Recognizing that "So may the outward shows be least themselves" (III.ii.73), he picks a lead casket with the inscription "Who chooseth me must give and

THE JEW OF LONDON

The plot of *The Merchant of Venice* may have been influenced by the trial of Roderigo López, a Jewish doctor from Portugal who served as Queen Elizabeth I's personal physician. He was executed in 1594 after being convicted of participating in a Spanish plot to murder the queen. A reference to Shylock as a wolf (*lupus* in Latin) in Act IV is thought to be a pun on the name López. Another similarity between López and Shylock is that both had enemies named Antonio—in López's case, Antonio Perez, a pretender to the throne of Portugal.

See color plate 6, vol. 2.

hazard all he hath" (II.vii.9). Through this wise choice he wins Portia, who has already fallen in love with him. Bassanio's friend Gratiano, who has accompanied him to Belmont, announces that he has just become engaged to Nerissa. Just then Salerio (friend to Antonio and Bassanio), Lorenzo, and Jessica arrive with the news that Antonio is unable to repay the money he owes Shylock and must therefore sacrifice a pound of his flesh. Portia declares that if Bassanio will marry her immediately, she will send him back to Venice with Gratiano and all the money he needs to help his friend. Portia leaves her house in the care of Lorenzo and Jessica. Then, disguising herself as a lawyer and Nerissa as a clerk, she departs secretly for Venice to help save Antonio.

In court the duke of Venice hears Shylock's case against Antonio. Still furious over all the abuse he has suffered, Shylock is determined to collect his promised collateral, notwithstanding Bassanio's offer to give him three times the sum he is owed. The disguised Portia's eloquent speech on "the quality of mercy" (IV.i.184–205) also fails to move him. She then declares that Shylock's contract fully entitles him to a pound of flesh, but not one drop of blood. If he sheds any blood in cutting the pound of flesh from Antonio's breast, she says, under Venetian law he will lose his entire estate. Denied his revenge, Shylock agrees to accept the money instead, but Portia insists that since he has demanded justice, he will get nothing else: a pound of flesh and not a bit more. Disgusted, Shylock turns to leave. But then Portia springs her second trap: she reminds him of a law that says if anyone who is not a citizen of Venice seeks to take the life of a citizen, he will be punished with death and the loss of all his possessions. Since Shylock is not a citizen of Venice (because Jews were denied citizenship anywhere in Europe at that time), he is subject to this penalty.

Others now have the opportunity to respond to Portia's speech about mercy. The duke at once spares Shylock's life and says that half of the moneylender's fortune will go to the state and half to Antonio. Shylock asks the duke to let him die because he no longer has the means to support life. The duke appeals to Antonio to show mercy, and he does—but his "mercy" is highly problematic for modern audiences. He agrees to let Shylock keep half his fortune on two conditions: first, he must convert to Christianity, and second, he must agree to leave all his wealth to his daughter and son-in-law when he dies. The duke supports Antonio, and Shylock is forced to agree to these terms. Saying he is ill, he leaves the court with a promise to sign the deed of gift that Nerissa (still disguised as a law clerk) will bring him.

Bassanio gratefully tries to repay the young lawyer who has saved his friend's life, but Portia refuses the money. When Bassanio insists on giving the youth something, however, she asks him for his wedding ring. Bassanio refuses, saying his wife has made him promise never to lose this token of their vows. When Antonio begs him to surrender it, however, Bassanio reluctantly sends Gratiano to deliver it. When Portia receives the ring, Nerissa tells her that she will persuade her husband to give up his ring too. The two women know that they will have great fun later at their spouses' expense.

The last act largely restores the mood of romantic comedy that the trial scene has threatened to destroy. As Lorenzo and Jessica sit together enjoying a beautiful moonlit night, Portia and Nerissa return to Belmont, once again dressed as women. Soon afterward their husbands arrive with Antonio. The fun begins when Portia and Nerissa "discover" that their husbands no longer have their rings. They claim that Bassanio and Gratiano must have betrayed them and given the rings to other women. The two wives, therefore, swear to take revenge by sleeping with the lawyer and his clerk at the first opportunity. Antonio pleads with Portia to give her husband another chance, saying that as he once pledged his body, he will now pledge his soul to guarantee Bassanio's trustworthiness. Portia then gives Bassanio a new ring, asking him to take better care it than he had of the last, and Nerissa does the same with Gratiano. The two men are astonished to find that the rings are identical to the ones they received earlier. Portia reveals how they obtained them and then delivers the happy news to the others, telling Lorenzo and Jessica that Shylock has left them all his possessions and informing Antonio that his ships have miraculously come home safely. On this note the play ends happily—for all except Shylock.

TEXT AND SOURCES. Shakespeare assembled the plot of his play from a variety of sources, mostly Italian, although it is unclear whether he read these accounts in the original language. The "pound of flesh" plot came from *Il pecorone* (The Dunce), a collection of stories by the little-known Italian writer Giovanni Fiorentino. The choice of three caskets came from a popular story that appeared in several collections, most notably the anonymous *Gesta Romanorum*, published in 1472 and translated into English in 1577. The Jessica-Lorenzo subplot was from *Il novellino* by the Italian novelist Masuccio Salernitano. Shakespeare combined the various narrative strands to create a complex drama that deals with various kinds of bonds, those linking parent and child, husband and wife, friend and friend, master and servant, debtor and creditor, and ultimately one human being with all others.

COMMENTARY. Nearly every character in this complex drama raises questions for modern viewers—beginning with Antonio and the play's opening line, "In sooth, I know not why I am so sad." The play never offers an explanation for Antonio's melancholy, but some commentators speculate that it has much to do with Bassanio. The script appears to hint that Antonio has an unrequited* homosexual desire for Bassanio. Although this is never clearly stated, the two characters are sometimes played with this situation as a subtext.

Bassanio's relationship with Portia is as ambiguous* as his relationship with Antonio. When he asks his friend for money to travel to Belmont, he refers pointedly to Portia's wealth, suggesting that her estate may provide him with the means to repay the loan. Some critics therefore see Bassanio as merely a gold digger looking for a rich heiress to bail him out of his financial difficulties. If his love for Portia can be questioned, however, his sincere devotion to Antonio is quite clear, so much so that

* *unrequited* not returned

* *ambiguous* unclear; able to be interpreted in more than one way

Portia appears to suspect Antonio of having too strong a hold on her new husband. Her bold and clever action to save Antonio is surely motivated by a sincere wish to help the friend her husband values so highly, but at the same time it places Antonio in her debt. The trick she plays with the rings is an even more emphatic device to establish her supremacy, and that of her marriage, over a relationship between two male friends. Portia is one of Shakespeare's most active and intelligent heroines, but not necessarily one of the most likeable. Not only does she sometimes act very superior, but her ethnic slurs against the prince of Morocco and several of her other suitors do little to endear her to modern audiences.

Most complicated and confusing of all the major characters, however, is Shylock. Shakespeare may originally have conceived of him as a comic villain in the tradition of the VICE in medieval morality plays. The image of a Jewish moneylender as pure villain would almost certainly have been influenced by the portrayal of Barabas in Christopher Marlowe's *The Jew of Malta*, written around 1588. Shakespeare's character, however, moves beyond this stereotype. Unlike Barabas, Shylock has a clear motivation for his deep-rooted hatred of Antonio and his fellow Christians, who frequently mock and attack him. His underlying humanity is powerfully expressed, particularly in the "Hath not a Jew eyes" speech in Act III. Indeed it may be argued that *The Merchant of Venice* is a play about anti-Semitism, and one that proves far more critical of "Christian example" than of any behavior that characterizes Shylock and his fellow Jews.

PERFORMANCE HISTORY. Although *The Merchant of Venice* is frequently performed in England, where it is a required text for high school students, it seldom appears on stage or in the classroom in the United States. Many producers and educators do not want to risk offending Jewish audiences by presenting a play in which the "villain" is Jewish and the "heroes" are all anti-Semitic. Others, however, have addressed this problem by emphasizing the more sympathetic aspects of Shylock's nature. The complexities of this character make the role a particular challenge for actors.

During the 1600s and early 1700s, Shylock was presumably played as a comic villain like Marlowe's Barabas. (At the Oregon Shakespeare Festival in the 1930s and 1950s, Angus Bowmer gave a very effective "historical" portrait of a comic Shylock, complete with red beard and wig and a putty nose.) When Charles Macklin took over the role in 1741, he played a more terrifying villain, as Maria Edgeworth indicates in a scene from her novel *Harrington*. Portrayals of Shylock became more appealing in the 1800s, probably beginning with Edmund Kean's representation of the Jew as one "more sinn'd against than sinning" (*King Lear*, III.ii.59). This interpretation reached a high point in Henry Irving's production, which added a new scene in Act II in which Shylock returns home from dinner and knocks on his door in vain, unaware that Jessica is not there to let him in.

Twentieth-century productions varied in their presentation of Shylock. Key differences can be seen in the way various actors have handled the courtroom scene (IV.i) in which Shylock is forced to convert to

Christianity. In the National Theater production directed by Jonathan Miller in London in 1970, Lawrence Olivier's Shylock gave a horrendous offstage scream after his exit in this scene. By contrast Patrick Stewart's Shylock in the 1978 Royal Shakespeare Company production was far less sympathetic: interested primarily in money, he cared little about being forced to convert. In 1999 at the Shakespeare Theater in Washington, D.C., Hal Holbrook played a Shylock who accepted Antonio's terms with great pain, and the trial scene ended in a near brawl between Jewish and Christian characters. Portrayals of Jessica have also changed over time. In some productions of the late 1990s, she was shown having second thoughts about her betrayal of her father and her conversion to Christianity.

If Shylock is indeed a villain, it is well to remember that just as the heroes of this play are not altogether likeable, the vengeful moneylender at its center is not entirely unlikeable. The play is full of paradoxes*, reflecting the true complexity of human behavior and motivation. This ambiguity, along with the play's many beautiful verse speeches, may explain why *The Merchant of Venice* continues to attract readers and playgoers alike. (*See also* **Actors, Shakespearean; Pageants and Morality Plays.**)

* **paradox** apparent contradiction

MERCHANTS

See *Trade.*

MERMAID TAVERN

Taverns were, and still are, an important part of English life. Originally serving as inns for travelers, taverns became popular as restaurants during Shakespeare's time. Elizabethan taverns offered private rooms that patrons could rent for eating and drinking, gambling, making business deals, or even making love. Some of these private rooms had names, such as the Angel, the Dolphin, and the Rose. People who rented them knew that they would be undisturbed by all but the *drawer* (the Elizabethan word for "waiter").

Several groups regularly rented tavern rooms. One of these was a literary group, known as the Friday Street Club, that met on the first Friday of every month at the Mermaid tavern. Located on Bread Street in an area of London known as Cheapside, the Mermaid became the gathering place for actors, playwrights, and other literary and artistic figures. Members of the Friday Street Club included Shakespeare, the poet and playwright Ben JONSON, and the comedy writers Francis Beaumont and John Fletcher. The tavern must have provided some lively times, because on one occasion Beaumont recalled, "What things have we seen / Done at the Mermaid!"

The innkeeper of the Mermaid, William Johnson, was a good friend of Shakespeare's and served as a financial agent for the playwright's purchase of the BLACKFRIARS Gate-House, which later became a theater. (*See also* **Elizabethan Theaters; Falstaff, Sir John.**)

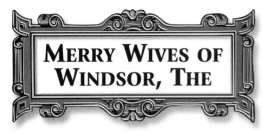

MERRY WIVES OF WINDSOR, THE

Among Shakespeare's comedies, *The Merry Wives of Windsor* is notable for its detailed portrayal of Elizabethan country life. Although the play is considered by many scholars to be one of Shakespeare's lesser works, it has remained popular with audiences for centuries because of its delightful characters and its broad physical comedy.

PLOT SUMMARY. The action focuses on the efforts of Sir John Falstaff, a scheming old knight, to seduce Mistress Page and Mistress Ford in the hope of gaining access to their husbands' money. Outraged by Falstaff's audacity, the women determine to retaliate by playing a series of hilarious pranks on the "greasy knight." In addition, Mistress Ford wishes to teach a lesson to her jealous husband. The play's subplot involves three suitors who are competing to marry Mistress Page's daughter, Anne.

After luring Falstaff to her home, Mistress Ford orders the lecherous knight into a small basket and covers him with dirty linen to conceal him from her husband, who has arrived in a jealous rage. While Master Ford fumes and accuses her of adultery, Mistress Ford commands her servants to carry the basket outside and dump its contents into the Thames. Because Falstaff remains unrepentant, the wives make another appointment to meet him. This time when Master Ford arrives, the wives persuade Falstaff to disguise himself in the clothes of an old woman. Although he again escapes, Falstaff is beaten by Ford, who mistakes him for a local witch.

The wives tell their husbands of their campaign to embarrass Falstaff, and after Master Ford apologizes for mistrusting his wife, the group plans a final prank on the unruly knight. Luring Falstaff into the woods, the conspirators emerge disguised as fairies and torment the cowardly knight by pinching him and burning him with candles. When the "fairies" reveal their true identity to Falstaff, he admits that he has been outdone by the wives: "I do begin to perceive that I am made an ass" (V.v.119). Meanwhile Anne Page has circumvented her parents' attempts to arrange her marriage and has wed Fenton, her true love. Accepting the situation, Mrs. Page invites the whole group, including her new son-in-law and Falstaff, to her home to "laugh this sport o'er by a country fire" (V.v.242).

SOURCES AND HISTORY. According to legend, Queen ELIZABETH I was so charmed by the character of Falstaff in *Henry IV, Part 1* and *Part 2,* that she asked Shakespeare to write a play featuring Falstaff in love. Indeed, there is some evidence to suggest that *The Merry Wives of Windsor* premiered in 1597 at a royal ceremony hosted by the queen. Some scholars believe that the play is an adaptation of an anonymous work titled *The Jealous Comedy* (1593).

COMMENTARY. The play marks the final appearance of Sir John Falstaff, one of Shakespeare's most popular characters. Instead of portraying the unflappable Vice figure of his previous plays, however, Shakespeare presents Sir John as a bumbling character long overdue for a comeuppance.

Interestingly, *The Merry Wives of Windsor* provides a preview of Shakespeare's later works, in which determined women control the action. As strong, independent characters, Mistresses Ford and Page foreshadow

See
color plate 9,
vol. 2.

Shakespeare's greatest heroines, such as Beatrice in *Much Ado About Nothing* and Rosalind in *As You Like It*. (*See also* **Falstaff, Sir John; Humor in Shakespeare's Plays; Marriage and Family; Music Inspired by Shakespeare; Plays: The Comedies.**)

Scholar R. A. Foakes observed in 1984 that *A Midsummer Night's Dream* is as complex a comedy as *Hamlet* is a tragedy. Four sets of characters are woven together in a story that includes the royalty of ancient Athens, the rulers of a kingdom of FAIRIES, and four very appealing young people in love. Shakespeare's plot involves a total of nine lovers in ever-shifting romantic pairings. It challenges theater and film directors to create imaginative fantasy worlds, with music, dance, and spectacle. For today's audiences it raises such issues as gender, power, and sex, opening the door to a multitude of critical interpretations.

PLOT. The play opens with Theseus, the duke of Athens, planning his wedding to Hippolyta, queen of the Amazons, whom he has recently defeated in battle. The proceedings are interrupted by Theseus's courtier Egeus, who asks the Athenian lord to force Egeus's daughter, Hermia, to marry Demetrius, the husband he has chosen for her. Hermia wishes to marry another gentleman, Lysander. Theseus sternly insists that under the law she must either wed Demetrius, die for disobeying her father, or spend the rest of her life as a nun. He gives her four days to consider her decision. After everyone else leaves, Hermia and Lysander resolve to flee from Athens and marry in secret (much like the young lovers in *Romeo and Juliet*, which Shakespeare wrote at about the same time). Through Hermia's friend Helena, the jealous Demetrius learns of their plan and decides to follow them. Meanwhile Helena—who is in love with Demetrius—announces that she will follow him.

The four lovers make their way through a forest that turns out to be haunted by fairies. Oberon and Titania, the fairy king and queen, have come from India to bless the wedding of Theseus and Hippolyta. When they first appear on stage, however, they are quarreling over a young Indian boy whose mother, Titania's friend, died while giving birth to him. Oberon wants the boy for a servant, and when Titania refuses him he decides to punish her. He sends his servant Puck, the "merry wanderer of the night," to bring a flower whose juice will act as a love potion. Oberon intends to place the love juice on Titania's eyelids as she sleeps, causing her to become infatuated with the first creature she sees. While Puck is on his errand, the fairy king overhears the lovesick Helena pleading with the scornful Demetrius. Moved by Helena's sorrow, Oberon sends Puck to place some of the juice on Demetrius's eyes so that he will fall in love with Helena. As it happens Puck mistakes Lysander for Demetrius, and when the drugged Lysander awakes, he sees Helena and falls in love with her. Leaving Hermia asleep on the forest floor, he pursues Helena through the woods.

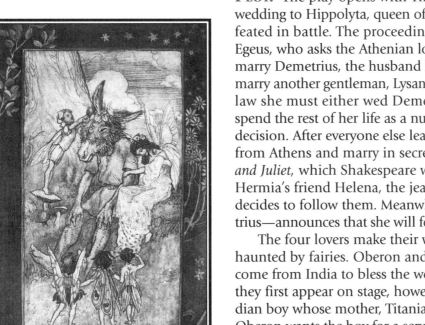

In one of the most humorous scenes in *A Midsummer Night's Dream,* the queen of the fairies falls in love with Nick Bottom, a simpleminded weaver wearing the head of a donkey. This illustration (by Arthur Rackham, ca. 1900) shows the transformed weaver being attended by the fairy queen's servants.

Meanwhile a subplot has developed around a group of "rude mechanicals," or craftsmen, who are preparing an entertainment for Theseus's wedding. Peter Quince the carpenter casts the amateur actors in what is described as "the most lamentable comedy, and most cruel death of Pyramus and Thisbe." Bottom the weaver wants to play all the parts but eventually agrees to limit himself to the role of Pyramus. The craftsmen meet in the forest to rehearse near the bed of the sleeping Titania, whose eyes Oberon has enchanted with the love potion. An amused Puck plays a practical joke on them by placing the head of a donkey on the unsuspecting Bottom. The weaver's friends then flee in terror, crying "Bless thee, Bottom . . . Thou art translated" (III.i.118–19). At this point Titania awakens and under Oberon's spell falls in love with the ass-headed Bottom. She spirits him away to her private bower, creating one of the most enduring images in all of Shakespeare, a rustic ass-headed man asleep in the arms of the beautiful fairy queen.

After the delighted Puck reports his mischief to Oberon, the four young lovers enter in great confusion. Demetrius and the drugged Lysander compete for Helena, who believes that they are mocking her and protests at their cruelty. Hermia, meanwhile, is shocked and hurt by Lysander's behavior and blames Helena for the betrayal. Oberon orders Puck to undo his mistake, and Puck lures the four exhausted lovers into another part of the wood. There as they sleep he removes the enchantment from Lysander's eyes. Oberon, who has finally persuaded Titania to give up her Indian boy, releases her from the love spell, and Puck removes Bottom's ass's head. Oberon and Titania dance to celebrate their reconciliation, then disappear as dawn approaches.

Theseus, Hippolyta, and their servants enter the wood for a morning hunt and discover the four sleeping lovers. Egeus angrily demands again that his daughter marry Demetrius, but Demetrius reports that he now loves Helena and abandons his claim to Hermia. Theseus therefore overrules Egeus, and the whole party exits to a triple wedding. Bottom then awakens, reflects on the strange "dream" he has had, and decides to have Quince turn it into a ballad. He rejoins his friends, and that evening the simple workmen present their hilariously earnest version of "Pyramus and Thisbe" as part of the court wedding festivities. The three couples then retire, and the fairies enter to bless the palace and its sleeping lovers with a song and dance. After all the fairies but Puck have left the stage, he concludes the play with an epilogue. Addressing the audience, Puck says that if any part of the play has displeased them, they should simply think of what they have experienced as a dream.

SOURCES. For the plot of *A Midsummer Night's Dream*, Shakespeare artfully combined material from a variety of sources, most of which were well known in his day. The "translation" of Bottom, the story of Pyramus and Thisbe, and Titania's name probably came from OVID's *Metamorphoses*, which had been translated into English in 1567 by Arthur Golding. Various details about Theseus, the legendary founder of Athens, probably came from PLUTARCH's LIVES and from "The Knight's Tale," one of Geoffrey Chaucer's *Canterbury Tales*. Shakespeare may also have drawn

THAT MISCHIEVOUS AND KNAVISH SPRITE

Puck is identified early in the play as Robin Goodfellow, a familiar figure from English folklore. A witty prankster, he plays such tricks as skimming all the fat off the milk so that it cannot be made into butter. But he is also a friendly spirit, providing help with household chores in exchange for a gift of food. Like all the fairies, Puck is described as very tiny—small enough to disguise himself as a roasted crab apple. He is also capable of traveling "swifter than the wind," disappearing and reappearing faster than the eye can follow.

on Chaucer's "The Merchant's Tale," which includes materials on a fairy king and queen. The playwright probably took the name of Oberon from the French romance* *Huon of Bordeaux*, and other fairy lore seems to have come from popular legends and older plays.

EARLY MUSICAL VERSIONS. From the Restoration* until 1816 the only performances, of *A Midsummer Night's Dream* presented in the theater were operatic adaptations. According to the traditions of classical* theater, fairies and other supernatural figures were too unrealistic to be acceptable in a drama, so they were confined to poetic and musical works.

In 1692 London audiences saw *The Fairy Queen,* a semiopera in which each act ends with a spectacle resembling a MASQUE. Henry Purcell wrote some of his most sublime music for this version, which celebrated the marriage of the recently crowned Queen Mary to William of Orange. The final masque occurred in a spectacular garden, where the Greek god Hymen sang praises of the first couple, symbolized on stage by two orange trees and depicted as models of domestic harmony. Half a century later, three operatic renderings of the play appeared at the Drury Lane theater under the famous actor-manager David Garrick. The most successful of the three was the one that least resembled Shakespeare's play.

An operatic adaptation at Covent Garden in 1816, by Frederic Reynolds and Sir Henry Rowley Bishop, was filled with British nationalism. It ended not with Pyramus and Thisbe and the fairy blessing but with a spectacle the playbill described as "A GRAND PAGEANT, commemorative of The Triumphs of Theseus." This pageant was actually a celebration of Britain's recent defeat of Napoleon, with Theseus representing the Duke of Wellington. In Romantic* art and poetry Theseus was portrayed as the protector of Western civilization, a role that England, in a new era of colonial expansion, would soon take on.

VICTORIAN PRODUCTIONS. Actress-manager Eliza Bartolozzi (Madame Vestris) restored the full text of Shakespeare's play in her elaborate 1840 staging at Covent Garden. Her production was a tribute to the recently married Victoria and Albert, who came to see it in February 1841. Vestris played Oberon, and with such success that the king of fairies was played by women throughout the rest of the 19th century. A female Oberon was more ethereal (airy), and therefore closer to the Victorian idea of what a fairy should be like. Victorians were very fond of fairy lore, which appeared in paintings, music, pantomimes, and illustrated fairy tales, and they may have seen this fantasy world as an attractive alternative to the harsh realities of their industrial society. Later Victorian productions, such as Charles Kean's (1856) and Sir Herbert Beerbohm Tree's (1900), included elaborate and realistic sets for the city of Athens and the enchanted forest.

Felix Mendelssohn's famous score for the play was created for an 1843 production at court in Potsdam, commissioned by Prussia's King Friedrich Wilhelm IV. The Romantic movement in Germany had adopted the English Shakespeare as an important influence, so the occasion celebrated both German culture and the patron* king. The performance was

* *romance* story of love and adventure, the forerunner of the modern novel

* *Restoration* referring to the period in English history, beginning in 1660, when Charles II was restored to the throne
* *classical* in the tradition of ancient Greece and Rome

* *Romantic* referring to a school of thought, prominent in the 1800s, that emphasized the importance of emotion in art

* *patron* supporter or financial sponsor of an artist or writer

staged by the prominent writer and Shakespeare scholar Ludwig Tieck, using August Wilhelm von Schlegel's translation. Tieck's personal theory about *A Midsummer Night's Dream* was that Shakespeare had designed it for a court wedding that Queen Elizabeth attended. Scholars have subsequently suggested 11 weddings as possible occasions for the play's first presentation, but there is only slight evidence for any of them. Another problem with Tieck's theory is that Shakespeare's acting company depended primarily on the large audiences in public playhouses for its income.

MODERNIST PRODUCTION AND CRITICISM. Modernist* productions broke from the Victorian taste for elaborate stage pictures. In 1914 Harley Granville-Barker presented a less realistic, more symbolic setting and shocked audiences with gilded* fairies, some of whom looked more like Cambodian temple dancers than the Victorian ballet fairies that audiences had come to expect. Granville-Barker and directors after him focused on the poetry and the swift movement of the play. Variations on Victorian and modernist interpretations continued to appear through the 1950s, however, with both types generally presenting the play as a delicate and innocent tale of universal love. German director Max Reinhardt, who staged the comedy some 13 times in Europe and America, directed a film for Warner Brothers in 1935 with William Dieterle. One of the first great Shakespearean screen productions, it featured Mickey Rooney as Puck, Victor Jory as Oberon, and James Cagney as Bottom. The film's atmosphere of fantasy provided an escape during the difficult years of the Great Depression. It offered remarkable illusions of a fairytale forest, but it also contained a few images that suggested a disturbing dream.

After World War II, Shakespearean criticism explored the many contrasts in the play: reason and imagination, illusion and reality, order and disorder, fickleness and faithfulness. In an essay written in 1959, C. L. Barber linked the play to traditional pagan* rituals celebrating fertility. Barber saw the wild energy of the midsummer festivities as contained, at the end of the play, by marriage vows. Polish critic Jan Kott, on the other hand, read the play as a grim nightmare of government power and raw sexuality (1962).

Both criticism and theatrical productions began to explore Freudian* possibilities in the play. In recent decades Oberon and Titania, in particular, have been played with a high degree of sexual energy. Scholars and directors have imagined them ruling over the night and the wild setting of the forest as Theseus and Hippolyta rule over the daytime and the controlled society of Athens. In many productions both couples have been played by the same pair of actors. A notable production by the ROYAL SHAKESPEARE COMPANY, directed by Peter Brook in 1970, broke with many traditions. Brook staged the play in a dazzling white box, with Oberon and Puck on trapezes. The production celebrated young love and sexuality, echoing the period of youthful rebellion that had dominated the late 1960s. Brook's contemporary exploration of the script influenced several later Shakespearean productions.

* *modernist* referring to a literary and artistic style that emphasized new and different forms of expression appropriate to modern society
* *gilded* coated with gold

* *pagan* referring to ancient religions that worshiped many gods, or more generally, to any non-Christian religion

* *Freudian* based on the theories of Sigmund Freud, a doctor in Vienna during the late 1800s and early 1900s who developed the practice of modern psychotherapy

110

POSTMODERN PRODUCTIONS AND CRITICISM. In the 1980s and 1990s, interpretations of *A Midsummer Night's Dream* focused strongly on issues of gender and power. In 1983, for example, critic Louis Montrose described the play as a reflection of the anxieties about sexuality that characterized Shakespeare's time. Elizabethan culture was male-dominated in every respect but one: it was headed by a powerful woman, Queen Elizabeth. Some productions have presented Theseus and Oberon as brutally controlling Hippolyta and Titania. Others have suggested confusion about gender identity and sexuality. The role of Puck—who can be treated as male, female, or neither—has been played in ways that underline the uncertainties about gender relations in the play.

Over the course of its history, *A Midsummer Night's Dream* has been read as a story of blissful love, of imperial power, and finally as reflecting a world in which perceptions are often misleading and identity is seen as unstable. In general this play has shown a remarkable ability to be adapted to each era's concepts of love, power, sex, and the supernatural. (*See also* **Actors, Shakespearean; Directors and Shakespeare; Music Inspired by Shakespeare; Play Within the Play; Shakespeare on Screen.**)

MILITARY LIFE

Queen Elizabeth I did not maintain a professional standing army; in fact she used military forces far less often than did the English kings whom she followed. Most of her military actions were small campaigns to subdue Irish rebellions or to assist Protestant armies fighting on the European continent. Even so, the military had a strong presence in English life. Many Englishmen volunteered or were made to serve in temporary military companies and were thus well acquainted with military life. Those who did not serve probably had experienced recruitment drives and had received some military training. Not surprisingly, military life was a common theme in many of Shakespeare's plays, especially the English histories.

RANKS OF THE ENGLISH MILITARY. The top-ranking military authorities were the monarch and the Privy Council, a select group of royal advisers. They would appoint a commander, usually a high-ranking nobleman, for a particular campaign. The commander was normally assisted by several corporals, also likely to be aristocrats, reflecting the common belief among the nobility that military service was their duty and command their rightful role.

The key link in the chain of command was the captain. Captains were in charge of the basic units of men called companies. Their assisting officers might include a lieutenant, two sergeants (drill instructors), and several corporals, as well as a flag bearer (for battlefield communications), a drummer (for company morale), and a surgeon. The company itself consisted of about 150 soldiers.

Captains controlled the pay, equipment, clothing, and feeding of the men in their company, and many were known to abuse the system

to enrich themselves. Some captains, for example, maintained as few officers and soldiers as possible while still claiming to have a full complement in their company. Since government pay clerks gave all of a company's wages to the captain for distribution, an unscrupulous officer could keep much of the extra money for himself. A typical captain's roster of men was so unreliable that the king and his council had only a very rough estimate of the nation's available forces.

RECRUITING SOLDIERS.

Because England had no standing army, citizens were expected to form local militias* to defend the country against invasion. Every 4 years the government held a muster, in which all able-bodied men between the ages of 16 and 60 were called up for counting and military training. Musters were also called during times of crisis.

* *militia* army of citizens who may be called into action in times of emergency

Volunteers were usually few in number, so when England was involved in a foreign war, soldiers had to be "pressed" into service. During a press (forced recruitment) local officials submitted the names of potential soldiers to the captains who came through town to fill their companies. Citizens who could afford to bribe the officials were often able to avoid the press. For this reason poor people and peasants filled most companies.

A famous recruitment occurs in *Henry IV, Part 1* when the fat, cowardly knight Sir John FALSTAFF receives a commission to gather a company of men to fight the rebels who are threatening the crown. Falstaff begins by recruiting (or threatening to recruit) family men and prospective husbands, men of some means who are likely to resist going to war and who have the means to buy their way out. Falstaff accumulates more than £300 in bribes, but he still has to put together a company. He does so by gathering vagabonds, beggars, and other sorry souls, a generally unimpressive lot. Furthermore, instead of outfitting his men with the money given to him for that purpose, Falstaff insists that they will "find linen enough on every hedge" (IV.ii.47–48), suggesting that they help themselves to the laundry spread out to dry by unsuspecting villagers.

MILITARY SERVICE.

The life of a soldier during wartime was generally miserable. Captains seeking to increase their riches pocketed the money intended for their soldiers' equipment, food, and clothing, leaving the troops largely unprovided.

War itself was a dangerous occupation, especially for poorly equipped and inadequately trained soldiers. Hard-hearted captains failed to protect their men because casualties enabled them to collect the wages of the dead soldiers. In addition the lack of sanitation in the military camps resulted in numerous deaths from disease.

IN THE NAVY.

As an island nation, England maintained a standing navy for two reasons: to build and maintain its warships and to protect its trading vessels. Merchant vessels and crews could be pressed into service during emergencies. Life for sailors was less grim than that for soldiers. The English navy was better trained and more highly disciplined than the army, and sailors could supplement their regular earnings by committing acts of piracy against Spanish ships and colonies.

SHAKESPEARE'S PORTRAYALS OF MILITARY LIFE. Military campaigns and their commanders abound in Shakespeare's plays. Shakespeare's most complete portrait of a greedy and irresponsible captain is Sir John Falstaff, who appears in three plays, but with such roguish charm and wit that audiences enjoy him in spite of his unscrupulous and cowardly behavior. At the other extreme is Prince Hal, who plunges bravely into battle, defeating and killing his enemy Hotspur (in *Henry IV, Part 1*) in single combat. Two plays later, Hal has become Henry V. In the work that bears his name, he inspires his men (outnumbered by the French five to one) before the Battle of Agincourt with these words: "We few, we happy few, we band of brothers; / For he to-day that sheds his blood with me / Shall be my brother" (IV.iii.60–62).

Shakespeare depicted the Elizabethan virtues of loyalty and discipline not only in his portraits of nobles but also in his portrayals of common soldiers. At the same time, he understood the complaints of the ordinary soldier against his superiors. In *Othello*, for example, IAGO has been passed over for promotion. He denounces Cassio, who was promoted instead, for knowing too much of military theory and too little of real battle. (*See also* **Arms and Armor; Warfare.**)

MIRANDA

* *protagonist* central character in a dramatic or literary work

* *chastity* quality of moral virtue achieved by abstaining from unlawful sexual activity

* *betrothal* mutual promise to marry in the future

Miranda is the daughter of Prospero, the protagonist* in one of Shakespeare's last plays, *The Tempest*. She has lived with her father on an island for 12 years, since the age of 2. The only other inhabitants of the island are Ariel (a spirit who helps Prospero work his magic spells) and Caliban (the half-human monster whom Prospero has enslaved).

The play's action begins when Prospero causes his enemy, the king of Naples, to be shipwrecked on the island with his son and several other members of his court. Miranda, who has never seen other people, falls in love with the prince, Ferdinand. To test his loyalty to Miranda, Prospero pretends to disapprove of the match. He imprisons Ferdinand and forces him to stack thousands of logs. Miranda visits her beloved in secret and offers to help him, but he refuses her assistance. Eventually Miranda, having "no ambition / To see a goodlier man" (I.ii.483–84), and the prince pledge their undying love for each other.

The name *Miranda*, created by Shakespeare, means "admirable" (to be marveled at) in Latin. It reflects both Miranda's own virtue and the uncritical wonder with which she views the shipwrecked arrivals to the island. Her chastity*, compassion, and honesty are expressions of her innocence. Her character is most directly contrasted with that of Caliban, whose uncivilized nature is usually portrayed as savage; the play reveals that he had once tried to rape Miranda.

At the betrothal* of Miranda and Ferdinand, a troupe of goddesses perform a MASQUE in which Miranda fulfills the ancient role of woman as the fertile source of birth and life. This theme of renewal is expressed in the play's happy conclusion and in Miranda's return to society, where she

will do her part to perpetuate the royal dynasty of Naples. (*See also* **Gender and Sexuality; Marriage and Family; Tempest, The.**)

MONEY

See *Banking and Commerce; Coins and Currency.*

MORALITY AND ETHICS

* *classical* in the tradition of ancient Greece and Rome

The behavior of Shakespeare's heroes and villains reflects Elizabethan attitudes about morality and ethics. The Elizabethan code of ethics was drawn from a combination of classical* philosophy and Christian doctrine concerning virtue and vice.

MORAL TEACHINGS. Scholars of the Middle Ages commented extensively on the writings of ancient philosophers, and the study of these works reached new heights during the Renaissance. One of the best-known works on the subject of morality was the *Nichomachean Ethics* by the ancient Greek philosopher Aristotle. Aristotle's most influential idea was probably the concept of the "golden mean." According to this concept, too little or too much of anything is harmful. True virtue lies in moderation, finding and following the mean, or midpoint, between deficiency and excess. Elizabethans defined *temperance* as the virtue of avoiding extremes, and they regarded it as the moderator among all other virtues.

Renaissance philosophers adopted this ancient perspective by viewing it through the lens of Christian doctrine. Many of the virtues celebrated by the ancients, such as justice, are recognized in the Christian moral system. Other ancient virtues were viewed differently within a Christian context. Pride, for example, is not considered virtuous if it opposes God's will. Some virtues, such as holiness, are specifically Christian and are not part of the ancient moral framework. It is difficult to define the Christian belief system of the Elizabethan age because Christianity itself was newly divided at the time between Catholicism, which had dominated most of Europe throughout the Middle Ages, and Protestantism, which had arisen fairly recently. Some basic principles, however, are part of the overall structure of Christianity and remain essentially the same across different branches.

* *Old Testament* first part of the Bible, whose teachings are accepted by Jews and Christians

* *New Testament* second part of the Bible, whose teachings are accepted by Christians

* *medieval* referring to the Middle Ages, a period roughly between A.D. 500 and 1500

The primary virtue in Christianity is love; God, defined as love, serves as a model for ideal human love. While the Old Testament* outlines elaborate guidelines for behavior in a variety of situations, the New Testament* sums up this complex code of morality in the statements "love thy God" and "love thy neighbor" (*neighbor* now refers to all people). Like other aspects of morality, Elizabethan views of love were influenced by classical beliefs. The ancient Greeks recognized two kinds of love: *eros,* or sexual love, and *philia,* friendly or "brotherly" love. Aristotle defined *philia* as a love between equals, but medieval* philosopher Thomas Aquinas

later argued that *philia* could exist in an unequal relationship, such as that between man and God.

Perhaps the most influential medieval work concerning human love was *On Christian Doctrine* by Saint Augustine, a philosopher who became bishop of Hippo (a city in Africa). Augustine distinguished between right love, or *caritas* (charity), and wrong love, or *cupiditas* (cupidity). This two-sided view of love was linked to the idea that every human being has both a mortal body and an immortal soul, which can either exist in harmony or be divided by conflict. Right love, associated primarily with human reason, meant loving everything for the sake of God. Wrong love, connected primarily with the senses, was loving anyone or anything without reference to God. This view influenced the entire Elizabethan moral system. To act in accordance with God's will was seen as a moral choice, and to violate God's will was immoral. Those who practiced right love would live together in harmony. It followed, then, that a realm's political stability rested on its moral strength and unity. This ethic for Elizabethans was challenged, however, by new ideas that placed pragmatism, or practicality, over morality.

HONOR AND DUELING. The Elizabethan concept of honor, like the Elizabethan concept of love, was influenced by both classical and Christian ideals. Aristotle defined honor primarily as a good reputation, something that depended on the opinions of others rather than a virtue that came from within. For Aristotle, outward glory was not a virtue in itself but a reward for virtuous or heroic behavior. The Christian ideal of honor, by contrast, was one that pertained to internal human worth or goodness. It arose from such virtues as brotherly love and patience, regardless of whether those virtues were recognized by others. The Elizabethan view of honor concerned both outward and inward merit. A "gentleman" or "gentlewoman" was not only a person of high birth but also a person known to be "gentle" or noble in spirit. Honorable behavior, however, was different for different people. It varied, for example, according to gender. For a man, honor or honesty meant being true to his word. For a woman, to be "honest" was to be chaste, sexually pure before marriage and faithful to her husband afterward.

Shakespeare's plays illustrate the multiple meanings of honor, especially the tension between inward and outward honor. In *Julius Caesar*, for example, Mark Antony ironically calls Caesar's murderers "honorable men" (III.ii.83), hinting that it is possible to have a good reputation and yet be inwardly faulty. In *King Lear*, by contrast, Edgar shows a noble spirit that endures even when he is stripped of all his earthly glory. While these two plays focus on inward honor, the idea of outward honor figures more prominently in *Henry IV, Part 1*. Various characters in this play seek to gain honor—that is, high reputation—through glorious deeds in battle, but the witty FALSTAFF argues that honor of that kind is not worth risking one's life for because it is nothing but "a word." Considering only the outward aspect of honor, Falstaff concludes that it will not endure because "detraction will not suffer it" (V.i.139), permit it to survive unchallenged.

Falstaff's remark raises an important point about the Elizabethan obsession with honor. Because honor depended on outward reputation as

well as inward virtue, it was vulnerable to "detraction"; that is, it could be taken away by others. It was therefore important for people to protect their honor against attacks from others. In extreme cases Elizabethan men, especially those of noble birth, would fight to the death to defend their honor. A trial by personal combat was known as a duel. Bloody swordplay in the name of honor was commonplace in England and in western Europe during the 1500s. For example, between 1590 and 1610 one-third of the French nobility perished in duels, even though such activities were illegal.

The practice of dueling exemplifies the conflicts within the Elizabethan code of honor. In theory an honorable duel was consistent with the Christian values of godly truth, justice, and wisdom. In common practice, however, duels were more often fought over outward honor, that is, reputation, for causes that could hardly be considered noble. Duels of this type conflicted with the Christian doctrines of brotherly love and submission to God's will. Seeking private revenge for a personal injury also tended to undercut the public justice system, which was supposed to be the primary means of settling disputes.

According to popular opinion a duel was usually accepted, even expected, as a means of redressing a personal injury. If a gentleman was "given the lie" (accused of lying), honor demanded that he avenge this insult by force of arms. But the rules for honorable dueling, as set down by Vincentio Saviolo (a fencing master from the Italian city of Padua), attack this popular view as a corruption of the original institution of the duel. According to Saviolo, the true purpose of the honorable duello is to defend truth and justice in God's name. To be honorable, a duel must be necessary. A man should not defend his honor with weapons if he can clear his name through nonviolent means, such as a court case. Under this interpretation, fighting a duel simply to satisfy a personal desire for revenge is the exact opposite of honorable behavior. It is yielding to a base, animal instinct rather than using reason to guide one's actions. (*See also* **Astronomy and Cosmology; Duels and Feuds; Gender and Sexuality; Law; Love; Philosophy; Religion; Social Classes.**)

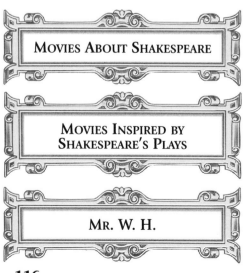

MOVIES ABOUT SHAKESPEARE   See *Shakespeare on Screen; individual works.*

MOVIES INSPIRED BY SHAKESPEARE'S PLAYS   See *Shakespeare on Screen; individual plays.*

MR. W. H.   See *Sonnets.*

MUCH ADO ABOUT NOTHING

Written around the middle of Shakespeare's career, *Much Ado About Nothing* is a comedy with some serious undertones. Much of the play's humor centers on wordplay, and the title is itself a pun. The word *nothing* was pronounced in a way that was similar to *noting*, which means eavesdropping. Many scenes in the play involve conversations being overheard—and frequently misinterpreted—by other characters. These misunderstandings are a source of humor, but they also serve as a focus for serious social commentary.

PLOT. The play is set at the home of Leonato, governor of the Italian city of Messina. Don Pedro, the prince of Aragon, has been fending off an uprising led by Don John, his illegitimate* half brother. The play opens with the news that the two men have made peace and are on their way to Leonato's house, accompanied by the soldiers Claudio and Benedick. Claudio immediately falls in love with Leonato's daughter Hero, and the prince promises to help him court her. Benedick, however, is scornful of marriage, as is Beatrice, Hero's cousin. Leonato explains that "there is a kind of merry war" between Beatrice and Benedick, but the jests they exchange in their "skirmish of wit" hint at the emotional scars of a possible past relationship between them.

That night at a masked ball Don Pedro successfully woos Hero on Claudio's behalf, although Don John—who resents Claudio's success on the battlefield and his intimacy with Don Pedro—tries to convince Claudio that the prince is wooing Hero for himself. Claudio believes this at first, giving the audience a hint at how easily deceived he is. To pass the time until Claudio's wedding, Don Pedro devises a plan to make a love match between Beatrice and Benedick. Claudio and Don Pedro arrange for Benedick to overhear a conversation in which they remark that Beatrice is madly in love with Benedick but refuses to admit it because she knows he will reject her. Then Hero and her maid Ursula play out a similar conversation for Beatrice to overhear. Both Beatrice and Benedick realize that there is truth in what has been said and privately acknowledge their feelings for each other.

The night before the wedding, Don John comes to Don Pedro and Claudio and tells them he has proof that Hero is unfaithful. He has them stand outside her window and overhear a conversation between Hero's servant Margaret and Don John's friend Borachio, who is romantically involved with Margaret. Margaret appears at the window dressed in Hero's clothing and converses with Borachio about what the observers take to be the secret encounters they have had. Convinced by this evidence, Claudio and Don Pedro plan to expose Hero's shame the next day. Later that night two watchmen overhear Borachio boasting to a friend about his meeting with Margaret. They arrest him and take him to Leonato, who tells them to question the prisoner themselves, because he is busy preparing for the wedding.

Standing before the altar, Claudio calls Hero "an approved wanton" and refuses to marry her. Don Pedro supports his claim, and the two leave together. Leonato is inclined to believe the princes' accusations, but the friar performing the ceremony is convinced that Hero is innocent. He persuades Leonato to pretend she is dead, hoping to move Claudio to regret his harsh words. Left alone with Beatrice, Benedick declares his love for her and asks her to "bid me do any thing for thee" (IV.i.288). "Kill Claudio," she replies. Benedick is shocked at first, but he eventually agrees when she convinces him of Hero's innocence. He tells Claudio that Hero is dead and challenges him to a duel.

Meanwhile Dogberry, the well-meaning captain of the watch, has questioned Borachio. Finding him guilty of slandering Hero, he brings him before Leonato. In front of Claudio and Don Pedro, Borachio confesses his crime and expresses remorse for causing Hero's death. He tells them that Don John, who has fled the city, was responsible for the plot and that Margaret was an unknowing participant in it. A guilt-stricken Claudio promises to do anything in his power to make amends. Leonato demands that Claudio marry his niece the following morning. The "niece" appears with a veil covering her face, and Claudio swears to accept her as his wife. When she removes the veil, he sees in astonishment that his bride is Hero. Beatrice and Benedick then confess their love for each other and agree to marry, although they joke that they do so only out of pity. To complete this resolution a messenger brings news that Don John has been captured and is being brought back to Messina.

SOURCES AND COMMENTARY. The central plot device of *Much Ado About Nothing,* a lover wrongly convinced of his beloved's unfaithfulness, is an old theme dating back to ancient Greece. It was used in several Renaissance works, including Ludovico Ariosto's *Orlando Furioso* (1516), Matteo Bandello's *Novelle* (1554), and Sir Edmund SPENSER's *The Faerie Queene* (1590). In most versions of the tale, the two lovers are of different

In *Much Ado About Nothing,* Beatrice and Benedick deny that they are in love, preferring instead to exchange humorous insults. In this scene, from a 1991 Royal Shakespeare Company production, the lovers are presented with poems they have written to each other.

social classes. Shakespeare eliminated class inequality from the love-and-betrayal plot he devised, but he explored the idea in more subtle ways elsewhere in the play.

conventional following established practice

The central figures in the play's main plot, Claudio and Hero, are both conventional* characters who conform to the values of their society. Hero is an obedient daughter who makes no objection to her father's insistence that "if the prince do solicit you [for marriage] . . . you know your answer" (II.i.66–68). Claudio's interest in her is based almost entirely on her appearance—"she is the sweetest lady that ever I looked on" (I.i.187–88)—and the only information he seeks to confirm his choice is whether she is Leonato's only heir. Knowing so little of her character, Claudio is quick to believe Don John's accusations against her. His pride then forces him to reject her, because it is unacceptable to him to take a wife who is not a virgin.

Most audiences find the less conventional Beatrice and Benedick a more memorable couple. The clever wordplay in their battles of wit provides better entertainment than the near-tragic story of Hero and Claudio. Beatrice is one of several noteworthy heroines in Shakespearean comedies who do not conform to ordinary Elizabethan ideas of womanhood. In a time when women were expected to be either virtuous, silent, and obedient or faithless, vicious, and shrewd—with nothing in between—Beatrice is charming, intelligent, and independent. She resists the idea of marriage as the only suitable goal for women and urges Hero to challenge her father's control over her choice of a husband saying "let him be a handsome fellow, or else . . . say, 'Father, as it please me'" (II.i.54–56). She also rebels against the role assigned her in society. When Claudio deserts Hero, Beatrice cries out, "O God, that I were a man! I would eat his heart in the market-place . . . [but] I cannot be a man with wishing, therefore I will die a woman with grieving" (IV.i.306–23).

Beatrice and Benedick openly criticize Messina society, but they remain capable of living within it while rejecting its assumptions. Don John, by contrast, is an outsider by definition—a bastard whose social status is limited by his birth. His first major scene reveals how cut off he feels from others: "it better fits my blood to be disdain'd of all than to fashion a carriage to rob love from any" (I.iii.28–30). He is unwilling to gain social acceptance by pretending to be something he is not. His dissatisfaction expresses itself as an unfocused desire to harm the people Messina views as admirable. Although Don John expresses a particular resentment toward Claudio, he is willing to do anything that will "build mischief." Benedick's promise of "brave punishments" for him at the end of the play makes it clear that Don John will never again be accepted in Messina society.

Dogberry and his companions are also outsiders because of their low social and economic class. The other characters view them, and many productions treat them, merely as a source of humor. They misuse words and misunderstand the words of others, but they also succeed in exposing Don John's plot, which baffled the major characters. By arresting the "arrant knaves," they confirm Dogberry's opening claim that they are "good men and true." Yet when they first attempt to talk to Leonato before the wedding, he dismisses their efforts with "Neighbors, you are tedious"

(III.v.18). Only because they eventually succeed in bringing their charges against Borachio does the play end as a comedy and not a tragedy.

Another "low" character of interest is Margaret. Like Beatrice she rebels against her social status. Wearing Hero's dress for her conversation with Borachio may express a secret wish to gain her friend's higher social position. She admires the "rare fashion" of Hero's wedding gown and speaks with awe of an exquisite gown worn by the duchess of Milan, perhaps hinting that she longs for similar finery. In the same scene she assumes Beatrice's cloak of wit much as she put on Hero's dress, engaging in sexual puns that embarrass the innocent Hero. A later scene shows her defeating Benedick in a battle of wits and expressing her desire to rise in social status: "Why, shall I always keep below stairs?" (V.ii.9–10). When her role in Don John's plot is revealed, Leonato insists that she was "in some fault for this" (V.iv.4). Rather than lay the blame entirely on Claudio and Don Pedro, his social superiors, he excuses their "error" and focuses on Margaret's participation in the trick Don John played on them.

PERFORMANCE HISTORY. *Much Ado About Nothing* was apparently well received from its earliest performances. It was performed at court in 1613, and a 1640 edition of Shakespeare's poems observed in its introduction "Let but Beatrice / and Benedick be [seen], lo, in a trice / The Cockpit Galleries, Boxes all are full." In the 1660s manager William Davenant borrowed material from *Much Ado* for an adaptation of *Measure for Measure*, which he called *The Law Against Lovers.* Charles Johnson indulged in similar borrowing for his *Love in a Forest,* an adaptation of *As You Like It,* in 1723. In the late 1700s and early 1800s, such noteworthy actors as David Garrick and Charles Kemble assumed the role of Benedick, but Henry IRVING's performance of the part in 1882 was overshadowed by Ellen Terry's exquisite Beatrice. John Gielgud directed the play at Stratford in 1949 and throughout the 1950s. His interpretation of the work, with himself as Benedick and Peggy Ashcroft as Beatrice, was felt by many to be definitive (authoritative and complete).

Many modern productions of *Much Ado About Nothing* have altered the time and place of the play's setting. In a 1976 production by the ROYAL SHAKESPEARE COMPANY, director John Barton chose to relocate Messina in British-occupied India. Dogberry was played as an Anglo-Indian caught between cultures, so that his misguided attempts to speak elegantly reflected the difficulty of adjusting to a foreign language.

Judi Dench's studio production for the Renaissance Theatre Company in 1988, with Kenneth Branagh as Benedick and Samantha Bond as Beatrice, changed the play's setting to England in the 1800s. Setting the play in this class-conscious era highlighted its issues of social class and gender. The best-known screen version of *Much Ado About Nothing* is the visually stunning 1993 film directed by Kenneth Branagh, with himself as Benedick and Emma Thompson as Beatrice. Branagh made heavy cuts in the text, reducing Margaret's role to a single line and blurring the importance of Dogberry and the watch. (*See also* **Actors, Shakespearean; Gender and Sexuality; Plays: The Comedies; Shakespeare's Plays, Adaptations of; Social Classes.**)

MUSEUMS AND ARCHIVES

Numerous museums, archives, and other research institutions aid scholars in the study of Shakespeare's life, work, and influence. These institutions contain collections that range from first editions of Shakespeare's works to the account books that belonged to London theater owners. Most of these collections are in academic libraries, accessible only to qualified scholars.

SHAKESPEAREAN COLLECTIONS IN THE UNITED STATES. The Folger Shakespeare Library, located in Washington, D.C., houses one of the most complete collections of works by and about Shakespeare. It has more early folios and quartos* than any other museum or archive: 79 copies of the FIRST FOLIO (including fragmentary copies), 58 of the Second, 24 of the Third, and 37 of the Fourth Folio. Especially noteworthy are a one-of-a-kind copy of *Titus Andronicus* dating to 1594 and a portion of a first edition of *Henry IV, Part 1*. In addition to original plays and poems, the Folger also houses the largest collection of English adaptations of Shakespeare, including a version of the *Henry IV* plays dating from about 1623. Other early theater-related material includes prompt books* dating to the 1600s, playbills, and sketches of costumes. The collection also contains letters, manuscripts, pictures, and other mementos from famous Shakespearean actors, such as David Garrick and Edmund Kean.

The Folger Shakespeare Library is open only to scholars. Since 1936 it has awarded fellowships to scholars from around the world to conduct research on Shakespeare's life, times, and works. The library publishes facsimiles and reprints of some of its more important early literary and historical works.

Another notable Shakespearean collection in the United States belongs to the Henry E. Huntington Library and Art Gallery in San Marino, California. The Huntington Library owns first-edition quartos of all of Shakespeare's plays except *Titus Andronicus*. In addition, it has several copies each of the First through Fourth Folios. One of the Second Folios in the collection is a well-known version called the Perkins Folio, with notes that scholars once believed were written by Shakespeare. Eventually these annotations were shown to be forgeries.

SHAKESPEAREAN COLLECTIONS IN GREAT BRITAIN. The Bodleian Library at the University of Oxford is one of the oldest reference libraries in Great Britain. Sir Thomas Bodley, a collector of medieval* texts, founded the library in 1602. Since then its collection has grown from around 2,000 books and manuscripts to more than 4 million. Included in that total are 43 early quartos of Shakespeare's works, two First Folios, three Second Folios, one Third Folio, and two Fourth Folios. In addition, it boasts original manuscript copies of an early biography of Shakespeare by John Aubrey and of Simon Forman's *Booke of Plaies*, which contains the earliest performance records of *Macbeth, The Winter's Tale,* and *Cymbeline*. The Bodleian Library also has manuscripts for other Elizabethan plays, including one with songs that Shakespeare used in *Macbeth*.

The British Library in London houses an extensive Shakespeare collection that formerly belonged to the British Museum. Separated from the

* **quarto** referring to the format of a book or page; a sheet of paper folded twice, yielding four leaves or eight pages

* **prompt book** annotated copy of a play, which contains instructions for entrances, exits, music, and other cues

* **medieval** referring to the Middle Ages, a period roughly between A.D. 500 and 1500

museum in 1972, the British Museum's library was reorganized as the British Library Reference Division. The Shakespeare-related materials in this collection are among the most diverse in the world. Among them are more than 60 original quartos of the playwright's works, donated by such famous figures as the actor David Garrick and England's King George III. The library also holds several copies of the First, Second, and Third Folios. One of the institution's most exciting documents is a manuscript that is thought to contain writings in Shakespeare's own hand.

The Shakespeare Institute at the University of Birmingham focuses on the environment in which Shakespeare lived and worked and on his influence on other writers. Founded in 1951, the institute maintains a wide variety of materials about all aspects of European life and culture in the 1500s and 1600s. Unlike other collections, the institute's archive is not built primarily around original copies of early works. Instead it features more than 20,000 microfilm copies of books and manuscripts, most dating from between the years 1500 and 1660. The Shakespeare Institute has a complete collection of all known English plays up to 1700, as well as many Latin plays and English songbooks from the same period. It also sponsors a Summer Shakespeare School every year and an International Shakespeare Conference every two years. Both events take place in Shakespeare's hometown of STRATFORD-UPON-AVON, approximately 20 miles from the university. (*See also* **Actors, Shakespearean; Printing and Publishing; Prompt Book; Quartos and Folios; Shakespeare's Works, Adaptations of.**)

MUSIC IN ELIZABETHAN THEATER

See color plate 15, vol. 1.

Elizabethan playwrights used music for several purposes. Sometimes music merely provided a pleasant diversion from the main action. At other times it was the key element in a scene for communicating mood, commenting on action, or revealing a character's feelings or motivations. Shakespeare made ample use of music in his work, incorporating it into more than 500 passages in his plays and poems. His writings reveal a fondness for music as well as a good understanding of its technical aspects.

SINGERS AND MUSICIANS. The acting companies of Shakespeare's day had access to a wide range of singers and musicians. Boy actors—employed to play the female roles—often had choir training and some instrumental skills as well. Among the talents expected from a company's clown were singing and dancing, and most lead actors could perform at least simple songs, alone or in a chorus.

A variety of musical instruments accompanied the singers and provided background melodies for plays. The most common types of instruments in Elizabethan theaters were woodwinds (flutes and fifes), string instruments (lutes and violins), drums, horns, and trumpets. Organs, virginals (similar to modern pianos), and other keyboard instruments were seldom used in theaters. Musicians typically performed offstage, often in

a music room that was located above the stage. Not all theaters had music rooms, however, and sometimes musicians were located on stage, behind the stage, or even under it.

INSTRUMENTALS AND SONGS. Shakespeare often used instrumentals (music without words) to convey a certain mood or reveal something about a character's personality. In *Twelfth Night,* Duke Orsino responds to a melody by exclaiming, "If music be the food of love, play on" (I.i.1). His reaction indicates his sentimentality.

Shakespeare also employed a wide variety of Elizabethan songs for different occasions. These included celebratory songs, serenades, lullabies, and songs for MASQUES, the elaborate entertainments popular among the upper classes. Several songs in his plays are purely for entertainment value, but most of the music serves specific dramatic functions. Songs

Music was an important part of Elizabethan theater. The musicians in this painting from 1596 are shown playing some of the popular instruments of the day, including a flute, a violin, and a lute.

sometimes mark places where the action is interrupted or indicate that a period of time has passed between two scenes.

Some songs serve as essential dramatic elements of scenes in which they appear. In *The Merchant of Venice,* for example, a song plays as Bassanio considers which casket—gold, silver, or lead—contains the portrait of Portia, which, if chosen, will gain him her hand in marriage. The lyrics speak of the deceptive power of outward appearances, a hint that the lead casket in this instance may be more valuable than the others, and they include words that rhyme with *lead,* providing additional clues about the correct choice. (*See also* **Acting Companies, Elizabethan; Music Inspired by Shakespeare.**)

MUSIC INSPIRED BY SHAKESPEARE

The earliest major musical composition inspired by a Shakespeare play was written by English composer Henry Purcell in 1692 for *The Fairy-Queen,* an adaptation of *A Midsummer Night's Dream.* After that, Shakespeare's plays inspired no really significant music until the 1800s, when the Romantic* movement made the playwright well known throughout Europe. From the mid-1800s on, the plays proved a rich source of inspiration for many important composers.

OPERA. Over the course of the 19th century, many operas were drawn from Shakespeare's plays. Among the most popular of these were Charles Gounod's *Roméo et Juliette* (1867), Ambroise Thomas's *Hamlet* (1868), and Otto Nicolai's *Die lustigen Weiber von Windsor (The Merry Wives of Windsor)* (1849). The only operas of a quality and importance comparable to their Shakespearean sources are Giuseppe Verdi's *Otello* (1887) and *Falstaff* (1893). Verdi's early *Macbeth* (1847) is a remarkable work, but *Otello* and *Falstaff,* his last two operas, benefit from the librettos* written by Arrigo Boito as well as from the mastery Verdi had achieved over a lifetime.

In *Otello,* Boito brilliantly adapted Shakespeare's tragedy to the forms and conventions* of Italian tragic opera. He concentrated the action and reduced the characters to their essential qualities, making IAGO satanic* and DESDEMONA angelic. His libretto enabled Verdi to develop the action and the characters in detail in the music, a task the composer accomplished with great power and subtlety. For the comic opera *Falstaff,* Boito simplified the plot of *The Merry Wives of Windsor* but gave it greater depth and richness by incorporating the many-sided FALSTAFF of *Henry IV, Parts 1* and *2.* The 80-year-old Verdi responded with astonishingly rich and energetic music, full of witty detail and great affection for the characters.

Shakespeare's plays continued to inspire significant operatic works in the 1900s. Samuel Barber's *Antony and Cleopatra,* written for the opening of the New York Metropolitan Opera House at Lincoln Center in 1966, used a libretto fashioned directly from Shakespeare's words. So did Ralph Vaughan Williams's *Sir John in Love* (1929), based on *The Merry*

* *Romantic* referring to a school of thought, prominent in the 1800s, that emphasized the importance of emotion in art

* *libretto* text for an opera

* *convention* established practice

* *satanic* characteristic of Satan, or the devil

See color plate 14, vol. 2.

* *overture* orchestral concert piece written as a single movement; also an introduction to a musical dramatic work
* *incidental music* instrumental music written to accompany a play

1692
Henry Purcell,
The Fairy Queen
(musical adaptation).

1827
Felix Mendelssohn,
overture to
*A Midsummer
Night's Dream.*

1880
Peter Tchaikovsky,
fantasy overture to
Romeo and Juliet.

1887
Giuseppe Verdi,
Otello (opera).

1893
Giuseppe Verdi,
Falstaff (opera).

1935
Sergei Prokofiev,
Romeo and Juliet
(ballet).

1957
Leonard Bernstein,
West Side Story
(musical adaptation).

1690
1740
1790
1840
1890
1940
1990

Wives of Windsor, and Benjamin Britten's *A Midsummer Night's Dream* (1960). Although *Pyramus and Thisby*—the PLAY WITHIN THE PLAY performed by the "rude mechanicals," or low characters—is presented as a hilarious parody of Italian opera, the atmosphere of Britten's opera is often eerily disturbing. The fairy world the composer created is ruled by a somewhat sinister OBERON.

ORCHESTRAL MUSIC. Shakespeare's plays inspired music for the concert hall as well as for the operatic stage. In 1826 at the age of 17, Felix Mendelssohn composed his concert overture* *A Midsummer Night's Dream.* This composition was intended to provide an independent impression of the play rather than an introduction to it. Mendelssohn portrays in music the collision of the play's separate worlds: the society of Athens and the woods outside the city. The piece opens with four woodwind chords that set the magical mood. The composer then introduces musical themes that represent the fairies, the Athenian court, the four lovers wandering through the woods, the rude mechanicals (including braying noises for the character of Bottom, transformed into a donkey), and the hunting horns of Duke Theseus. These themes first appear one by one and then in various combinations until a repetition of the four opening chords brings the overture to a harmonious conclusion. Sixteen years later Mendelssohn incorporated the overture into a set of incidental music* he wrote for the play.

Mendelssohn's overture was the first of many orchestral pieces based on Shakespeare's plays. Perhaps the best of those that followed in the 1800s are Hector Berlioz's "dramatic symphony" *Roméo et Juliette* (1839) and Peter Ilyich Tchaikovsky's "fantasy overture" on the same subject (1880). The design of Berlioz's symphony reflects the composer's special interest in the separation of the young lovers from the society around them. Although the piece contains vocal and choral movements, including an extended finale in which Friar Lawrence (a bass) lectures and unites the feuding families (the chorus), the lovers "speak" only through the instruments of the orchestra. The most noteworthy 20th-century piece is Sir Edward Elgar's *Falstaff* (1913), a "symphonic study" of the character as seen in the *Henry IV* plays that ingeniously uses the full forces of the modern orchestra.

OTHER STAGE MUSIC. To date, only one major ballet score has been based on Shakespeare: Sergei Prokofiev's full-length ballet *Romeo and Juliet* (1935). The scenario Prokofiev crafted from the play provides ample opportunity for large dance numbers but always keeps the story of the lovers prominent through a series of recurring musical themes, each associated with a particular character.

Leonard Bernstein's *West Side Story* (1957), a musical based on *Romeo and Juliet,* points the way to exciting new possibilities for composers seeking inspiration in Shakespeare's work. The plays will undoubtedly continue to provoke many kinds of wonderful music. (*See also* **Art Inspired by Shakespeare; Music Inspired by Shakespeare; Shakespeare's Works, Adaptations of.**)

MYTHOLOGY

See *Gods and Goddesses.*

NATURE

Shakespeare uses nature throughout his plays. Whether characters flee to natural settings, are lost at sea, or exposed to the elements, most seem to resolve their problems and then return to their daily lives transformed by the experience.

INTO THE WOODS. As the city of LONDON grew and became England's cultural center, some Elizabethans longed for a return to nature, which to them symbolized innocence and simplicity. Like many writers in the late 1500s, Shakespeare frequently set up a conflict in his plays between urban life and country life. He has several of his characters flee to the forest to escape the rules and restrictions of court life. Their responsibilities, however, often pull them back to the royal court. As with most of the subjects he wrote about, Shakespeare carefully examined nature from many angles.

Shakespeare's forests are magical places, often the perfect location for romantic escapades. The Forest of Arden in *As You Like It*, for example, is a somewhat idealized world where shepherds and shepherdesses live in harmony with the elements. In Arden nature offers a sanctuary where the main characters, accustomed to a sophisticated life at court, are freed from many of the corrupting influences of the wealth, social class, and power that defined their daily lives at home.

The characters in *As You Like It* react to nature in different ways. Touchstone, the clown, prefers the comforts of the royal court: "Aye, now am I in Arden, the more fool I. When I was at home, I was in a better place" (II.iv.16–17). The exiled duke, on the other hand, enjoys his new-found life of hunting, eating, and singing. He considers civilization, where people are deceitful and insincere, more dangerous than the wilds of the forest: "Are not these woods / More free from peril than the envious court?" (II.i.3–4).

In the Forest of Arden, Shakespeare emphasizes both sides of the natural world: nature can be pleasant and beautiful or wild and unpredictable. The forest in *As You Like It* is unlike any found in Europe. There are lions, snakes, and even palm trees in this imaginary locale. Arden is an imperfect place, however, because it is not exempt from "the icy fang / And churlish chiding of the winter's wind" (II.i.6–7).

A DREAM PLAY. Most Elizabethans believed that supernatural creatures, such as FAIRIES, inhabited nature, and this magical side of nature takes center stage in *A Midsummer Night's Dream*. The play is set in a dream world where fairies dance in the moonlight and supernatural occurrences are commonplace. This is the land of OBERON, king of the fairies, a place where Athenian woods become the backdrop for all the joy, pain, and jealousy of love.

The fairies in these woods are mischief makers. They cause the play's characters to fall in love, and they even replace one man's head with that of a donkey. This world, too, is imperfect. PUCK, Oberon's jester, reminds the audience that although fairies may appear to be good, they are also attached to darker powers, to the unknown side of nature:

> Now it is the time of night
> That the graves, all gaping wide,
> Every one lets forth his sprite,
> In the church-way paths to glide.
> And we fairies, that do run
> By the triple Hecat's [the moon goddess's] team
> From the presence of the sun,
> Following the darkness like a dream,
> Now are frolic.
>
> (V.i.379–87)

OUT TO SEA. The violent forces of nature, such as storms at sea, also appear in Shakespeare's plays. The dramatist's depiction of the shipwreck that opens *The Tempest* was based on a popular account of the destruction of a ship that had sailed for Virginia in 1609. Stories about this dangerous voyage through uncharted seas to the New World influenced the playwright. Accounts of other voyages to the Americas provided descriptions of vegetation and animal life there.

As always, Shakespeare used his sources to create powerful drama. The storm, which is the catalyst of all the action in *The Tempest*, is conjured by PROSPERO, the magician who lives on an island. It causes a shipwreck, but because Prospero controls the elements, none of the ship's passengers are harmed. Prospero's island is a magical place, inhabited by supernatural creatures, including Ariel, the nature sprite, and CALIBAN, the savage offspring of a witch. In some ways Ariel and Caliban represent two sides of human nature: the spiritual and the animal.

As interest in the natural world grew among Elizabethans, many became attracted to the concept of the noble savage, the idea that man, by returning to nature, could find his true identity. Through Caliban, Shakespeare examines the popular notion that humanity might benefit by moving back to nature. Caliban is sometimes seen as an uncivilized monster because he lacks the refinements of culture. Shakespeare emphasizes Caliban's rebellious nature by letting the audience know that he has tried to rape MIRANDA, Prospero's daughter. The playwright also portrays him as a creature who has been oppressed by Prospero, and who has learned to speak verse and respond sensitively to Ariel's music.

The sea's power is also an important theme in Shakespeare's *Pericles*. Shipwrecks and exposure to the elements form a significant part of the play's atmosphere. The action occurs near the Aegean Sea in the eastern Mediterranean. During the course of the play, the violent waves seem to take everything from Pericles; he loses his wife in a shipwreck, and pirates capture his daughter. In the last act, however, a storm blows his ship off course to a city where he is reunited with his family. The action in *Pericles*

mirrors the cycle of nature: birth, death, and rebirth. (*See also* **Arden, Forest of; Prose Technique; Settings; Weather and the Seasons.**)

NAVIGATION

Navigation is the art of determining one's location at sea and setting a course to a specific destination. During Shakespeare's lifetime, advances in navigation enabled English merchants and explorers to travel farther from home than ever before.

Because England is surrounded by water, travel beyond its borders was done by ship. A common method of navigation used by ship pilots was to stay close to the coastline, looking for familiar landmarks and using their knowledge of local currents and hazards, such as reefs and rocks. Familiarity with the coastline was usually passed along by word of mouth, but some written and printed guides for sea captains also appeared. Widespread use of the printing press made maps and charts more readily available, especially those charts known as portolans, which used a complex network of lines to indicate sailing distances and directions between points on the map.

When sailing across open waters out of sight of land, mariners often referred to Polaris, the so-called North Star or polestar, as a rough indication of north. Another common technique was known as dead reckoning, in which the navigator estimated the ship's speed, made corrections for winds and currents, and tried to calculate the vessel's approximate

Elizabethan sailors used several instruments to aid navigation. In this 16th-century wood-cut a sailor uses an instrument called a quadrant to measure the altitude of the sun and thereby determine his location at sea.

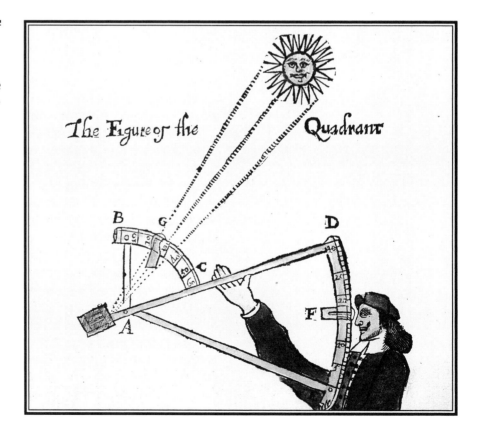

latitude, its distance north or south of the equator. This method was inexact, however, and often led sailors off course.

Navigators used several instruments to track their locations. The magnetic compass had a magnetized needle floating in a bowl of water; the needle pointed toward the closer of the earth's two magnetic poles. Another early instrument was the astrolabe, a tool used to measure the sun's height above the horizon. Once the altitude was calculated, navigators consulted a chart and matched the sun's height with the current date to find the latitude.

Several Elizabethan navigators published books on the art of navigation. William Bourne's *Booke Called the Treasure for Travoilers* (1574) provided readers with the mathematical knowledge necessary to study navigation. In *The Seamans Secrets* (1595) English captain John Davys wrote about the uses of the shadow-staff, a tool he invented for the measurement of the sun's altitude. The shadow-staff greatly aided navigators because, unlike the astrolabe, it could accurately measure the sun's altitude from the deck of a ship in rough seas. (*See also* **Exploration; Ships; Transportation and Travel.**)

NURSES AND MIDWIVES

Expectant mothers in Elizabethan England relied on midwives to help deliver their children. Once the children were born many mothers hired wet nurses to breast-feed them. People of the time held divided opinions on the practice of wet-nursing. Some criticized mothers who refused to breast-feed, claiming that such refusals stemmed from a woman's fears that her breasts would be unattractive afterward. Even so, many upper class women hired wet nurses.

Families gave careful consideration to the selection of a wet nurse. The nurse not only had to be healthy but also of good moral character, because Elizabethans believed that personal qualities were transmitted through breast milk. For this reason many mothers chose to nurse their own children, because one could never be sure of another person's character. Some wet nurses lived in the children's homes, but most took care of the infants in their own dwellings, where the birth parents occasionally visited the children. When the children were weaned, typically around the age of two, they were returned to their own households.

In an age with few physicians and hospitals, the job of assisting women in childbirth usually fell to midwives. A midwife was typically a reliable local woman who had experience in overseeing deliveries. Some midwives claimed to use magic and witchcraft to aid in the birth of children because superstitions regarding deliveries were widespread. Ringing church bells, for example, was supposed to ease a difficult labor, as was tying a bell rope around a woman in labor. In an age when pregnant women and infants often died during childbirth, midwives who knew how to handle problem deliveries were highly valued, even if some of their methods relied on supernatural remedies. (*See also* **Marriage and Family; Medicine.**)

I n *A Midsummer Night's Dream*, Oberon is the king of the FAIRIES. He uses his supernatural powers to ensure that four conflicted lovers, who are the focus of the play, are properly paired. When Oberon appears in Act I, he seems quarrelsome and hot-tempered. He orders his wife, Titania, to hand over a "little changeling boy." According to Elizabethan folklore, fairies sometimes stole healthy infants and replaced them with scrawny children, who were referred to as changelings. When Titania refuses to obey his command, Oberon orders PUCK, a mischievous fairy, to fetch a love potion and prepare to retaliate. While Titania is sleeping, Oberon puts a magic ointment on her eyes, causing her to fall in love with the first creature she sees when she awakes. When Titania opens her eyes, she instantly falls in love with Nick Bottom, a foolish weaver. Adding to Titania's humiliation is the fact that Puck has replaced Bottom's human head with that of a donkey.

Oberon's essentially good nature is revealed when he expresses remorse for his trick and releases Titania from the spell—after she surrenders the changeling boy. In addition, Oberon directs Puck to use the love potion to ensure that Demetrius falls in love with Helena, a maid he had previously rejected. At the conclusion of the play, Oberon bestows his blessing on the marriages of Demetrius and Helena and two other happy couples.

Oberon was a well-known character in Elizabethan folklore. The most likely source for Shakespeare's portrayal of him was *Huon of Bordeaux*, a French adventure tale from the 1200s. (*See also* **Dreams; Magic and Folklore; Supernatural Phenomena.**)

O phelia is the daughter of Polonius, the sister of Laertes, and the beloved of Hamlet in the play that bears his name. She is also one of the most sympathetic and tragic of all Shakespearean characters. Reacting to what others demand of her, Ophelia is generally ignored, used, and then left to fend for herself, something she is incapable of doing.

In Act I, Scene iii, Laertes warns his sister that Hamlet's feelings for her are temporary and that she should protect her honor and be wary of the prince's declarations of love. Polonius enters and demands that she reveal the details of her relationship with the prince. Showing little concern for his daughter, beyond her usefulness as a source of information, Polonius forbids her to see the prince again. Being an obedient daughter, Ophelia returns Hamlet's love letters. This rejection, combined with his mother's infidelity, causes Hamlet to turn on the unfortunate Ophelia and curse all women, dismissing her with the well-known line "Get thee to a nunn'ry" (III.i.136–37). The word *nunnery*, which usually refers to a convent, had another meaning in Shakespeare's time. It was Elizabethan slang for a brothel*, which makes Hamlet's command to her doubly harsh. (On the other hand he may simply want her to be safe and out of harm's way.)

See color plate 13, vol. 2.

* *brothel* house of prostitution

Ophelia's "mad scene" is one of the few challenges Shakespeare provided for women. In Act IV, Scene v, of *Hamlet,* Ophelia portrays her madness by singing bawdy tunes and twining flowers in her hair.

Ophelia has no way of knowing which meaning Hamlet intends. Her confusion and grief at his rejection are compounded when Hamlet accidentally kills Polonius, who had been hiding behind a curtain to eavesdrop on him. After this deed Ophelia is tormented by the conflict between her loyalty to her father and her concern for the man who killed him. This inner turmoil eventually drives her insane, and she next appears wandering about and talking madly of unfulfilled love, death, and funerals.

Ophelia drowns in Act IV when the tree limb she is climbing on breaks and she falls into a pond. Although the circumstances of her death indicate that it was an accident, the queen reports that Ophelia made no attempt to save herself. To many, among them the priest who presides over her funeral and the grave digger who prepares for her burial, it appears that she has committed suicide

Ophelia symbolizes the innocence of youth destroyed by the corruption around her. A tragic victim of the actions of others, this loving creature is driven insane by events over which she has no control. Used and abused by the men in her life, she is ultimately abandoned by both Hamlet and her father, and her brother returns too late to be of any aid or comfort to her.

Interestingly, some scholars have suggested that Ophelia's name may have been chosen or transmitted in error. The name, which means "succor" (aid) in Greek, seems inappropriate for this pathetic creature. Shakespeare may have meant to give her the name *Aphelia,* which means "innocence." (*See also* **Hamlet; Madness; Plays: The Tragedies.**)

ORLANDO

Orlando is one of the principal characters in the comedy *As You Like It.* His love for the heroine ROSALIND is the main focus of the play. When Orlando first appears, he is at odds with his older brother Oliver, who has cheated him out of his inheritance and plans to kill him. After surviving one attempt on his life (and falling in love with Rosalind), Orlando flees to the Forest of Arden with his faithful servant Adam. In the forest he meets Duke Senior, the leader of a group of exiled noblemen, and Ganymede, who is actually Rosalind disguised as a boy.

While in the forest Orlando decorates trees with love poems dedicated to Rosalind. The idealistic notions expressed in these verses reveal that Orlando has much to learn about authentic love. Participating in a role-play with "Ganymede," he pretends to woo the youth as if Ganymede were Rosalind. It is evident that Orlando's love has matured when he remains steadfastly dedicated to Rosalind despite Ganymede's attempts to discourage him.

It is Orlando's reconciliation with his brother, however, that truly signals his readiness for love. At one point he encounters Oliver sleeping in the forest and notices a lion nearby. Rather than allow the lion to kill his wicked brother, Orlando risks his own life and drives it away. When Oliver

Othello

mends his ways and finds true love with Celia (Rosalind's best friend), Orlando tells Ganymede he realizes that love is more than just a state of mind or romantic thoughts. Convinced that Orlando's feelings have ripened into a real love for her, Rosalind reveals her true identity, and the two marry at the end of the play. (*See also* **Arden, Forest of; Disguises; Pastoralism.**)

OTHELLO

* *Moorish* referring to invaders from North Africa who conquered Spain during the Middle Ages

* *ensign* low-ranking military officer

Most of Shakespeare's tragedies focus on characters of noble or royal rank. These plays tend to be more political than personal, because the events that affect the main characters will also determine the fate of an entire kingdom. *Othello*, by contrast, is more personal than political. Its hero, a Moorish* general, is tricked into believing that his wife is unfaithful to him. He murders her, then learns of her innocence, and kills himself in a fit of grief and shame. Deeply personal and intensely dramatic, *Othello* is recognized as one of Shakespeare's most powerful tragedies.

SOURCE, PLOT, AND CHARACTERS. Shakespeare's source for *Othello* was an Italian story by Giambattista Giraldi, or Cinthio, published in 1565. The central figure in Cinthio's tale is a beautiful Venetian woman, whose name, *Disdemona*, means "the ill-fated one." Against the wishes of her family, she marries a Moorish captain and goes with him to his military post in Cyprus (an island in the eastern Mediterranean). The Moor's ensign*, Disdemona's rejected suitor, deceives her husband into believing she has betrayed him with another officer. The Moor and his ensign beat her to death, then attempt to make her death appear accidental. Disdemona's relatives eventually avenge her by killing her husband, and the ensign dies under torture.

Shakespeare altered Cinthio's story in several ways. Some of the changes were designed to speed up the action. For example, he replaced the long, drawn-out aftermath of Cinthio's story with a single, fast-paced scene in which the Moor murders DESDEMONA, her innocence is revealed, he kills himself, and his ensign is taken away to be tortured and executed. Most of Shakespeare's changes, however, involved the characters, who are far more vivid and complex than Cinthio's. The nameless Moor of the original source becomes Othello, a noble general who is admired and praised for his courage. By the end of the play, however, this heroic figure becomes so brutal in his language and actions that he is almost unrecognizable to those who once loved and admired him.

Desdemona's devotion to her husband is almost superhuman, as is her courage in marrying him over the objections of her father, the Venetian senator Brabantio. Elizabethan drama tended to portray young women who elope with their lovers as sympathetic characters and the fathers who oppose them as comical. But Shakespeare turns even the bigoted Brabantio into a tragic figure, having him die of a broken heart after Desdemona's elopement. He parts from Othello with the warning, "Look to her, Moor. . . . She has deceiv'd her father, and may thee"

(I.iii.292–93). Brabantio's warning foreshadows the play's ending, possibly planting the first seeds of suspicion in Othello's mind.

Perhaps the most significantly altered character is IAGO, the villain. The villain of Cinthio's story was motivated by love for Disdemona, but Shakespeare's Iago is motivated primarily by hatred. He deeply resents both the successful Othello and his lieutenant, Cassio, who has been promoted in Iago's place. He also suspects both men of having affairs with his wife, Emilia. His plan to persuade Othello that Desdemona has betrayed him with Cassio satisfies his desire to ruin both men. As it happens, Iago gives so many reasons for his actions that it is hard to identify any one of them as his true motive. In one of the most famous comments on the play, Samuel Taylor COLERIDGE called Iago's explanations of his actions "the motive-hunting of motiveless malignity."

Even the minor characters in the play are vividly drawn. The villain in Shakespeare's source was not only married but had a young daughter. Shakespeare omits the daughter but develops the character of Iago's wife, Emilia, who is torn between her passion for Iago and her devotion to Desdemona. Although Emilia yearns for her husband's affection, she does not trust him, and she is scornful of men in general. After Desdemona's death she shows heroic courage by exposing the murder at the cost of her own life. The handsome Cassio is innocent of adultery but is ashamed of his real love affair with Bianca. Also, instead of making Iago a rejected suitor of Desdemona, Shakespeare creates a minor character to fill that role. Roderigo is a silly young Venetian completely ruled by Iago, who has convinced him that Desdemona will take him as her lover if he gives her expensive presents—which Iago instead keeps for himself. Iago eventually persuades Roderigo to help him kill Cassio. When this attempt fails, he stabs Roderigo to keep him silent.

COMMENTARY. For much of its history, critics saw *Othello* as a straightforward story of a marriage destroyed by jealousy. Rather than pay attention to the plot, they tended to focus on the play's poetic language. Many critics have been particularly drawn to Othello's spellbinding descriptions of his travels and his exotic life—the same stories, as he relates, that won him Desdemona's love. The beauty of Shakespeare's language, for some readers, makes the unrelieved tragedy of its plot almost bearable.

Scholars have frequently viewed *Othello* in symbolic terms. Emphasizing the contrasts between the black Othello and the white Desdemona, they have seen these two characters as examples of opposite natures. Othello is associated with "the sun where he was born" (III.iv.30), while Desdemona is linked to the moon, a symbol of chastity*. The other major character, Iago, self-consciously refers to himself in diabolical* terms. These images make it possible to read *Othello* as an outgrowth of the morality plays* of the Middle Ages, in which the forces of good (Desdemona) and evil (Iago) struggle for the hero's soul. Iago's "motiveless malignity" makes sense if he is viewed as the VICE, a character in morality plays who represented human villainy and whose primary function was to lead the hero astray. Despite his evil nature, the Vice often appealed to

* *chastity* quality of moral virtue achieved by abstaining from unlawful sexual activity
* *diabolical* characteristic of the devil
* *morality play* religious dramatic work that teaches a moral lesson through the use of symbolic characters

133

audiences because of his witty humor. In the same way, the sheer cleverness of Iago's schemes and the depth of his evil have fascinated audiences.

Later scholars began to explore the play's connection to social issues. In the 1800s Othello's blackness triggered readers' concerns regarding the issue of slavery. In the 1900s the plot echoed a host of social concerns, ranging from racism and social inequality to wife abuse and psychopathic behavior. Scholars have also used the play to explore the political issues surrounding colonialism. The play shows Venice, a colonial power, sending a black general to its colony Cyprus to repel an invasion from Turkey, which the natives of Cyprus may well support. Some productions have highlighted this issue by making Bianca, Cassio's mistress, a native of Cyprus. In other stagings she is portrayed by a black actress. Modern scholars tend to look at the play in realistic rather than symbolic terms, rejecting a romantic view of the characters. Actors used to emphasize Othello's grief and remorse in the final scene, but modern productions are more likely to stress the brutality of the murder.

In recent years English and American criticism has been dominated by the question of how Othello's race affects the drama. Critics have examined the attitudes of other characters, and even of Othello himself, to determine how they react to Othello's skin color. They have also explored the impact of those attitudes on Othello—for example, whether his status as an outsider in Venice makes him more vulnerable to suspicion. Even the question of whether the "Moor" should be seen as having black or brown skin can affect the way the play is read.

Sex, as well as race, is an issue of continuing interest in the play. Desdemona is much younger than Othello, and she openly expresses her sexuality: "I [did] love the Moor to live with him" (I.iii.248). Desdemona's youth and sexual vigor may be seen as a source of anxiety to a husband who is "declined into the vale of years" (III.iii.265–66), possibly making him more inclined to suspect her unfaithfulness. Scholars have also wondered whether Iago's jealousy over Emilia is due to sexual impotence. Some have suggested that his resentment toward Othello and Cassio springs from repressed homosexual desires. Many have noted that the play's military setting creates an artificial, dehumanizing environment in which all the women are out of place.

OTHELLO ON THE STAGE. Shakespeare's leading actor, Richard Burbage, was the first actor to play Othello, and it was apparently one of his most famous roles. Some scholars believe that Iago was first played by a comic actor—perhaps John Lowin, who in 1604 would have been about 28 years old, Iago's stated age. Several successful performances have taken advantage of the opportunities for comedy in Iago's interaction with the audience.

One question in stage productions of *Othello* is whether the lead role must always be played by a black actor. The African American actor Ira Aldridge played Othello in England as early as 1825 but found even greater success in Germany and Russia, which at that time was engaged in a nationwide debate over the abolition of serfdom. The most famous of all stage Othellos was Paul Robeson, the black actor and singer. He played

LET HUSBANDS KNOW

Though a minor figure in the plot, Emilia has one noteworthy speech near the end of *Othello*. Arguing that women should not be sexually faithful to cruel husbands, she protests against all the abuses men inflict on their wives: "[They] pour our treasures into foreign laps; / Or else break out in peevish jealousies, / Throwing restraint upon us; or say they strike us, / Or scant [waste] our former having [money]" (IV.iii.88–91). Some find her remarks coarse and worldly, a contrast to the purity of Desdemona. Modern readers, however, may see Emilia as a feminist who recognizes but cannot prevent the injuries a male-dominated world inflicts on women.

In *Othello*, Desdemona is unjustly accused of adultery and then murdered by her jealous husband. In this illustration from an 1892 edition of Shakespeare's works, Othello contemplates the murder of his sleeping wife.

the role in London in 1930, then in a famous production on Broadway and on tour from 1943 to 1945, and finally in STRATFORD-UPON-AVON in 1959. Some viewers were offended to see Laurence Olivier, a well-known white actor, take the role of Othello in a 1964 production at the National Theatre (directed for the stage by John Dexter and for video by Stuart Burge). Olivier's performance, however, was a classic in many ways. He was the first to consider Othello's negative traits, showing him not as the noble victim of a fiendish villain but as a man who falls victim to his own pride.

Since the 1960s British and American directors have generally assumed that a black actor should play Othello, and Jonathan Miller's 1981 production for BBC-TV was much criticized for casting Anthony Hopkins in the title role. Miller's rendering of the tragedy drew on Renaissance art for its visual effect but treated the characters from a modern point of view, as ordinary people rather than larger-than-life figures of good and evil. It ends with the sound of giggling from the psychopathic Iago (Bob Hoskins) ringing down the empty corridors of the palace. In the late 1900s there were various casting experiments with black Iagos and Desdemonas, and in 1997 a white Othello (Patrick Stewart) played with a mainly black cast at the Shakespeare Theater in Washington, D.C.

OTHELLO ON FILM. With its attractive settings in Venice and Cyprus, its emphasis on color contrasts, and its unusual use of "point of view," *Othello* has been a popular subject for film since the early 1900s. Orson Welles's 1952 film is a recognized classic, though it is heavily cut and often hard to hear. Many directors have been influenced by Welles's symbolism of

labyrinths, mirrors, and floating gauzy curtains to indicate the disturbed state of Othello's mind.

Two of the most interesting later screen treatments are based on stage productions. Janet Suzman's 1990 film, based on her own stage production at the Market Theatre in Johannesburg, South Africa, contrasts a large and vicious Iago with a small Othello, played by African actor John Kani. Suzman's Iago, who appears to be motivated by racism, utterly destroys the weaker Othello. The other film, a television version by Trevor Nunn, is based on his staging of the play for the Other Place at Stratford, England, in 1989. Haitian-born opera star Willard White gives a fine performance as Othello, with Ian McKellen as a repressed, utterly convincing Iago and Imogen Stubbs as one of the most lively and lovable of all Desdemonas.

The first version of the play since Welles's to be made specifically for film is Oliver Parker's (1995). Like Welles, Parker cut the script heavily and stressed the play's sexual subtext. Iago (Kenneth Branagh) seems to hate Othello (Laurence Fishburne) out of envy for his sexual potency. The beautiful French Desdemona (Irène Jacob) seems as isolated as Othello, and Emilia (Anna Patrick), who genuinely loves Iago, becomes a tragic figure when in the final scene she is finally forced to recognize what kind of man he is.

ADAPTATIONS OF OTHELLO. *Othello* was one of the first plays to be performed abroad as Shakespeare's popularity grew in the late 1700s. Iago's evil and Desdemona's undeserved suffering were so shocking that translators often adapted the play rather freely, producing French and German versions with happy endings.

See color plate 14, vol. 2.

During the 1900s many stagings and films either adapted or otherwise borrowed from the story of *Othello*. The movie *A Double Life* (1947) is one of several to illustrate the devastating effect that playing the jealous Othello can have on an actor when his own wife is playing Desdemona. Other adaptations have viewed the story in the light of modern concerns about race and gender. In Charles Marowitz's *An Othello* (1972), a militant black Iago warns Othello of the white men who will use and betray him. Anne-Marie MacDonald's *Goodnight, Desdemona; Good Morning, Juliet* (1988) is a comedy about a feminist scholar's attempt to release tragic heroines from the role of victim. More grimly, *Desdemona: A Play About a Handkerchief* by Paula Vogel (1993) makes its heroine more comfortable in Bianca's brothel* than with her overidealizing husband. In *The Nature of Blood* (1997), Caryl Phillips combines Othello's story with the persecution of Jews in Venice during the Middle Ages and the 1940s. This adaptation suggests the importance of understanding and love between persecuted minorities who have sometimes been hostile toward each other.

Othello has inspired operas by Rossini (1816) and Verdi (1887) and a rock musical by Jack Good called *Catch My Soul* (1970), with Othello as a traveling evangelist in Santa Fe. Among a number of ballets, the best known is *The Moor's Pavane* by José Limón (1949), which is still frequently performed. (*See also* **Domestic Tragedy; Music Inspired by Shakespeare; Shakespeare on Screen; Shakespeare's Works, Adaptations of.**)

* **brothel** house of prostitution

THE PLAYS

Plate 1
This poster, created by Edmund Dulac for a 1911 production of *Macbeth* at His Majesty's Theatre in London, presents the famous scene in which Macbeth confronts the three witches. These "secret, black, and midnight hags" are supernatural creatures with the ability to predict the future. Their prophecies, however, are vague and confusing, leading Macbeth to believe he cannot be harmed when in fact his downfall is imminent.

Plate 2

In 1996 Baz Luhrmann updated Shakespeare's *Romeo and Juliet* for the screen. Instead of 16th-century Verona, Italy, Luhrmann's *Romeo + Juliet* is set in 20th-century Verona Beach, California. Luhrmann translated the play into modern terms with sets, props, and costumes, while keeping most of Shakespeare's language intact. In this scene, Romeo (Leonardo DiCaprio) is immediately love-struck by Juliet (Claire Danes) when they meet at a costume party hosted by her family.

Plate 3

The 1998 film *Shakespeare in Love* is a fictional account of the writing of *Romeo and Juliet*. The screenplay, written by Marc Norman and Tom Stoppard, includes many sly references to lines, characters, and events in Shakespeare's life and works. In this scene, Shakespeare (Joseph Fiennes) rehearses with Edward Alleyn (Ben Affleck), the leading actor of the Admiral's Men, and Hugh Fennyman (Tom Wilkinson), a wealthy backer who has been given a minor role by way of a bribe.

Plate 4

The Royal Shakespeare Company's 1984 production of *Twelfth Night* starred Zoe Wanamaker as Viola, a young gentlewoman who disguises herself as a youth when she is shipwrecked in an unfamiliar land. She takes a job in the household of Duke Orsino (played by Miles Anderson), who employs her as messenger to his beloved, the scornful Lady Olivia. Matters grow more complicated as Viola falls in love with Orsino and Olivia with the disguised Viola—a tangle of love affairs that take the remainder of the play to sort out.

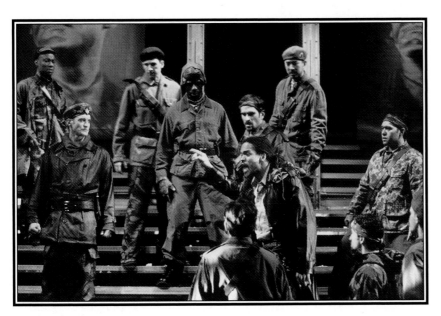

Plate 5

Shakespeare's *Coriolanus* is about a great Roman warrior whose excessive pride leads to his dishonor and death. In this modern-dress production of the play at The Shakespeare Theatre in Washington, D.C., in 2000, Coriolanus (Andrew Long) meets his enemy Tullus Aufidius (Keith Hamilton Cobb) in the presence of a company of soldiers.

Plate 6
In 2000 the Utah Shakespearean Festival in Cedar City won a Tony award for best regional theater in the United States. In this scene from their 2000 production of *The Merchant of Venice,* the duke introduces Portia to the court. Portia, disguised as a young lawyer, saves the merchant, Antonio, while ruining and humiliating Shylock.

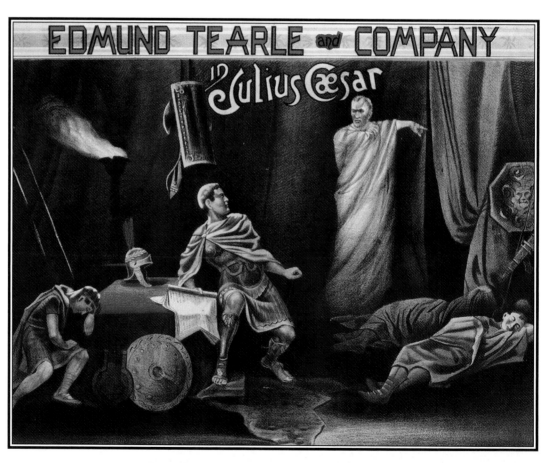

Plate 7
Edmund Tearle was one of several American actors who attempted—generally without much success—to establish their reputations on the London stage in the late 1800s. In 1892 his acting company produced *Julius Caesar* at the Olympic Theatre in London, appearing for seven performances in the month of April. This poster advertising the production illustrates the scene in which Caesar's ghost (played by Gow Bentinck) confronts Brutus (played by Tearle) with the declaration that they will meet at Philippi, the battlefield on which Brutus later dies.

Plate 8

The most celebrated American actor of the mid-1800s was Edwin Booth. He adapted his beautiful speaking voice to a broad range of Shakespearean roles, from tragic heroes like Othello to villains such as Shylock in *The Merchant of Venice.* Booth was also the first American to gain fame in England as a Shakespearean actor. This playbill from an 1863 production of *Hamlet* at the Boston Theatre gives Booth top billing for his appearance in the title role.

BOSTON THEATRE

LESSEE AND MANAGER . . . . . . Mr WYZEMAN MARSHALL
STAGE MANAGER . . . . Mr J G HANLEY

THE MANAGER IS PLEASED TO ANNOUNCE AN ENGAGEMENT
FOR A LIMITED NUMBER OF NIGHTS, WITH THE

EMINENT TRAGEDIAN,

EDWIN BOOTH

WHO WILL APPEAR ON

MONDAY AND TUESDAY EVENINGS,

OCTOBER 26th AND 27th, 1863,

— IN —

SHAKSPERE'S CLASSICAL TRAGEDY

— of —

HAMLET!

PRINCE OF DENMARK.

Hamlet..........Edwin Booth
Ghost of Hamlet's Father.Mr W. H. Whalley
King Claudius........Mr W. H. Hamblin
Laertes.................Mr J. G. Hanley
Polonius................Mr W. H. Curtis
Horatio.................Mr E. W. Beattie
Rosencrantz...........Mr W. H. Danvers
Guildenstern.............Mr E. Barry
Osric.................Mr N. T. Davenport
Marcellus..............Mr C. M. Davis
Bernardo................Mr F. O. Savage
Player King............Mr J. Biddles
Second Actor..........Mr Jeffries
Francisco.................Mr J. Taylor
First Gravedigger.........Mr W. Scallan
Second Gravedigger........Mr J. Jeffries
Priest................Mr F. O. Savage
Queen Gertrude........Mrs Anna Cowell
Ophelia.. (HER FIRST APPEARANCE IN BOSTON)...Miss Cranston
Player Queen............Mrs Stoneall
Lords, Ladies, Pages, &c.

Regular Dramatic Performance EVERY SATURDAY NIGHT

PRICES OF ADMISSION.

Boxes, Parquet and Balcony . . . . 50 Cents
Family Circle. . . . . 25 Cents | Gallery . . . . 15 Cents
Private Boxes. . . . . 6 Dollars

DOORS OPEN AT 7 . . . . TO COMMENCE AT 7 1-2 O'CLOCK

Notice.—A Box in the Second Tier has been assigned for the use of Colored People, who will be admitted to that part of the Theatre only.

F. A. Searle, Printer—Journal Building—118 Washington St., Boston.

Plate 9

The action in Shakespeare's two *Henry IV* plays occurs in two main settings—the royal court and the Boar's Head tavern. These two locales represent the two competing forces in the life of Prince Hal, the plays' central character. Hal recognizes that his duty lies at the court with his father, but he is tempted by the wild and easy lifestyle of the tavern, presided over by the rowdy, drunken Sir John Falstaff. In this 1991 production, Falstaff (Robert Stephens) carouses with his companions, including the prostitute Doll Tearsheet (Joanne Pearce).

Plate 10

The Comedy of Errors, Shakespeare's earliest comedy, features a pair of long-separated twin brothers (both named Antipholus) and their servants (another pair of long-separated twins, both named Dromio). In this scene from the 1992 New York Shakespeare Festival production of the play, Adriana (played by Marisa Tomei) receives some surprising news from one of the Dromios.

Plate 11

In *The Life and Death of King John,* one of Shakespeare's history plays, the king orders the murder of his nephew, Arthur. In the Shakespeare Theatre's production in 1999, Philip Goodwin played King John and Derek Kahn Thompson played Arthur.

Plate 8

The most celebrated American actor of the mid-1800s was Edwin Booth. He adapted his beautiful speaking voice to a broad range of Shakespearean roles, from tragic heroes like Othello to villains such as Shylock in *The Merchant of Venice.* Booth was also the first American to gain fame in England as a Shakespearean actor. This playbill from an 1863 production of *Hamlet* at the Boston Theatre gives Booth top billing for his appearance in the title role.

BOSTON THEATRE

LESSEE AND MANAGER .... Mr WYZEMAN MARSHALL
STAGE MANAGER .... Mr J. G. HANLEY

THE MANAGER IS PLEASED TO ANNOUNCE AN ENGAGEMENT
FOR A LIMITED NUMBER OF NIGHTS, WITH THE

EMINENT TRAGEDIAN,

EDWIN BOOTH

WHO WILL APPEAR ON

MONDAY AND TUESDAY EVENINGS,

OCTOBER 26th AND 27th, 1863,

IS

SHAKSPERE'S CLASSICAL TRAGEDY

OF

HAMLET!

PRINCE OF DENMARK.

Hamlet.........	Edwin Booth
Ghost of Hamlet's Father	Mr W. H. Whalley
King Claudius	Mr W. H. Hamblin
Laertes	Mr J. G. Hanley
Polonius	Mr W. H. Curtis
Horatio	Mr E. W. Beattie
Rosencrantz	Mr W. H. Danvers
Guildenstern	Mr E. Barry
Osric	Mr N. T. Davenport
Marcellus	Mr C. M. Davis
Bernardo	Mr F. O. Savage
Player King	Mr J. Biddles
Second Actor	Mr Jeffries
Francisco	Mr J. Taylor
First Gravedigger	Mr W. Scallan
Second Gravedigger	Mr J. Jeffries
Priest	Mr F. O. Savage
Queen Gertrude	Mrs Anna Cowell
Ophelia, (HER FIRST APPEARANCE IN BOSTON)	Miss Cranston
Player Queen	Mrs Stoneall
Lords, Ladies, Pages, &c.	

Regular Dramatic Performance **EVERY SATURDAY NIGHT**

PRICES OF ADMISSION.

Boxes, Parquet and Balcony .... 50 cents
Family Circle............... 25 Cents | Gallery .... 15 Cents
Private Boxes........................... 6 Dollars

DOORS OPEN AT 7....... TO COMMENCE AT 7 1-2 O'CLOCK

Notice.—A Box in the Second Tier has been assigned for the use of Colored People, who will be admitted to that part of the Theatre only.

F. A. Searle, Printer—Journal Building—118 Washington St., Boston.

Plate 9

The action in Shakespeare's two *Henry IV* plays occurs in two main settings—the royal court and the Boar's Head tavern. These two locales represent the two competing forces in the life of Prince Hal, the plays' central character. Hal recognizes that his duty lies at the court with his father, but he is tempted by the wild and easy lifestyle of the tavern, presided over by the rowdy, drunken Sir John Falstaff. In this 1991 production, Falstaff (Robert Stephens) carouses with his companions, including the prostitute Doll Tearsheet (Joanne Pearce).

Plate 10

The Comedy of Errors, Shakespeare's earliest comedy, features a pair of long-separated twin brothers (both named Antipholus) and their servants (another pair of long-separated twins, both named Dromio). In this scene from the 1992 New York Shakespeare Festival production of the play, Adriana (played by Marisa Tomei) receives some surprising news from one of the Dromios.

Plate 11

In *The Life and Death of King John,* one of Shakespeare's history plays, the king orders the murder of his nephew, Arthur. In the Shakespeare Theatre's production in 1999, Philip Goodwin played King John and Derek Kahn Thompson played Arthur.

OVID

43 B.C.–A.D. 18
Roman poet

Ovid was one of the greatest ancient Roman poets. Having gained fame as a poet during the reign of the Roman emperor Caesar Augustus, Ovid enjoyed success until A.D. 8, when he was banished from Rome because some of his love poems had allegedly led the emperor's daughter to commit adultery. Ovid spent the rest of his life in an isolated fishing village along the Black Sea.

Ovid's poems, which feature tales from Greek and Roman mythology, had a major influence on Shakespeare's works. Among the poet's finest works is the *Metamorphoses*, a collection of poems linked by the theme of transformation. The *Metamorphoses* was the source for Shakespeare's poem *Venus and Adonis*, which tells the story of Venus's love for a handsome young mortal named Adonis. Shakespeare altered Ovid's story, in which Adonis reciprocates Venus's love, by having the mortal reject the goddess. The *Metamorphoses* also influenced Shakespeare's plays. In *Titus Andronicus*, for example, the story of Lavinia's rape and mutilation—in which her hands and tongue are cut off—was borrowed from Ovid's masterpiece. In fact Lavinia is finally able to communicate what happened to her by turning to the story of Philomela in her nephew's copy of the *Metamorphoses*.

Ovid's other works also influenced Shakespeare. The *Fasti*, for example, was a primary source for Shakespeare's *The Rape of Lucrece*, a poem about the rape of a Roman woman by a prince. In addition, traces of *Heroides*, a collection of love letters, appear in the conversation between Jessica and Lorenzo in Act V of *The Merchant of Venice*. (*See also* **Shakespeare's Sources.**)

PAGEANTS AND MORALITY PLAYS

* *medieval* referring to the Middle Ages, a period roughly between A.D. 500 and 1500

* *allegorical* referring to a literary device in which characters, events, and settings represent abstract qualities and in which the author intends a different meaning to be read beneath the surface

* *genre* literary form

Pageants and morality plays were two types of theatrical performance that entertained and educated Elizabethan audiences. The pageant was a dramatic procession held to honor a member of the nobility, while the morality play was a form of medieval* drama that instructed people how to live a virtuous life. In both pageants and morality plays, the hero or heroine encountered a series of allegorical* figures, learning important lessons about morality and goodness along the way. Despite these similarities, however, the two genres* had different purposes and settings.

PAGEANTS. The most famous pageant of Shakespeare's lifetime celebrated the coronation of Queen ELIZABETH I. The queen was the center of attention, parading through London with an impressive array of courtiers, maids, and trumpeters. Silk and velvet tapestries hung from the buildings, and along the way the procession passed a series of arches where actors delivered moral messages. At the first arch actors portraying Elizabeth's royal ancestors established her legitimacy. At the next arch actors representing the seven cardinal virtues (faith, hope, charity, justice, fortitude, prudence, and temperance) defeated the seven deadly sins (anger, avarice, envy, gluttony, lust, pride, and sloth). At other arches

Pageants and Morality Plays

Morality plays date back to the Middle Ages. They were usually performed on wagons or scaffolds that were set up in the town square and could be moved easily from place to place.

children proclaimed the queen's honor, and actors calling themselves Time and Truth presented her with a Bible.

MORALITY PLAYS. The morality play developed in the 1300s and reached its peak in the 1500s. In a typical morality play a character representing mankind makes his way toward death. Along the journey he is tempted by Satan and by characters representing various types of sins. Shaking off these demons with the help of the virtues and angels, the hero eventually meets death with the assistance of grace, repentance, and redemption.

Although essentially a medieval dramatic form, the morality play continued to influence Shakespeare and other Elizabethan writers. Some of Shakespeare's villains, such as Richard III and IAGO, are descended from the VICE. Like this character from the morality tradition, they possess a complex blend of wit, charm, and humor that enables the audience to enjoy the battle between good and evil. The comic aspect of the Vice is also found in some of Shakespeare's characters, such as Sir John FALSTAFF, who offers witty moral lessons to Prince Hal—the hero of *Henry IV, Part 1* and *Part 2,* even as he attempts to lead him astray. The hero of a morality play must transcend temptation and folly to achieve salvation. In Shakespeare's later use of the morality tradition, whether or not the central character succeeds in overcoming the forces of evil often marks the difference between comedy and tragedy. (*See also* **Masques; Medievalism.**)

PAMPHLETEERS

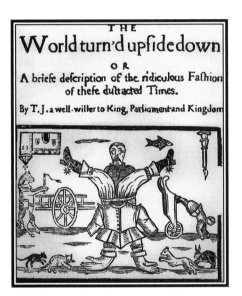

Many pamphleteers attacked aspects of their society that they perceived to be immoral or foolish. This pamphlet, by John Taylor (published using only the initials T. J.), mocks the "ridiculous fashions" of the 1600s.

In 1592 the playwright Robert Greene lay on his deathbed. Dying in poverty after a life spent with criminals and prostitutes, Greene wrote an autobiographical essay titled GROATSWORTH OF WIT, which was subsequently sold as a pamphlet. In bitter words he warns playwrights not to trust actors and refers to William Shakespeare as an "upstart crowe"—an arrogant newcomer—who thinks he is "the onely Shakes-scene in the countrey." Greene's pamphlet offers the first published reference to Shakespeare as a playwright.

Greene was one of many Elizabethan pamphleteers—writers of short booklets that featured authors' opinions on issues of the day. Like modern editorial writers, pamphleteers exposed wrongdoing by well-known figures or offered criticism on the arts. These pamphlets were an important source of information both in LONDON and in the countryside.

Other successful pamphleteers in Shakespeare's day included Anthony Munday and Thomas Nash. Born in London and trained as a child actor, Munday learned the print trade when he was about 16 years old. In 1578 he was sent to France and Italy to spy on Catholic refugees, and over the next few years he produced a series of anti-Catholic pamphlets. In 1584 he published *A Watchword to England*, a warning against "traitors and treacherous practices." Munday also wrote for the theater, and some critics believe that his plays influenced Shakespeare's works. His depiction of a heartless moneylender in his first book, *Zelauto* (1580), for example, may have inspired Shakespeare's portrait of SHYLOCK in *The Merchant of Venice*.

For centuries Thomas Nash has been identified with biting satire. Nash was one of the University Wits, a group of pamphleteers and playwrights who were educated at Cambridge and Oxford. The University Wits—and their sarcastic criticisms—became hugely popular in the 1580s. Nash strongly opposed the Puritan movement in England. Through his pamphlets he engaged in a long satirical debate about Puritanism with the writer Gabriel Harvey. The published feud caused such a stir that in 1599 the entire matter was declared a public scandal and the archbishop of Canterbury insisted that Nash's pamphlets be burned.

Although he had attacked popular theater in an earlier pamphlet (which he cowrote with his friend Robert Greene), Nash later published *Pierce Penniless*, a pamphlet defending Elizabethan drama. *Pierce Penniless* offers the earliest commentary on a production of Shakespeare's *Henry VI, Part 1*, and also may have influenced some lines in *Hamlet*, such as Prince Hamlet's advice on acting found in Act III. (*See also* **Literature and Drama.**)

PARLIAMENT

See *Government and Politics.*

PASSIONATE PILGRIM, THE

In 1599 William Jaggard, a publisher, collected love poems composed by several writers. Hoping to profit from Shakespeare's reputation, which had grown considerably after the publication of *Venus and Adonis* and *The Rape of Lucrece*, Jaggard printed the playwright's name on the title page of the poetry collection. Out of the 20 poems that appear in *The Passionate Pilgrim*, only 5 seem likely to have been written by Shakespeare: two sonnets and three verse passages from *Love's Labor's Lost*. To make matters worse Shakespeare appears to have known nothing about the collection and evidently had not authorized the use of his name or his poems. Nevertheless, the book became so popular that Jaggard published a second edition.

In 1612 Jaggard published a third edition of *The Passionate Pilgrim* and again put Shakespeare's name on the title page. In the third edition, however, Jaggard made the mistake of adding nine new poems by the playwright Thomas Heywood. In his *Apologie for Actors*, also published in 1612, Heywood protested against what Jaggard had done. In addition Heywood mentioned that Shakespeare was displeased over the misuse of his name and that the playwright was "much offended with M. Jaggard (that altogether unknowne to him) presumed to make so bold with his name." Jaggard took the criticism seriously and promptly removed Shakespeare's name from the title page of *The Passionate Pilgrim*. (*See also* **Poetry of Shakespeare; Shakespeare's Canon.**)

PASTORALISM

* *genre* literary form

Residents of crowded, noisy Elizabethan cities often associated the countryside with a quieter, simpler way of living. This popular image of rural life was expressed in a literary genre* known as pastoralism. Originating in ancient Greece with such writers as Theocritus, pastoralism regained popularity during the 1500s and significantly influenced Shakespeare's works.

Works in this genre, called pastorals, typically include a country setting, a love story, and kind-hearted shepherds. Among the earliest and finest English language pastorals is *The Shepheards Calendar*, which was written by Edmund SPENSER around 1579. Other early English pastorals include Robert Greene's *Menaphon* (1589), Sir Philip Sidney's *Arcadia* (1590), and Thomas Lodge's *Rosalynde* (1590), which was the source for Shakespeare's *As You Like It*.

Like most pastorals *As You Like It* is set in the countryside, in this case the Forest of Arden. The relationship between Rosalind and Celia in the play represents idealized friendship, which is a standard element of pastorals. Of course Shakespeare was never satisfied with simply following conventions, and *As You Like It* also contains passages critical of pastoralism's oversimplified view of the world. Touchstone, a cynical jester, reminds the audience of the hardships of country life. When Touchstone, who is accustomed to the comforts of the royal court, arrives in the Forest of Arden he says, "Ay, now am I in Arden, the more fool I. When I was at home, I was in a better place" (II.iv.16–17). Shakespeare also satirizes another pastoral tradition—the wise peasant. A rural maiden named Audrey is portrayed as an illiterate simpleton.

A section of one of Shakespeare's later plays, *The Winter's Tale,* follows the pastoral pattern more closely. Scholars believe that the main source of the play was Robert Greene's novel *Pandosto,* published in 1588. (*See also* **Arden, Forest of; Nature.**)

PATRONAGE OF THE ARTS

Shakespeare presented two of his major poems as tributes to his patron, Sir Henry Wriothsley, earl of Southampton. Some critics have speculated that Southampton was the mysterious "Mr. W. H." to whom the first edition of Shakespeare's *Sonnets* was dedicated.

Patronage of the arts was an arrangement by which wealthy Elizabethans provided artists or writers with financial support and other assistance. As an expression of gratitude, writers often included flattering dedications to their patron in their works.

In Shakespeare's day the most prominent patron of the arts was Queen ELIZABETH I. The queen's support extended far beyond money. As monarch she could also grant titles of nobility and various other honors. Her successor, King JAMES I, was especially good to Shakespeare. He placed the playwright's acting company under his direct patronage. In *Henry IV, Part 2,* Shakespeare acknowledged the value of influential supporters when he wrote, "A friend i' th' court is better than a penny in purse" (V.i.30–31).

The identity of a literary patron is usually made clear by a dedication at the beginning of a volume. The most famous patron of literature in Shakespeare's day was Mary Herbert, the countess of Pembroke. The poets Ben JONSON, Edmund SPENSER, and Samuel Daniel all praised her in their works. The countess was also a talented writer and translator. Her translation of Robert Garnier's *Marc-Antoine* (1578) provided source material for Shakespeare's *Antony and Cleopatra.* Many scholars believe that the countess's son, William Herbert, the earl of Pembroke, was the person to whom Shakespeare dedicated his *Sonnets:* "To the onlie begetter of these insuing sonnets Mr. W.H. . . . "

Among the most generous patrons of the arts was Henry Wriothesley, the 3rd earl of Southampton. A highly educated man who loved literature, Southampton is often considered to be Shakespeare's greatest patron. Shakespeare dedicated two of his major poems, *Venus and Adonis* and *The Rape of Lucrece,* to the earl. It is also believed that Southampton once gave Shakespeare £1,000, perhaps in gratitude for the dedications.

Acting companies also needed patrons to survive in Elizabethan England. George Carey, the 2nd Lord Hunsdon, was the chief patron of the Chamberlain's Men, Shakespeare's acting company during Elizabeth's reign. From 1597 to 1603 Lord Hunsdon's financial support enabled the Chamberlain's Men to enjoy tremendous success. His father, Henry Carey, the 1st Lord Hunsdon, had also supported the Chamberlain's Men and was their patron when Shakespeare first joined the company in 1594. Lady Elizabeth Carey, wife of the 2nd Lord Hunsdon, was another generous patron, especially of poets. She was one of the people to whom Spenser dedicated his poem *The Faerie Queene.*

Another prominent patron of the arts was Robert Dudley, the earl of Leicester. The acting company that took his name, Leicester's Men, played

Pepys, Samuel

frequently at court and also toured the provinces, even performing in STRATFORD-UPON-AVON in the early 1570s. In 1574 Leicester's Men became the first acting company to receive the royal patent*. (*See also* **Acting Companies, Elizabethan.**)

* *patent* official document granting a right or privilege

PEPYS, SAMUEL

1633–1703
Diarist

* *Restoration* referring to the period in English history, beginning in 1660, when Charles II was restored to the throne

Samuel Pepys was the administrator of England's Royal Navy and an avid theatergoer. His thoughts and observations were collected in a book titled the *Diary*, which provides a vivid history of the performance of Shakespeare's plays during the Restoration* period.

Pepys's *Diary* covers the years from 1660 to 1669. Although Restoration theater was famous for numerous productions of Shakespeare's plays, many of those stagings were adaptations that altered the original script to meet the tastes of the day. For example, *Romeo and Juliet* had a happy ending, and the Fool was cut out of *King Lear*. In the years covered by his diary, Pepys attended 41 performances of 12 Shakespearean plays.

Excerpts from the *Diary* reveal Pepys's honest and opinionated reaction to the plays he saw. For example, in September of 1660 he attended a performance of *Twelfth Night* and wrote: "I took no pleasure in it at all." Two years later Pepys also responded negatively to *A Midsummer Night's Dream*: "it is the most insipid [dull] ridiculous play that ever I saw in my life." Pepys enjoyed *Macbeth* when he saw it in January of 1666: "To the Duke's house, and saw 'Macbeth' . . . a most excellent play in all respects." In April of 1667 Pepys saw *The Taming of the Shrew* at the King's playhouse and thought it had "some very good pieces in it, but generally is but a mean play."

Interestingly the *Diary* records Pepys's varying reactions to different productions of the same play. For example, he enjoyed a performance of *Macbeth* in April of 1667: "To the play-house, where we saw 'Macbeth,' which, though I have seen it often, yet it is one of the best plays for a stage . . . that ever I saw." In October of the same year, however, Pepys attended another production of *Macbeth* with a different and inferior lead actor: "Lord! what a prejudice it wrought [made] in me against the whole play, and every body else agreed in disliking this fellow."

Pepys held fast to some of his opinions throughout the years. In January of 1669, nine years after his negative response to a production of *Twelfth Night*, he wrote: "To the Duke of York's house, and saw 'Twelfth Night,' as it is now revived; but, I think, one of the weakest plays that ever I saw on the stage." (*See also* **Shakespearean Theater: 17th Century.**)

PERFORMANCES

Performances in Shakespeare's day were advertised on bills, posters tacked up on posts or distributed in the streets. Gatherers at the theater's main entrance and at the stairs leading up to the gallery seats collected admission fees. Just as flashing house lights in modern theaters indicate that it is time for audience members to take their seats, a

142

trumpet was sounded in the Elizabethan theater to alert both the spectators and the actors. The third trumpet call indicated the actual start of the performance.

The physical structure of the Elizabethan playhouse affected when and how plays were performed. Public playhouses such as the GLOBE had only torches and candles for lighting, so performances had to take place during the daylight hours. Plays usually began around 2 or 3 P.M. and ran for two or two and one-half hours, usually without an intermission. The only breaks in the action occurred at the ends of scenes. The actors left the stage, and the scenery, if there was any, was changed. Sets were usually minimal, however, so scene changes were quick and generally did not interrupt the performance. This practice changed somewhat when Shakespeare's plays began to be performed at private, indoor playhouses such as BLACKFRIARS. There it became customary to include breaks in the performance, usually at the end of Acts I and III, during which music was played or sung.

Because the scenery was fairly limited, the actors had to set the scene with language. This task was relatively easy because Elizabethan playhouses, unlike modern theaters, placed almost no space between the actors and the spectators. In fact in the private playhouses it was common for wealthy audience members to sit directly on the stage. The actor's proximity to his listeners helped him communicate more intimately. Actors also used speech to provide background information about characters or setting, the sort of detail that is often printed on the program in a modern theater. Players often spoke directly to the audience in the form of a prologue at the beginning of a play (or at the beginning of a scene) or an epilogue at the end. Prologues helped explain the play's action and identify the characters and settings. Epilogues were usually presented as an apology for any flaws in the play and as a plea for applause.

In public playhouses a work was often followed by a humorous piece known as a JIG. The jig, a farce* written in verse, was usually recited by a clown. Over time the jig grew into a complete production number. It featured as many as four players and often included music and dancing. (*See also* **Dramatic Techniques; Elizabethan Theaters; Fools, Clowns, and Jesters; Globe Theater; Playhouse Structure; Settings; Shakespearean Theater: 17th Century.**)

See color plate 13, vol. 1.

* **farce** light dramatic composition that features broad satiric comedy, improbable situations, stereotyped characters, and exaggerated physical action

PERICLES

One of the most popular plays of its time, *Pericles* is the first of Shakespeare's romances, or late tragicomedies. These plays have adventure-filled plots in which the main characters endure terrible trials before being rewarded with happiness at the end. The themes Shakespeare developed in *Pericles* would go on to play a major role in *The Winter's Tale* and *The Tempest,* two of the playwright's most impressive creations.

The source for the story of *Pericles* is the ancient legend of Appolonius of Tyre, as retold by the medieval* poet John Gower. Shakespeare includes

* **medieval** referring to the Middle Ages, a period roughly between A.D. 500 and 1500

Gower himself in the play as a narrator whose function is to explain the series of disconnected episodes that make up the plot. Over the course of the play, Pericles finds, loses, and regains love. He meets the woman who will become his wife, Thaisa, after being shipwrecked in her father's kingdom, but he later becomes separated from her during a storm at sea. Their daughter, Marina, raised by two friends, is sold into slavery at a brothel*. Believing that his wife and daughter are both dead, Pericles falls into despair. He is revived from his deathlike grief when he is shipwrecked in the land of Mytilene and finds his way to the house of the governor, Lysimachus, who has taken Marina under his protection. Marina's sweet singing restores Pericles to his former self, and he realizes that she is his long-lost daughter. He then has a vision in which the goddess Diana instructs him to visit her temple at Ephesus. Once he travels there, he is reunited with Thaisa, who has become a priestess at the temple. To complete the happy ending, Marina and Lysimachus become engaged.

In many ways the story resembles a fairy tale. Its characters are either very good or very evil, and there are hints of magic in the wondrous restorations of Thaisa and Marina, both believed to be dead. *Pericles* closely resembles the miracle plays of the Middle Ages, in which the hero patiently endures the trials of life and the pain of death and is rewarded with eternal bliss in the afterlife. Unlike most Shakespearean heroes, the title character is passive rather than active. His suffering and his eventual restoration to happiness can be seen as expressing the idea that humans cannot control their destiny.

Few scholars believe that Shakespeare wrote all of *Pericles*. The play does not hold together well, and parts of it are poorly written. Many claim that Shakespeare did not contribute at all to the first two acts. Some think that he wrote *Pericles* with a coauthor, while others see the play as the half-finished revision of another playwright's work. Rough as it is, however, *Pericles* established the form for Shakespeare's romances. Many of its themes, particularly the idea of restoration and rebirth, appear in his later, more polished romances. As a group the romances also share some features of MASQUES, among them music and dancing. (*See also* **Fate and Fortune; Plays: The Romances.**)

* brothel house of prostitution

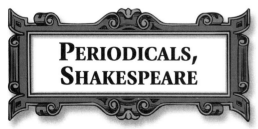

PERIODICALS, SHAKESPEARE

Over the last four centuries Shakespeare has attracted the interest of scholars and critics throughout the world. Many of the most important studies of his works appear in periodicals, and a number of those periodicals are devoted solely or primarily to Shakespeare. Of these, most are scholarly in emphasis, written by and for academics in colleges and universities, but some are designed for a more general readership. In recent years several new publications have appeared, and those that can be obtained by school libraries will often contain materials that students and their teachers will find useful.

The oldest periodical by far is the *Shakespeare Jahrbuch*, short for *Jahrbuch der Deutschen Shakespeare-Gesellschaft* (Yearbook of the German

Shakespeare Society), which has been published annually since 1865. The *Jahrbuch* includes occasional articles in English, but its primary purpose is to reflect scholarship, performance, and other Shakespearean-related projects in Germany.

Another annual, *Shakespeare Survey,* is one of the most prestigious periodicals in Great Britain. Founded in 1948 as an arm of the Shakespeare Institute at the University of Birmingham and published by Cambridge University Press, this illustrated journal covers Shakespearean productions in the United Kingdom, with most of its space devoted to STRATFORD-UPON-AVON and London. Each issue of the *Survey* features a specific theme (such as the Elizabethan theater or Shakespeare in his own age) and contains a helpful overview of past studies on that and related topics. Many of the essays in a particular volume of *Shakespeare Survey* originate from the biennial International Shakespeare Conference at the Shakespeare Insititute. Over the years a number of these articles have offered fascinating indications of emerging trends in the way influential thinkers are approaching the poems and plays.

The most prominent Shakespearean journal in the United States is *Shakespeare Quarterly.* An outgrowth of the *Shakespeare Association Bulletin,* which began in 1924 as a newsletter for the initial Shakespeare Association of America, the *Quarterly* assumed its current identity in 1951. In 1972 when a new organization acquired rights to the name of its original sponsor, the *Quarterly* became affiliated with the Folger Shakespeare Library in Washington, D.C. It is now a copublication of the Folger and George Washington University. Over the years *Shakespeare Quarterly* has covered Shakespeare in performance, and from the mid-1970s to the mid-1980s it compiled reports on theater productions around the globe. Its coverage now tends to be more analytical and is generally limited to major acting companies in the English-speaking world. In addition to articles and book reviews, the *Quarterly* provides the most comprehensive international Shakespeare bibliography in existence, an indispensable resource with valuable annotations for most entries.

Another major American journal is *Shakespeare Studies,* published annually by Fairleigh Dickinson University Press. First published at the University of Cincinnati in 1965, *Shakespeare Studies* is widely admired for its lengthy articles and unusually thorough reviews of books and periodicals.

Since 1950, when *The Shakespeare Newsletter* was started at Kent State University in Ohio, this periodical has done the most to keep readers current on what is happening in scholarship, performance, and other aspects of what has been called "the Good Will Industry." In 1965 it moved its offices to the University of Illinois at Chicago, and since 1992 it has been produced at Iona College in New York.

Over the years many other Shakespeare periodicals have appeared. *Hamlet Studies* is a journal, emanating from the University of Delhi in India, whose title suggests how specialized Shakespearean scholarship has now become. *Shakespeare Bulletin,* formerly the *Bulletin of the New York Shakespeare Society,* is notable for its analyses of current stagings of the plays. *Shakespeare and the Classroom* is a venture with connections to Shakespeare's Globe on the Bankside. *Shakespeare and Schools* comes from

England's Cambridge Institute of Education. The *Shakespeare on Film Newsletter* has established itself as the most authoritative source of information on and criticism of film and television renderings of the playwright's works. *Shakespeare Worldwide* is a Tokyo-based annual, formerly known as *Shakespeare Translation*, that addresses the problems involved in adapting Shakespeare's works to languages other than English. *The Upstart Crow*, a journal that began at the University of Tennessee in Martin and is now edited at Clemson University in South Carolina, contains essays, notes, poems, and thought-provoking ideas concerning the playwright's work. Of particular interest to teachers and students is a magazine known simply as *Shakespeare*, which is copublished by Cambridge University Press and Georgetown University and which features articles, interviews, and profiles written by and for classroom instructors at the precollege level.

This overview is by no means exhaustive. It makes no reference to Web-based services, for example, or to the numerous magazines and newsletters that go out to theater subscribers, in part because periodicals come and go with such rapidity these days. But perhaps this survey will provide an introduction to a burgeoning area of activity.

PERSONAL HYGIENE

Among the most common misconceptions about Elizabethan life are those that involve matters of personal hygiene. For example, it is a popular myth that Queen ELIZABETH I never bathed. In truth she bathed every two weeks and even took a portable bathtub with her when she traveled. Although the queen bathed more often than most people did, many Elizabethans took personal cleanliness seriously and used several methods to ensure good hygiene.

Baths were usually taken in a large wooden tub, which was placed before the fireplace for warmth. Taking a bath was considered a luxury by most of the poor, some of whom washed in rivers or ditches. Wealthy people, on the other hand, had servants to help them bathe. Drafts were one of the main concerns of bathers because they feared that a cold breeze would cause them to become ill. Therefore, the chamberlain, or main servant, would prepare his master's bath by hanging scented sheets throughout the room to keep out drafts. He would then place sponges in the tub for the master to lean against or sit on. When the master was ready for his bath, the servant would help him remove his clothes and then wrap him in a sheet to keep him warm. During the bath only the part of the master being washed with one of the soft sponges was exposed. After the bath the chamberlain would rinse his master with warm, scented water and then dry him with a soft towel and help him to bed. Wealthy women were similarly cared for by their personal servants.

Because the majority of Elizabethans bathed infrequently, perfumes, flowers, and various herbs were used to keep bodies and bedchambers smelling fresh. Many Elizabethans believed that foul odors caused melancholy, or depression. (*See also* **Sanitation**.)

PETRUCHIO

etruchio is KATHARINA's husband in *The Taming of the Shrew.* Readers have varying reactions to his "taming" of the willful Katharina. Elizabethan audiences almost certainly saw it as causing a positive transformation from an unhappy, rebellious daughter to a happy, obedient wife. Many modern readers, however, see Petruchio as a brutal husband who utterly crushes the lively spirit of his wife.

These differing interpretations are possible because Petruchio does not abuse Katharina in obvious ways, such as beating her for her disobedience. Instead he manipulates her psychologically. One of his methods for winning over his hot-tempered spouse is to give her a taste of her own medicine by playing the part of the comic tyrant. His behavior in effect holds up a mirror that shows Kate the unpleasantness of her own. At the same time he continually praises her "sweet nature," no matter how rudely she behaves. His words of praise hint at the rewards she might gain by being truly sweet-tempered.

Some of his methods, however, are more extreme. Petruchio deprives Katharina of food, clothing, and sleep, all the while insisting that he is only doing what is best for her. He insists on strict obedience, even requiring her to support him in obviously untrue statements—for example, that the sun is the moon or that an old man is a young woman. Eventually he succeeds in persuading Katharina to submit to his authority. At her sister's wedding in the play's final scene, Petruchio wins a bet with two other husbands over whose wife is the most obedient.

Petruchio (played by Howard Keel) playfully spanks his rebellious wife, Katharina (Katheryn Grayson), in a scene from *Kiss Me, Kate,* a musical based on *The Taming of the Shrew.*

Philosophy

* *dowry* money given to a woman's
husband at their marriage

Critics of Petruchio's character tend to point out that he specifically states his intent at the beginning of the play, to find himself a wealthy wife. These readers believe that Petruchio is interested only in Katharina's dowry*, not in her. As Petruchio and Katharina exchange insults at their first meeting, however, their battle of wits appears to suggest a genuine chemistry between them. If Petruchio is indeed attracted to Katharina for her high spirits, then the goal of his "taming" is presumably not to crush them but only to help her find a more socially acceptable way to express them.

Those who approve of Petruchio argue that for most of the play he is merely acting a role. He pretends to be a wild, domineering husband as part of his plan to tame Kate but does not intend to remain so. This view is supported by the fact that most of Petruchio's wild behavior is not played out on the stage but related by other characters. The audience must therefore think about Petruchio's actions, instead of simply watching them, and is more likely to see them as clever tricks rather than as a reflection of the character's true nature.

PHILOSOPHY

* *humanist* referring to a philosophy that
emphasizes the value of everyday life and
individual achievement

Audiences and critics have long tried to understand Shakespeare's philosophy—his ideas and opinions about religion, politics, ethics, and other topics. Although his poems and plays are rich in philosophical content, they do not necessarily reveal his personal views. They are not statements of belief but works of art, constructed to influence and move their audiences. The closest a modern reader can come to examining Shakespeare's mind is to consider in what light his works present their complex issues to his audience.

ELIZABETHAN THOUGHT. Shakespeare's plays are products of Elizabethan culture, and his first audiences viewed them against the background of Elizabethan thought. The major influences on Elizabethan belief systems were the writings of ancient philosophers, the teachings of Christianity, and the humanist* ideas of the Renaissance.

The most influential ancient thinkers were probably the Greek philosophers Plato and Aristotle. Plato emphasized the existence of ideals that could not be directly observed in the physical world but could be contemplated through meditation. Plato's pupil Aristotle, by contrast, focused on careful observation of physical reality along with logical deduction. Elizabethan philosophy combined these two models with the notion that ideals could be transformed into reality. Shakespeare's contemporaries also admired such philosophies as Stoicism, the view that humans should control their passions and accept whatever life offered. Shakespeare expressed this idea in Hamlet's description of Horatio (whose name suggests *ratio*, the Latin word for reason) as "a man that Fortune's buffets and rewards / Hast ta'en with equal thanks" (III.ii.67–68).

* *medieval* referring to the Middle Ages, a
period roughly between A.D. 500 and 1500

Elizabethans' knowledge of Christian beliefs was drawn primarily from the BIBLE, but the writings of medieval* Christian thinkers such as

148

A Tangled Web

Shakespeare's classic thinker, Hamlet, reveals the wide range of philosophies that influenced Elizabethan thought. He accepts the Christian doctrines that suicide is forbidden and that the king will go to heaven if he is killed while praying. Yet Hamlet's belief in personal revenge is more consistent with the ancient Roman code of honor and ignores the Christian requirement to forgive the sins of others. Meanwhile his careful investigation of the king's guilt is the mark of a scientific Renaissance mind, but one that would not have resolved, in theological terms, the identity of the Ghost (who could be a devil masquerading as an angel). These conflicting attitudes seem to contribute to Hamlet's uncertainty about how he should respond to his father's murder.

Saint Augustine of Hippo were also deeply influential. When Europeans rediscovered ancient Greek and Roman writings during the late Middle Ages, Christian philosophers such as Boethius and Thomas Aquinas struggled to reconcile Christian theology with the works of Aristotle. Traditional Christian thought continued to evolve throughout the Renaissance. New beliefs, such as humanism, arose in the context of the Protestant Reformation. Protestant attitudes toward morality differed from earlier Catholic beliefs. Protestants stressed the possibility of a personal relationship with God and emphasized the importance of faith more than good deeds.

LOOKING FOR SHAKESPEARE'S PHILOSOPHY. In his plays Shakespeare speaks only through his characters, whose opinions vary so much that they obviously cannot all be said to speak for the playwright. It is very tempting to believe that Shakespeare's own beliefs are uttered by the characters who seem positive and admirable, but even his villains often express noble ideas, even if they are not speaking sincerely. Similarly, his most likeable characters sometimes engage in behaviors that are morally questionable.

Instead of looking for Shakespeare's ideas in the words of his characters, readers may wish to consider the themes explored in the plays. Several themes—such as love, honor, and death—appear repeatedly in his work, but the playwright does not always consider them in the same way. The reader cannot assume, moreover, that Shakespeare kept returning to these ideas because of a personal interest in them.

As an artist he would consciously have chosen topics appropriate for the types of plays he was writing. For example, an audience gathered for a comedy would expect the hero to succeed and would see any barriers to his success as temporary (if sometimes amusing) complications. An audience attending a tragedy knew that the hero would fall despite his heroism, and his troubles would often be interpreted as the consequences of personal failings with moral significance. To understand a given play, the audience must recognize its structure and its value system. The ethical patterns of a Shakespearean play may reveal not what the playwright thought but how he wanted his audience to respond in a particular set of circumstances.

Unlike an essay, which attempts to persuade the reader through logical argument, a dramatic work uses conflict and emotion to guide the audience's reactions. It does this through the broad outline of the plot. In *Othello,* for example, the audience sees a character whose irrational jealousy destroys him and those closest to him. The audience cannot understand this play without recognizing its central premise that jealousy is self-destructive. Audience members may not all agree with this idea, but they must accept it as part of the story. Individual scenes may reinforce the play's overall theme in various ways, sometimes commenting on or contradicting each other. In the first scene of *King Lear,* for example, Gloucester speaks lightly of his relationship with his two sons, setting up the theme of father-child relationships that will shape the rest of the drama.

Shakespeare's plays almost never present a single, simple moral. Instead the playwright usually examines an ethical issue from several angles. Characters within a single play may have differing attitudes, and individual characters may change their minds over the course of the play. These contradictions, combined with the subtleties of Shakespeare's language, make his philosophy a fruitful subject for continuing debate. (*See also* **Astronomy and Cosmology; Fate and Fortune; Morality and Ethics.**)

PHOENIX AND TURTLE, THE

* *allegory* literary device in which characters, events, and settings represent abstract qualities and in which the author intends a different meaning to be read beneath the surface

* *stanza* section of a poem; specifically, a grouping of lines into a recurring pattern determined by meter or rhyme scheme

* *medieval* referring to the Middle Ages, a period roughly between A.D. 500 and 1500

* *elegy* poem that expresses sorrow for one who has died

Shakespeare's poem "The Phoenix and Turtle" is an allegory* on the extraordinary power of love. The poem tells of the deaths of two birds, the phoenix and the turtledove. The phoenix, a legendary creature from Greek mythology, was believed to live for 500 years. Only one existed at any given time, and when its life was complete it burned itself atop a pyre of twigs and then rose again from the ashes. Its long life and miraculous rebirth made the phoenix a traditional symbol of immortality. In Shakespeare's poem, however, the phoenix is treated primarily as a symbol of love. The turtledove, known in Elizabethan times as the turtle, symbolizes constancy, or faithfulness in love.

The 67-line poem is separated into three sections. The first five quatrains (four-line stanzas*) summon various birds to attend the funeral of the phoenix and the turtle. The next eight quatrains reveal that the two birds have burned themselves to death in order to achieve perfect union for all eternity. Reason, a character in the poem, acknowledges that its power is not as great as the power of love. This idea reflects a common Elizabethan belief that ideal love rises above logical thinking and represents a reality greater than that of the physical world. The final section of the poem is a funeral song composed by Reason that celebrates the phoenix and the turtle as the embodiments of truth and beauty: "Truth may seem, but cannot be, / Beauty brag, but 'tis not she, / Truth and Beauty buried be" (62–64).

"The Phoenix and Turtle" was initially an untitled poem and did not receive its current title until 1640. Because the poem is so unlike Shakespeare's other works, some early Shakespearean scholars doubted its authenticity. Most modern scholars, however, agree that Shakespeare wrote it, and they regard it as an important work. Although it has no known direct source, it bears similarities to tales by the ancient Roman poet OVID and the medieval* English poet Geoffrey Chaucer.

First published in 1601, the poem appeared in a collection titled *Love's Martyr*, which was compiled by the poet Robert Chester. *Love's Martyr* was dedicated to Sir John Salisbury, and some scholars believe that Shakespeare's poem refers to Salisbury and his wife. Other scholars are convinced that "The Phoenix and Turtle" is an elegy* for Anne Lyne, a Catholic executed for hiding and protecting priests. Another theory is that the poem refers to the supposed love affair between Robert Devereux, the earl of Essex, and Queen ELIZABETH I, who was often symbolically represented as a phoenix. (*See also* **Poetry of Shakespeare.**)

PLAY STRUCTURE

Modern editors divide Shakespeare's plays into acts and scenes. These divisions, together with line numbers, assist scholars, students, and other readers in discussing and quoting the works. The plays that were published during Shakespeare's lifetime, however, lacked such divisions. In general, only university-educated playwrights trying to imitate the ancient Roman dramatists included act and scene indications in the texts of their works.

Although most early editions of Shakespeare's plays did not include acts or scenes, there are signs that the dramatist may have used these divisions to structure his works. The Choruses* that appear in *Henry V* and *Pericles* strongly suggest that these scripts, at least, were divided into five acts. Additional evidence that Shakespeare may have sorted his plays into acts and scenes comes from plots—summaries of the action that were used by Elizabethan actors and stagehands. Seven of these summaries have survived from Elizabethan times. Plots were glued to two sides of a board that hung from a peg backstage, and solid or dotted lines drawn across the board divided the action into scenes. Perhaps the strongest evidence that Shakespeare divided his plays into sections, however, is the First Quarto* edition of *Romeo and Juliet* (printed in 1597), which features horizontal lines across the pages to break the play into acts and scenes.

Despite the evidence that Shakespeare's plays may have included acts and scenes, most scholars believe that there were no breaks during public performances at theaters such as the GLOBE. There are indications, however, that plays staged in private theaters such as the BLACKFRIARS featured act and scene divisions marked by pauses in the performances. CHILDREN'S COMPANIES often performed in such playhouses, and the boy actors may have needed to rest between acts. It is likely that the intervals between acts were often accompanied by music, for which the children's companies were famous.

* *Chorus* character in Elizabethan drama who recites the prologue and epilogue and sometimes comments on the action

* *quarto* referring to the format of a book or page; a sheet of paper folded twice, yielding four leaves or eight pages

PLAY WITHIN A PLAY

An unusual and striking feature of some of Shakespeare's dramas is the so-called play within a play. These secondary performances mimic several other dramatic forms, including MASQUES, pantomimes, comedies, and tragedies. They typically serve to comment on the action or to develop the plot.

One of Shakespeare's most famous plays within a play is in *Hamlet*. When a traveling company of actors arrives at the palace, the prince enlists them to perform a tragedy of revenge called *The Murder of Gonzago* before the royal court. Presented in Act III, the action begins with a "dumb show," or pantomime, in which a villain poisons a king and then consoles the queen. A scene with dialogue follows, and then the king's nephew poisons the murderer.

This play is intended to be a miniature of the main plot: Prince Hamlet's uncle (Claudius) has murdered his father (King Hamlet) and married the queen (Gertrude), compelling the younger Hamlet to contemplate revenge. The prince believes that his uncle's reaction to the

play will provide unmistakable proof about whether he murdered the king: "The play's the thing / Wherein I'll catch the conscience of the King" (II.ii.604–5). When Claudius reacts to the performance with panic and anger, Prince Hamlet is convinced of his uncle's guilt.

Shakespeare presents a play within a play in *A Midsummer Night's Dream* to celebrate the wedding of two characters, Duke Theseus and Queen Hippolyta. This farce, titled *Pyramus and Thisbe,* is acted with rowdy humor despite its serious subject: two lovers try to elope, but in the confusion caused by a lion they kill themselves in despair. The humor serves to remind the audience of the tragedy that might have occurred during the earlier elopement of the characters Lysander and Hermia.

Perhaps the most obvious example of Shakespeare's use of a play within a play is in *The Taming of the Shrew,* where the device is hardly secondary. It is in fact practically the entire play. Shakespeare begins with introductory scenes in which a nobleman plays a joke on a drunkard named Christopher Sly. The lord brings Sly into his manor and persuades him that he has suffered a bout of amnesia but is really a nobleman in his own home. The lord then hires a group of players to perform a comedy for Sly's amusement; their performance is *The Taming of the Shrew.*

Shakespeare occasionally used a play within a play to comment on the theater profession of his time. For example, the play within *A Midsummer Night's Dream* is a parody of buffoonish, clumsy performances of mediocre dramas. In Act II, Scene ii of *Hamlet,* Rosencrantz and Guildenstern comment that the popularity of the traveling players has suffered as a result of the success of the children's companies. A rivalry between companies of adult and child actors, called the war of the theaters, actually existed during Shakespeare's lifetime. Prince Hamlet also instructs his hired players in the techniques of proper acting, possibly reflecting Shakespeare's own opinions on the topic. (*See also* **Play Structure.**)

PLAYHOUSE STRUCTURE

In the early 1500s, plays were performed in the yards of inns and in the great halls of noblemen's houses. In 1576, however, a building called the Theater was constructed specifically for staging plays, and others soon followed. There were two basic types of performance spaces: public, open-air theaters, such as the GLOBE, and private, indoor theaters, such as the BLACKFRIARS. Although the playhouses differed to some degree, many shared the same basic structure.

PUBLIC THEATERS. The exterior of most public theaters was roughly circular in shape, with many flat sides to form a polygonal structure. All public theaters were built around an open courtyard, which enabled daylight to enter and illuminate the playhouse. The walls were usually made of wood, but one theater, the Swan, was constructed of concrete.

The main entrance of a playhouse led into the central courtyard, called the pit, where the less affluent audience members stood beneath the open sky. Along the inner walls were three stories of roofed galleries, where the

wealthy spectators sat on benches. The pit was typically about 55 feet wide, with the galleries rising about 35 feet above. Most theaters could hold 2,000 to 3,000 spectators. The entire interior was painted and decorated.

The stage extended from a back wall out into the center of the playhouse, enabling audience members to watch from the front and the sides. Measuring about 40 feet wide, the stage was partly covered by a roof, referred to as the *heavens,* held aloft by two large pillars. The stage itself was supported by several pillars about 5 feet high. The space below the stage, called the *hell,* served as a place from which actors playing the roles of ghosts or other supernatural beings could emerge or disappear.

A tall houselike building known as the superstructure stood at the rear of the stage. Typically, the first level of the superstructure was the tiring house, where actors dressed and changed costume. The upper stories, known as the upper stage, served as balconies, windows, or city walls during performances. The upper stories might also have housed musicians and equipment for creating sound effects. For example, from the upper tiers, cannonballs were rolled on boards to imitate thunder. At the top of the superstructure, a flagpole displayed the theater's banner on days when a performance was held. The color of the flag advertised the type of drama that was to be performed that day—black for tragedy, white for comedy, and red for history.

PRIVATE PLAYHOUSES. The most famous of the private, indoor theaters, Blackfriars, was located in a former monastery, or home for monks. The stage, which was about half the size of a public theater stage, stood at the end of a hall that measured about 66 feet long and 46 feet wide. Blackfriars held approximately 700 spectators, and the least expensive seating was the same price as the most expensive seat at the Globe. The most expensive seats were at the front, while the cheapest were benches at the back. Some spectators, usually important guests, sat on stools near the edge of the stage. (*See also* **Elizabethan Theaters; Households and Furnishings; Inn Yards.**)

See color plate 4, vol. 1.

PLAYS: THE COMEDIES

It is difficult to discuss Shakespeare's comedies as a group, largely because scholars do not all agree about which plays belong in this category. Nearly everyone sees *Love's Labor's Lost* and *A Midsummer Night's Dream* as comedies, but later works such as *Measure for Measure* and *The Tempest,* both of which have elements of comedy, are harder to categorize. Shakespeare's early comedies are quite different from his later ones. These differences in style reflect the development of the playwright's dramatic art, his ideas and interests, and the changing literary fashions of his time.

To follow the development of Shakespeare's comic style, it may be useful to group the comedies into three subcategories. The early plays include *The Comedy of Errors, The Two Gentlemen of Verona, The Taming of the Shrew,* and *Love's Labor's Lost.* The middle, or "mature," comedies are *A*

Plays: The Comedies

Midsummer Night's Dream, The Merchant of Venice, Much Ado About Nothing, As You Like It, and *Twelfth Night.* Finally, the late comedies (or "romances") are *Pericles, Cymbeline, The Winter's Tale,* and *The Tempest.* In addition to these, there are two or three so-called problem plays (*All's Well That Ends Well, Measure for Measure,* and perhaps *Troilus and Cressida*) that have the overall shape and style expected of a comedy but also contain many dark and unsettling elements that do not quite fit the spirit of the genre*.

SOURCES. During his youth Shakespeare undoubtedly had heard the old stories that were sung, recited, and performed as popular entertainment in the English countryside. Many of these dramatic performances formed part of the celebrations during FESTIVALS AND HOLIDAYS. In fact there is a strong connection between Shakespeare's comedies and ancient folk rituals that relate to spring, harvest, and Christmas. The title *Twelfth Night,* for example, refers to the final night of traditional Christmas festivities. Shakespeare often takes full advantage of these associations by incorporating elements of holiday entertainment into his comedies. *As You Like It* contains poetry writing and recitation, as ORLANDO clutters the trees in Arden with his love poems to ROSALIND. *A Midsummer Night's Dream* displays holiday performance in the form of the *Pyramus and Thisbe* skit staged by Bottom and his companions. Finally, almost every Shakespearean comedy celebrates the natural world by making it the place where important transformations occur.

Although Shakespeare borrowed freely from the tradition of popular entertainment, it was not the only influence on his comedies. Shakespeare was also familiar with the classical* tradition, which included the comedies of ancient playwrights as well as newer Italian and English plays that imitated the ancient style. The classical tradition thrived in universities and at the royal court, where comedies by Roman playwrights such as Plautus (ca. 254–185 B.C.) and Terence (184–159 B.C.) were often performed in their original Latin. Classical plays typically have complex plots and a satirical* tone. They usually feature stock characters, figures who are reused in many plays, such as old gullible fathers, young lovers, and tricky servants.

PLOTS. Shakespeare was the first English dramatist to successfully combine the popular and classical traditions. The tension between these two traditions is especially evident in early works such as *The Comedy of Errors.* This play is based primarily on *The Menaechmi,* a farce* by Plautus, which revolves around the unexpected meeting of identical twin brothers who have been separated at a young age and subsequently given the same name. The changes Shakespeare makes in adapting Plautus's plot reveal both his dramatic sense and his ties to popular tradition.

First, to heighten the potential for confusion, Shakespeare adds a second pair of identical twins (both named Dromio) as servants of the original twins (both named Antipholus). Second, he adds a subplot involving the separation and reunion of a husband and wife, the parents of the two Antipholuses. Long-delayed reunions were part of the tradition of popular romance, the tales of idealized love and adventure featured in widely read Elizabethan novels. Shakespeare also added a subplot in which one

* **genre** literary form

* **classical** in the tradition of ancient Greece and Rome

* **satirical** ridiculing human wickedness and foolishness

* **farce** light dramatic composition that features broad satiric comedy, improbable situations, stereotyped characters, and exaggerated physical action

Antipholus falls in love with the other's sister-in-law. These additions make this comedy much more emotionally satisfying than Plautus's, which ends with one of the twins auctioning off his wife (along with other possessions) before returning to his original home. In adapting Plautus's play Shakespeare multiplied not only the complexity of the plot but also its emotional possibilities. The repeated appearance of certain themes, such as reunion and the rekindling of enduring love, makes Shakespeare's comedies "romantic."

Although Shakespeare's early comedies were an important contribution to the Elizabethan stage, they fall far short of his later comic masterpieces. In *The Comedy of Errors* he makes the plot more complex largely to increase the opportunities for confusion and to heighten the sense of resolution at the end. In his mature comedies Shakespeare masterfully constructs plots that make effective use of characters and themes. In *As You Like It,* for example, the main plot (the courtship between the lovers Rosalind and Orlando) is echoed in subplots that depict courtships between less central characters. This arrangement certainly adds to the complexity of the action and the resolution of its ending, with four marriages instead of just one. It also works on a thematic level, showing how various characters understand love and act on their feelings.

CHARACTERS. In Shakespeare's early comedies, such as *The Two Gentlemen of Verona*, the characters tend to be fairly limited and conventional. Valentine and Proteus, two friends who have become rivals in love, may change their minds through the course of the play, but they never become more than stock characters like those in hundreds of other romances. In the middle comedies, however, Shakespeare creates the illusion that his characters' attitudes and behaviors spring from complex personalities rather than from plot requirements. In fact sometimes the

Many of Shakespeare's comedies feature bawdy humor. *The Merry Wives of Windsor,* in which the lusty knight Falstaff attempts to seduce two married women, is an example.

TRAGEDY TOMORROW, COMEDY TONIGHT

Many of Shakespeare's comedies are constructed in the tradition of ancient playwrights such as the Roman Plautus. The musical comedy *A Funny Thing Happened on the Way to the Forum,* by Stephen Sondheim and based on the plays of Plautus, captures much of the spirit of these old plays. Its opening song refers to the stock characters who traditionally appeared in the comedies of ancient Rome, saying, "Bring on the lovers, liars, and clowns!" It also mentions "Old situations, new complications," a reminder that these plays often depended on complex plot twists.

See color plate 6, vol. 2.

plot and the characters seem to be at odds. At one point in *Measure for Measure,* the plot calls for a criminal, Barnardine (a very minor character), to be executed in place of Claudio, one of the main characters. It is clear from the outset that this is his sole function in the play. When the time arrives for the crucial switch to be made, however, Barnardine bursts onto the stage declaring that he is too hung over to be executed. Having said his piece, he returns to his cell and is seen no more, leaving the officials to find another substitute for Claudio.

Probably the most consistently memorable characters in the comedies are Shakespeare's heroines. Women in Elizabethan England had few rights, and writers typically portrayed them as either patiently suffering wives and daughters or sharp-tongued shrews. Shakespeare was almost the only comic playwright of his day to create intelligent, independent, articulate, and decisive female characters. Most remarkable are the cross-dressing heroines who don male clothing to gain the greater freedom and power enjoyed by men. In their male disguises they generally prove wiser and cleverer than most of the real men around them. These female characters usually end up abandoning the freedom they enjoyed as "men" to enter traditional, male-dominated romantic relationships, but for many readers and audiences they remain empowering role models as well as one of the highlights of the comedies.

At times Shakespeare's ability to make his characters so lifelike can threaten the comic form of his plays. Even his villains have a certain kind of dignity that thwarts comic conventions. SHYLOCK in *The Merchant of Venice,* for instance, is part of a long line of Jewish stage villains and clowns like the ambitious and bloodthirsty Barabas of Christopher MARLOWE's *The Jew of Malta.* Shylock's role in the play is to threaten the life of Antonio, the title character, and the security of the Christian community. Shakespeare humanizes Shylock, however, giving him moving speeches that show his isolation and suffering in the face of disturbing prejudice. As a result his punishment at the end of the play—though required by the plot—inevitably provokes a more complex reaction from the audience than the downfall of the gleefully evil Barabas.

The clever comic resolution at the end of *The Merchant of Venice* cannot overcome the ever present sense of sadness that runs through the play. Shylock is broken, if not dead, and Antonio seems as haunted and alone as he did when he sighed "Indeed, I know not why I am so sad" in the play's first line. The notes of melancholy and uncertainty in *The Merchant of Venice* are deepened in the "problem plays" of the early 1600s. Written during the years in which Shakespeare produced his great tragedies, these plays are much less optimistic in tone than his earlier comedies. Probably the most striking example is *Measure for Measure,* a play in which the duke's court of law becomes the mirror of a shady underworld, and the manipulative duke uses forced marriages as a gentle form of punishment.

MAGIC. In his late comedies Shakespeare returns with vigor to the tradition of romance. These plays feature sea voyages, unfulfilled love, separation, and miraculous recovery, as in the scene at the end of *The Winter's*

Tale when the statue of Hermione (supposed dead for 16 years) seems to come to life. The romances produce a sense of wonder. In addition to the illusion of magic that concludes *The Winter's Tale,* the romances show actual magic worked both by humans (such as PROSPERO, the duke-turned-sorcerer in *The Tempest*) and by gods (such as Jupiter, who aids the main characters in *Cymbeline*).

Many readers have speculated about how these plays relate to Shakespeare's reflections on a long artistic career that was approaching its end. Some see them as a sign that Shakespeare had abandoned the idea of presenting real life on the stage and retreated into the world of imagination. Others see them as the ultimate achievement of a spectacular career, a ringing affirmation of the power of art to transform life. On a more down-to-earth level, the direction of Shakespeare's work probably had a great deal to do with the increasing popularity of MASQUES, elaborately staged productions performed at court that involved music and dancing. In *The Tempest,* Prospero has his spirit-servant Ariel present such a masque. When more pressing concerns in the real world distract him, Prospero allows the illusion to fade with the remark that life itself will fade away in the same way.

It is probably not worthwhile to speculate at length about how Shakespeare the man fits into the romances. At the same time it is a mistake to see them merely as airy delights. Like Shakespeare's earlier comedies many of the plays are concerned with issues of justice and government, love and morality, guilt and redemption. They refuse to let the audience experience the comfort and harmony of comic resolution without also glimpsing a bit of the sadness that the happy ending only partly replaces. (*See also* **Ceremonies and Rituals; Characters in Shakespeare's Plays; Disguises; Love; Plays: The Romances.**)

PLAYS: THE HISTORIES

Shakespeare wrote ten plays generally identified as histories. They cover a long period of English history, from the reign of King John (1199–1216) to that of Henry VIII (1509–1547), but the playwright did not write them in chronological order. The plays draw on a variety of historical sources, but they also contain material of Shakespeare's own invention. He used the continuing story of England to explore such themes as ambition, the conflict between public and private life, and the rightful source of power.

IDENTIFYING THE HISTORIES

The FIRST FOLIO edition divided Shakespeare's plays into three categories: comedies, histories, and tragedies. The publisher may have chosen these broad groupings for the sake of convenience, since each category contains a similar number of plays. These simple classifications, however, are not as straightforward as they initially appear. The full titles of some plays do not match their categories in the First Folio. *Richard II,* for example, was

ALSO KNOWN AS

Many of the history plays were first published with more interesting titles than those given in the First Folio. For example, *Henry VI, Part 2* was originally titled, "The First Part of the Contention betwixt the two famous Houses of Yorke and Lancaster, with the death of the good Duke Humphrey: And the banishment and death of the Duke of Suffolke, and the Tragicall end of the proud Cardinall of Winchester, with the notable Rebellion of Iacke Cade: And the Duke of Yorkes first claime unto the Crowne." It is hardly surprising that the First Folio editors decided to drop such a cumbersome title.

* *Tudor* referring to the dynasty that ruled England from 1485 to 1603

first printed as *The Tragedy of Richard II,* not as a history. Although the term *history* seems to suggest a factual account, some of the histories, most notably, *Richard III,* include supernatural figures and occurrences, such as the appearance of GHOSTS.

TEXTS. The First Folio lists ten plays as histories: *King John; Richard II; Henry IV, Part 1* and *Part 2; Henry V; Henry VI, Part 1, Part 2,* and *Part 3; Richard III;* and *Henry VIII.* The *Henry VI* trilogy was one of Shakespeare's earliest dramatic works, appearing in the theater between 1591 and 1592. The following season *Richard III* appeared, providing a conclusion to the *Henry VI* plays. Some writers group these histories together as a tetralogy (a group of four plays).

The next set of histories appeared over a period of several years. Shakespeare seems to have begun with *King John,* a stand-alone play that focuses on a period earlier than the rest of his histories, in 1594 or 1595. *Richard II,* first performed around 1595, is usually placed in a tetralogy alongside *Henry IV, Part 1* and *Part 2* (1597–1598), and *Henry V* (ca. 1600). These four plays are linked in several ways. Characters that appear in the later plays, such as the bishop of Carlisle, Owen Glendower, and Hotspur, are introduced or mentioned in *Richard II.* There are also prophecies in the earlier plays that are fulfilled in the later ones.

Henry VIII, which appeared around 1613, also exists independently of the other histories. Rather than dealing with wars and changing leadership, it focuses on conflicts between the king and a small number of powerful church leaders. Most scholars believe that Shakespeare wrote this play with John Fletcher, who also collaborated with him on *The Two Noble Kinsmen.*

SOURCES. The term *histories* refers specifically to Shakespeare's English history plays. Several of his other plays relate to events from the history of ancient Rome, but these are usually labeled tragedies. The Roman plays drew mostly on Thomas North's translation of PLUTARCH'S LIVES, while the English histories were based primarily on HOLINSHED'S CHRONICLES, which also provided material for several of Shakespeare's tragedies. The differing styles of the source materials give the English histories a very different tone from that found in Shakespeare's Roman plays.

The major source for the *Henry VI* plays was Edward Halle's *Union of the Two Noble and Illustre Famelies of Lancastre and York.* Born around 1498, Halle was a loyal supporter of Henry VIII, and many scholars argue that his account of the WARS OF THE ROSES was biased in favor of the Tudor* family. For a more balanced view it is possible to go back one step farther to Halle's primary sources. Historians before him had looked at events leading up to Richard II's death from different viewpoints, with some supporting the York family and others favoring the Lancastrians. Most historians, such as Polydore Vergil, combined material from Yorkist and Lancastrian versions, perhaps taking into account that the reigning dynasty might punish authors who wrote unfavorably of it.

Shakespeare's *Richard III* seems to have drawn upon the histories of both Halle and Holinshed. These writings, in turn, took material from Sir

Thomas More's *History of King Richard III*, which may itself have been a translation of a Latin work by John Morton, bishop of Ely, a devoted Lancastrian and an enemy of King Richard. Because Shakespeare's sources are drawn from other sources, all of which may have their own biases, the construction of Shakespeare's histories is far more complex than it may appear on first reading.

Scholars have suggested that the major source for *King John* was a play titled *The Troublesome Reign of King John*. *Richard II* may have been based on a lost play by the same author. Many of the history plays seem to assume that the audience will have some knowledge of the events involved, perhaps through these source plays and other stage histories, which were quite popular at the time. Elizabethans displayed considerable interest in the period from the death of Richard II, which represented a disruption of the established order, to the coronation of Henry VII, representing the return of order and stability. In addition to factual sources, Shakespeare's histories show a number of other artistic influences. The works of the

See color plate 11, vol. 2.

Many of Shakespeare's history plays deal with the struggle over succession that began when Henry Bolingbroke seized the crown from Richard II in 1399. The bloodiest struggle over the crown—the Wars of the Roses—was fought between the houses of Lancaster and York. This genealogical chart shows how both families traced their ancestry back to Edward III and how Henry VII, a Lancastrian, united the rival families when he married Elizabeth of York.

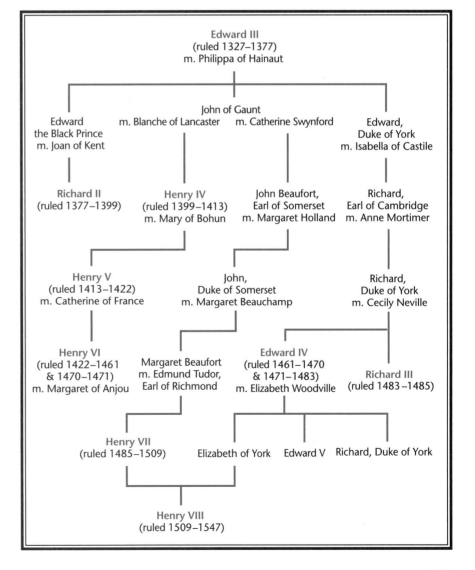

Roman playwright Seneca, for example, were probably a significant influence on some of Shakespeare's early works, such as *Richard III*. The violent plot and the appearance of ghostly characters in this play reflect the style of Seneca's tragedies.

THE PHILOSOPHY OF SHAKESPEARE'S HISTORIES

In writing the histories Shakespeare had to make his texts consistent with the known facts, such as when and where a battle occurred and who was victorious. These basic facts could be dramatized in different ways, however, and the way they were presented could influence the audience's reaction. It has long been held that Shakespeare's histories, as well as his other works, were structured to reflect the views of his society. To understand this claim it is necessary to understand the Elizabethan worldview and examine the sections of Shakespeare's histories that are said to support it.

ELIZABETHAN VIEWS. One of the dominant ideas in Elizabethan philosophy was the so-called great chain of being. According to this concept the entire universe formed a vast hierarchy*, with God at the top and all the world's creatures—from monarchs down to the lowest animals and plants—arranged beneath. This scheme, which placed kings closer to God than common people, was tied to the idea of divine right—the view that rulers were chosen by God and carried out God's will on earth. The divine right of kings, established long before the Elizabethan era, implied that anyone who helped depose* a monarch would suffer God's displeasure.

For many years it was generally believed that Elizabethans unquestioningly accepted the ideas of divine right and the chain of being. During the past several decades, however, this claim has been challenged. Many now see this hierarchical view of society as only one of many ideologies* that people held during Shakespeare's time. It was a view widely accepted by the rich and powerful and maintained by high-ranking officials of the church and the state because it helped them retain their power. Elizabethans of lower rank, however, may have found these concepts less agreeable or perhaps rejected them altogether. Some commentators now argue that there was no single Elizabethan ideology but rather a variety of worldviews as mixed and evolving as those of any other period.

As scholars reassess the ideas of Elizabethan society, they raise new questions about Shakespeare's views. Not surprisingly, critics in the past often interpreted Shakespeare's histories as supporting the notion of the chain of being. Because Shakespeare's sources—the writings of Halle and Holinshed—assumed that history unfolds according to God's will, many critics believed that Shakespeare held similar assumptions. It is clear that Shakespeare's histories illustrate the dangers of challenging an established ruler. Characters who attempt to overthrow a king generally do not prosper. Sometimes their punishment is swift, as in *Henry IV, Part I*, in which the rebellious Hotspur is killed by the king's son Prince Hal. It is worth remembering, however, that King Henry IV was the leader of a successful

* *hierarchy* ordered structure based on rank

* *depose* to remove from high office, often by force

* *ideology* belief system

uprising in *Richard II*. The two *Henry IV* plays show him as nervous and insecure in his power, challenged by rebellions such as Hotspur's and, more significantly, haunted by guilt. King Henry's punishment for challenging the established order is that constant difficulties trouble his reign.

NEW VIEWS. Some critics question the assumption that Shakespeare's histories support the dominant ideology of social order and the chain of being. Many of these commentators have wondered whether Shakespeare was simply using England's past as a convenient way to explore its present. For example, there are clear similarities between Richard II and ELIZABETH I. Like Richard, Elizabeth had no clear heir to her throne, a fact that caused much anxiety among her subjects. Many Elizabethans were also troubled by the fact that Elizabeth, like Richard, indulged her favorites at court. When *Richard II* was first printed in 1597, much of the scene in which Richard gives up his crown was omitted, conceivably because it was seen as hitting too close to home.

Many critics now argue that Shakespeare's histories, rather than upholding the "world order" view, put forward an alternative view. They see *Richard II* as depicting the breakdown of the traditional idea that political events in the human world occur according to God's will. King Richard, supposedly the ruler chosen by God, is weak, ineffective, and corrupt; Henry, who challenges him, is strong and disciplined. This play appears to offer a new view of the world and of political order. It appears that even in Shakespeare's time there were some who believed his plays did not support the dominant worldview. In *Piers Penniless*, a satirical* pamphlet penned in 1592, Thomas Nash defended the *Henry VI* plays from moralistic criticism. He claimed that the "valiant acts" of the heroic "forefathers" portrayed in Shakespeare's plays were set up as a contrast to the "effeminate days" of Elizabeth's reign. It would seem to follow from Nash's interpretation that Shakespeare's histories were intended to challenge, not support, the established ruler.

In *Richard II* and earlier histories, Shakespeare focuses the action on the title figure—the king. His later histories, however, paint a broader picture. In *Henry IV, Parts 1* and *2*, and *Henry V*, the playwright follows his sources less closely than in previous histories. He also introduces new events and characters that appear to be invented for purely theatrical purposes, such as the wonderful comic character of Sir John FALSTAFF. The mixture of styles, often combining the comic and the romantic, suggests that Shakespeare was drawing on a much greater variety of materials, not only historical chronicles but also popular sources such as ballads, fairy stories, and legends. By moving away from historical sources, Shakespeare was able to distance himself much more from the established ideology and from its implication that the monarch is a superhuman chosen directly by God. He humanized his kings and princes, exposing their struggles and weaknesses, in what many see as a breakdown of the traditional Elizabethan worldview.

Shakespeare's histories are often interpreted as attempts to learn from the past. Examining history can help answer such questions as how a monarch should rule and what qualities a ruler should have. The plays do

* *satirical* ridiculing human wickedness and foolishness

161

not use history to reinforce established ideas, as many Elizabethan writings did, but to explore a variety of ideas, both old and new. The histories therefore reveal a sense of both the dominant Elizabethan ideology, as found in Shakespeare's sources, and alternative views. Overall, they examine history in terms of the moral and political lessons that can be learned. (*See also* **Astronomy and Cosmology; History in Shakespeare's Plays: England; Philosophy; Playwrights and Poets; Royalty and Nobility; Shakespeare's Sources.**)

PLAYS: THE ROMANCES

* *genre* literary form
* *protagonist* central character in a literary work

* *Holy Grail* according to legend, the cup or platter used by Christ at the Last Supper

* *convention* established practice

Four of Shakespeare's late plays are customarily classified as romances. The term *romance* can have more than one meaning, however. One definition of a romance is an adventure story, but the adventure—the hero or heroine faces monsters, prisons, shipwrecks, fiendish villains, and other dangers—is only part of the enduring appeal of this genre*. For one thing the perils in a romance's world are not just physical but also psychological, often involving lost identities and unrelieved suffering. At the same time, the romance offers reassurance by guaranteeing that the protagonists* will eventually be rewarded, having their identities and fortunes restored and reuniting with their families and lovers. Their spectacular trials are bearable because this happy ending is a certainty.

SHAKESPEARE AND ROMANCE

The first literary work that might be classified as a romance is Homer's *Odyssey,* which was itself the end product of a long oral tradition. Categories of the genre include pastoral romances such as Sir Philip Sidney's *Arcadia* and Ludovico Ariosto's *Orlando Furioso,* set among shepherds and shepherdesses in the peaceful countryside, and chivalric romances, the stories of wandering knights on quests for love and the Holy Grail*. *Don Quixote,* by Miguel de Cervantes (a contemporary of Shakespeare), is both a parody and a celebration of the chivalric romance tradition. Many dramatists had adapted the form for the stage even before Shakespeare took up his pen. By Shakespeare's day the romance was the standard form for fiction.

ROMANTIC ELEMENTS IN EARLIER PLAYS. By the time Shakespeare wrote his late romances, pastoral and chivalric romances had been on the popular stage for so long that they had begun to seem old-fashioned. Critics from Shakespeare's time to the present have wondered why such an accomplished and sophisticated playwright turned to the moldy, overused stories and conventions* of the romance. It should be remembered, however, that the romance form was a major part of Shakespeare's literary background. It was everywhere in Elizabethan culture, both as a literary model and as a source of material—the tales told and retold during long winter evenings around the hearth. Shakespeare's interest in romance did

Written late in Shakespeare's career, the romances include elements of magic and wonder. This scene from *The Tempest* painted by William Hogarth in the 1700s, shows Prince Ferdinand of Naples shipwrecked on an island inhabited by the wizard Prospero; his innocent daughter, Miranda; and the half-human monster Caliban.

* *farce* light dramatic composition that features broad satiric comedy, improbable situations, stereotyped characters, and exaggerated physical action

not suddenly develop near the end of his career but is visible in even his earliest plays.

Shakespeare's first comedy, *The Comedy of Errors,* is primarily a farce*, following the conventions of ancient Roman comedy as practiced by Plautus. But the play opens and closes with the story of a family separated for years by a shipwreck and miraculously reunited, standard romance material. A similar plot device appears in *Twelfth Night,* where the action begins with a shipwreck that separates a pair of twins, a boy and a girl. A subplot in *The Merchant of Venice* is the romance-influenced tale of Portia's suitors, who must choose correctly among three caskets in order to win her hand. The most romantic of Shakespeare's comedies is probably *As You Like It,* an ingenious adaptation and parody of a popular pastoral romance. Elements of romance are seen not only in the comedies but also in the histories and the tragedies as, for example, in the test of love that King Lear imposes on his daughters.

FULL ROMANCES. If Shakespeare was no stranger to the romance tradition and was never afraid to borrow plot twists or devices to enhance his characters and settings from it, it may be unclear why only four particular plays—*Pericles, Cymbeline, The Winter's Tale,* and *The Tempest*—are usually singled out as romances. The reason is that these plays do not just casually mix some romance materials into the plot. Instead, they faithfully follow all the features and conventions of narrative romance, even those that seemed outdated. Also, in adapting his sources for these plays, Shakespeare did not seem to convert narrative material into dramatic with his usual skill and sophistication.

163

LOVE AND ROMANCE

In Shakespeare's day the word *romance* did not suggest a passionate love affair as it probably does to modern readers. Originally based on the Old French *romans,* which referred to the languages spoken in various parts of the Roman empire, the word *romance* came to mean a popular tale that was usually told in the local dialect (unlike a piece of formal writing, which was usually in Latin). By Shakespeare's time the word meant a tale told in verse, usually based on legend and involving heroism, love, and adventure. Because so many of these stories involved love, love stories came to be known as romances, and eventually the word took on its present meaning.

Until about 1950 many critics saw this as a flaw in the romances, perhaps a sign that Shakespeare was losing his artistic mastery or his interest in writing. Today most scholars see the lack of sophistication in these plays as a deliberate preservation of the innocent, primitive tone of the original sources. In modifying these stories for the stage, Shakespeare preserved the narrative quality of a tale drawn from the popular storytelling tradition. Along with it he captured the sense of magic and wonder felt by a listener—particularly when the listener is a child hearing stories told by adults—being transported into the world of the story without analyzing or criticizing it.

The romances invite the viewer to participate in the story, while at the same time recognizing it as an artificial creation. This tendency was already somewhat evident in Shakespeare's late comedies, sometimes known as the "problem plays" because they combine a comic story with a dark and cynical mood. The ending of *All's Well That Ends Well,* in which the main character reappears onstage after being presumed dead, can easily seem absurd and unrealistic. When performed well, however, it can also be deeply moving. Such stage "resurrections" are typical in the romances. They bring out contradictory feelings in the audience, who experience their emotional power while recognizing them as artificial and unconnected to real life.

THE FOUR PLAYS

The first two of the four romances, *Pericles* and *Cymbeline,* are generally viewed as only moderately successful. The last two, *The Winter's Tale* and *The Tempest,* are almost universally acknowledged as masterpieces. These judgments are not absolute, but they reflect a widely shared sense that as Shakespeare experimented with the romance genre, he grew surer of his goals and how to achieve them.

THE LESSER ROMANCES. Many have doubted that Shakespeare was the sole author of *Pericles.* Parts of the play have such flat writing and such clumsy staging that they are often seen as the work of another writer whose play Shakespeare stepped in to revise. The play is based on an ancient romance retold by poet John Gower in the late 1300s. Gower himself appears onstage as a narrator to introduce and comment on the story, which is presented as a series of adventures that befall the main characters. Pericles travels around the Aegean Sea for many years; loses his wife, Thaisa, and then his daughter, Marina; and falls into a deep depression. Marina, separated from her father, survives an assassination plot, a kidnapping by pirates, and an attempt to make her a prostitute, and is finally restored to Pericles. To complete the happy resolution Pericles and Marina are then reunited with Thaisa, who has been patiently awaiting their return in accordance with a prophecy of the goddess Diana.

The character of Gower emphasizes the nature of *Pericles* as a romance. He presents the story as an object of historical interest, "a song that old was sung" (I.i.1). His opening speech reminds the audience of the roots of the art of storytelling: "It hath been sung at festivals, / At ember-eves

and holy-ales, / And lords and ladies in their lives / Have read it for restoratives" (I.i.5–8). The word *restorative,* suggesting medicine, raises the story to the status of a secret potion or wonder drug, even for a sophisticated audience "born in these latter times, / When wit's more ripe" (I.i.11–12). The long-dead poet's presentation of this antique story serves as an introduction not only to *Pericles* but to all the romances. Speaking for Shakespeare the poet, taking up a form that may seem silly or outmoded, Gower calls to mind the healing power of the most ancient art forms.

Cymbeline was a far more ambitious project than *Pericles.* Set in Britain during the time of the Roman empire, its elaborate plot combines love, fidelity, betrayal, and adventure. It includes such spectacular elements as a princess in disguise meeting her long-lost brothers in the mountains of their homeland, an evil queen and her loathsome son, an extravagant Italian villain named Iachimo, and a prophetic dream in which the god Jupiter descends from the heavens "in thunder and lightning, seated on an eagle." The plot reaches its climax in a spectacularly complicated concluding scene, with identities revealed, families reunited, confessions made, forgiveness granted, and peace achieved between Britain and Rome. The size and ambition of this play are exhilarating but extremely difficult to present on the stage. A successful performance must clarify the overcomplicated plot while maintaining a difficult balance between the touching and the absurd.

THE GREAT ROMANCES. In *The Winter's Tale,* Shakespeare solved some of the structural problems of his first two romances, creating a plot that is somewhat easier to perform. It falls neatly into two halves, one tragic and one comic, that function together like a literal definition of tragicomedy (the dramatic genre closest in spirit to the narrative form of romance). The first half of the play is a tragic story of jealousy, madness, and death in which King Leontes, mistakenly suspecting his wife, Hermione, of unfaithfulness, banishes both her and their infant daughter from his court. The second half, which takes place about 16 years later, has all the elements of comedy, including romantic love and the restorative power of family. Not only is Leontes' long-lost daughter, Perdita, restored to him, but Hermione, supposed dead for many years, comes to life when he goes to see her statue.

The most remarkable feature of this plot is the break in its time line. According to classical* theories of drama, a play should be continuous in its time, place, and action, and this 16-year leap is a gross violation of the unity of time. Clearly aware that many would object to this, Shakespeare had the second half of *The Winter's Tale* introduced by the Chorus* representing Time, who points out that the unity of time is whatever he wishes it to be and therefore he may tell the story as he likes. The impishness of this dramatic move "relaunches" the play in a direction that combines merriment and wonder. The plot then resumes with a scene that combines tragedy and parody. Shakespeare preserves the fine balance between the touching and the absurd until the end of the play. If the famous statue scene works, the audience will be deeply moved by it, all the while

* *classical* in the tradition of ancient Greece and Rome

* *Chorus* character in Elizabethan drama who recites the prologue and the epilogue and sometimes comments on the action

165

knowing that their emotions are being manipulated. It is a rich dramatic moment that largely defines the mood of the romances.

The Tempest is the best known and most often performed of the romances, and it was probably the last to be written. Set on a "bare island" in the middle of nowhere, it goes out of its way to observe the same unities of time, place, and action that *The Winter's Tale* violated and mocked. The plot centers on the magician PROSPERO, who successfully controls the play's events and then at the end bids farewell to his art, a story many readers have viewed as a parallel to Shakespeare's own retirement from the stage. In addition to Prospero the island is peopled by strange and fascinating characters, among them CALIBAN—a half-human creature whom Prospero has made first a pet, then a slave—and Ariel, a spirit who serves him and aids him in his magic, all the while longing for freedom. The story also involves a plot against Prospero by Caliban and a pair of richly amusing clowns as well as a charmingly innocent love story between MIRANDA, Prospero's daughter, and Ferdinand, the son of his old enemy.

Because Prospero's magic controls events, there is little suspense in the story. Instead, the play focuses on music, poetry, and pageantry, including a MASQUE produced by Prospero to celebrate the young couple's engagement. When the magician must break off the spectacle in order to cope with Caliban's plot, he remarks in a famous speech (IV.i.146–63) that life itself dissolves as easily as this "insubstantial pageant." Prospero reflects on life and art in other scenes as well—such as his touching farewell to his magic, in which he vows to break his staff and drown his book—reinforcing the idea that the play may reflect Shakespeare's personal experiences. Perhaps the most moving scene of all is the epilogue, in which Prospero appears stripped of all his power, humbly asking the audience to understand and forgive him. Shakespeare wrote a powerful and demanding role in Prospero, as challenging for the actor as the great tragic roles of Hamlet and King Lear.

The romances are a curious mixture of wonder and laughter, pathos and parody, innocence and sophistication. They explore the very roots of art, the story as both an expression of human fantasies and a way of fulfilling them. Shakespeare examines such material both forcefully and tenderly, offering his readers and audiences a spectacular close to an extraordinary career. (*See also* **Pastoralism; Shakespeare's Sources.**)

PLAYS: THE TRAGEDIES

Scholars commonly organize Shakespeare's plays into four major groups: histories, tragedies, comedies, and romances. Ten plays are identified as tragedies. Many plays in the other three categories, however, contain elements of tragedy. Nearly every one of Shakespeare's plays contains some images of death and loss. At the same time, the plays known as tragedies often include comical passages and portrayals of love and joy. The category of tragedy, therefore, is not straightforward. Various factors contribute to the definition that sets Shakespeare's tragedies apart from his other plays.

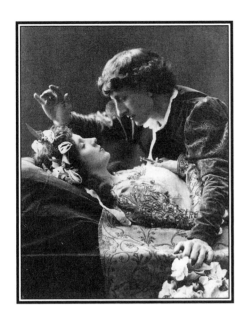

Shakespeare's early tragedy *Romeo and Juliet* is one of his most-loved works. The play's final scene, in which Romeo kills himself beside Juliet's tomb—not realizing that she is still alive—has moved many generations of audiences to tears.

* *genre* literary form

* *morality play* religious dramatic work that teaches a moral lesson through the use of symbolic characters

DEFINING THE TRAGEDIES

One of the difficulties in discussing Shakespeare's tragedies is deciding which plays actually fit into the category. While works such as *Hamlet* and *Romeo and Juliet* are clearly tragedies, others are more difficult to classify. For example, the Elizabethan writer Francis Meres describes the plays dealing with Richard II, Richard III, King John, and Henry IV as tragedies, whereas they are now identified as histories. Even more confusing is *Troilus and Cressida*, which early editions described variously as a tragedy, a history, and a comedy. *Cymbeline*, listed as a tragedy in the FIRST FOLIO, is now usually regarded as a romance. By contrast, *Julius Caesar, Antony and Cleopatra*, and *Coriolanus* are thought of as tragedies, even though they focus on figures and events from Roman history. Even *King Lear*, a classic example of a tragedy, was described as a "true chronicle history" on the title page of its first printed edition.

Another confusing aspect of Shakespeare's tragedies is that most of them contain elements of comedy. Some of these elements are confined to a single scene featuring a clown, such as the grave diggers in *Hamlet* or the porter in *Macbeth*, who was clearly intended to be played by a comic actor. Such characters appear on stage, perform their humorous scenes, and disappear from the action, allowing the tragic plot to continue. Other comic elements, however, center on characters who also contribute in a serious way to the tragedy. Mercutio, in *Romeo and Juliet*, delivers witty and lighthearted speeches early in the play, yet it is his death that gives the plot its first tragic turn.

Readers may therefore question the idea that Shakespeare actually saw tragedy as a distinct genre*, with specific qualities that set it apart from other genres. It is true that he seldom uses the words *tragedy* and *tragic* in the plays themselves. The plays identified as tragedies, however, do contain certain common elements. For example, the main character in a tragedy always dies. But this is not, by itself, sufficient to define the term. To explore the common elements of tragedy, it is useful to look at the heritage that influenced Elizabethan drama.

INFLUENCES ON ELIZABETHAN TRAGEDY

Shakespeare and other Elizabethan dramatists drew on two major traditions to create their tragedies. One centered on the writings of the ancient Greeks and Romans. The other was based on the morality plays* of the Middle Ages.

ANCIENT INFLUENCES. One major influence on Elizabethan dramatists was the *Poetics*, written by the ancient Greek philosopher Aristotle. This work contains an extended definition of tragedy. First, Aristotle claims, a tragedy is a serious, self-contained representation of a weighty subject. Second, it is written in "enriched," or poetic, language. Third, it is presented as "action," that is, as something happening in the present, rather than as a "narration" of something that happened in the past. Finally, it arouses the emotions of pity and terror in the audience and brings about

a *catharsis,* an ambiguous word often translated as "purging" or "purification." In other words, watching the tragedy cleanses the audience of negative or misguided emotions, making the viewers more clear-sighted and psychologically healthier as a result.

Aristotle goes on to claim that in order to arouse these emotions—pity and terror—the play must center on a tragic hero: someone who, like most viewers, is neither extremely virtuous nor extremely evil. The tragic hero should, however, be a person of high social standing, so that he falls from honor and prosperity into misery and, more often than not, death. His downfall results from a miscalculation or tragic flaw that becomes apparent during the course of the play. The definition of a tragic flaw, like that of a catharsis, is debatable. Some scholars have taken it to mean some sort of moral weakness or negative character trait, while others regard it primarily as an error of judgment.

Most of Shakespeare's tragedies, especially the most famous ones, appear to follow Aristotle's criteria. Othello, for example, is a character of high rank and reputation who has many virtues. The factor that causes his downfall and death is either a character trait (jealousy) or an error in judgment (trusting IAGO). Othello's suffering, and the suffering he causes others, arouses the emotions of pity and terror in the audience. This kind of straightforward analysis, however, is far too simple to explain a tragedy as complex as *Othello.* Even if this were not true, the fact remains that not all of the so-called tragedies follow so conventional a pattern.

Another ancient author who influenced Elizabethan tragedy was the Roman philosopher Seneca. Unlike Aristotle, Seneca wrote several tragedies himself. These plays were well known in Elizabethan England, studied in their original Latin in SCHOOLS AND UNIVERSITIES and available in an English translation that had been published in 1581. Seneca's plays are written in verse. His language is elaborate and vivid, and the events he depicts are so sensational that many critics find the overall effect of his dramas overwhelming. One of the most notable qualities in Seneca's writing is the way he shows the power of evil gradually destroying good. The evil he evokes is generally centered on a single person, but as the play proceeds it spreads to everyone and everything, with devastating results. Seneca's vivid descriptions of violent happenings have the power to shock even modern audiences used to the graphic violence of Hollywood movies. His influence is most clearly visible in Thomas Kyd's play *The Spanish Tragedy* (1589) and in Shakespeare's *Titus Andronicus* (1594).

MEDIEVAL INFLUENCES. During the 1900s many scholars began to question the extent of these ancient writers' influence on Elizabethan tragedy. Some focused instead on medieval* English plays that had been largely ignored by literary critics. Inspired by the Christian doctrines of the Middle Ages, these dramas focused on the terrors of hell, the trickery of Satan, and the suffering of Christ and the Christian martyrs*.

One important idea in these plays was the image of the "wheel of fortune." Fate was compared to a huge, ever-turning wheel on which all humans were bound. They could do nothing to control its turning, which

* *medieval* referring to the Middle Ages, a period roughly between A.D. 500 and 1500

* *martyr* one who suffers and dies rather than renounce his or her beliefs

could raise them up to happiness and prosperity or plunge them into misery and poverty. Tragic narratives based on this idea, which showed the falls of famous or distinguished men, were known as *de casibus* tragedies (short for *de casibus virorum illustrium*, or "on the downfalls of prominent persons"). These tales were designed to discourage the audience from thinking too much about earthly glory, which was sure to disappear, and to concentrate instead on preparing for the afterlife. The idea of the wheel of fortune appears in several of Shakespeare's tragedies. For example, in *King Lear*, the villain Edmund remarks just before he dies that "the wheel is come full circle" (V.iii.175).

Another aspect of the medieval morality plays that eventually found its way into Elizabethan drama is the figure known as the VICE, a tempter whose job was to recruit souls for the devil. Although he is evil, the Vice is also a curiously attractive character and a source of comic energy. The legacy of this figure can be seen in characters such as Edmund and Iago.

DEVELOPMENT OF SHAKESPEARE'S TRAGIC STYLE

Critics once claimed that Shakespeare's plays outlined the path of his career in a particular way. In the 1590s, according to this theory, Shakespeare was a young playwright experimenting and perfecting his art. Then in the early 1600s, he suffered some kind of depression that inspired him to write a series of tragedies. Toward the end of his career, he regained his inner peace and wrote the so-called romances. This view is now regarded with suspicion, partly because there is little evidence to support it and partly because it seems too neat and tidy for real life. It is clear, however, that Shakespeare's style evolved over the course of his career, especially with regard to the tragedies. Even his earliest tragedies are anything but simple; his later ones, however, are characterized by enormous complexity.

TWO REVENGE TRAGEDIES. The early play *Titus Andronicus* is a compelling revenge tragedy, a form that other Elizabethan playwrights had borrowed from Seneca. It follows a fairly standard pattern: one person takes revenge on a second person for an injury he has received. The second person then mounts a counterrevenge that is more grisly and violent than the first. The first person then responds even more horrifically, and so on to the end of the play. Unfortunately, the atrocities in *Titus Andronicus* are so bizarre that modern audiences have difficulty taking them seriously. Titus, for instance, is tricked into cutting off his own hand, while his daughter is raped and has her hands and tongue cut off. In due course he then murders the two rapists and serves them to their mother in a pie.

Hamlet also centers on an act of revenge, but in this later play Shakespeare takes a very different approach. He delays the bloodbath until the last act and instead focuses on revenge as an idea. Unlike Titus, Hamlet does not immediately plunge himself into bloody acts of retaliation at the request of his father's ghost. He contemplates his course and questions the justice of it; in the process he reflects on the very purpose of human existence.

A COMICAL TRAGEDY

One of Shakespeare's comedies, *A Midsummer Night's Dream,* contains a short play within the play, a tragedy described as "a tedious brief scene of young Pyramus and his love Thisbe; very tragical mirth." Theseus, the duke who is to watch this entertainment, complains about the contradictions of "Merry and tragical," but the phrase actually illustrates the difficulty of categorizing Shakespeare's plays. Both his comedies and his tragedies are likely to provoke laughter and tears at various times, so that any attempt to define the tragedies must also allow for their comical side.

See
color plate 2,
vol. 2.

TWO LOVE TRAGEDIES. It is not the case, however, that all of Shakespeare's early tragedies are simple. His two love-centered tragedies illustrate this point. *Romeo and Juliet,* an early play, is based on a poem called *Romeus and Juliet* written by Arthur Brooke. Shakespeare broadly follows the story, but he greatly enriches Brooke's characters and themes. For instance, Brooke takes a simple moral line, condemning the young lovers for their rashness and folly in marrying without their parents' consent. Shakespeare offers a more balanced view. He shows the young couple to be foolish and rash, but he also lets the audience witness their youthful enthusiasm, freshness, and overwhelming love for each other. The lovers' downfalls are presented not simply as the result of their own mistakes but also as calamities that reflect the follies of their elders and the workings of a cruel fate.

By the time Shakespeare wrote *Antony and Cleopatra* more than ten years later, his range and intellectual complexity had increased. As in most of his plays, the plot of this tragedy draws on a wide range of sources. Although there are a few passages that follow one of his sources almost word for word, the overall combination helps keep the play from being predictable or formulaic*. The finished product is far more complex and involved than the original material.

Unlike *Romeo and Juliet,* which is a "private" tragedy of two individuals, *Antony and Cleopatra* deals with two "public" figures. Their love for each other is combined with a desire for power. These two impulses, interacting and conflicting, eventually destroy the protagonists*. A similar conflict appears in most of Shakespeare's great tragedies, which typically focus on people who have public duties and are concerned with the exercise of power. From *Hamlet* to *Coriolanus* the dramatist explored the relationship between the "public" and the "private" sides of human life. The nature of this relationship, however, always remains ambiguous. Shakespeare provided no easily extractable moral statements, leaving the audience to find its own answers to the questions each play addresses. (*See also* **Education and Literacy; Fate and Fortune; Medievalism; Plays: The Histories; Playwrights and Poets; Shakespeare's Sources.**)

* *formulaic* according to a formula

* *protagonist* central character in a literary work

PLAYWRIGHTS AND POETS

Several major English playwrights and poets were active around the same time as Shakespeare. Not only did these writers influence one another, but many worked together to create works for the Elizabethan stage. Such collaborations were a common practice among dramatists of Shakespeare's day.

WRITERS OF THE LATE 1500s. When Shakespeare was beginning his career in the theater, John Lyly was England's most famous and fashionable playwright. Lyly's fame was based on his introduction of a new writing style, one that included an abundance of literary devices, such as metaphors* and similes*, and frequent references to ancient Greek and Roman mythology. Among Lyly's best plays are *Sapho and Phao, Gallathea,* and *Endimion.* Although his popularity declined after 1590, his

* *metaphor* figure of speech in which one object or idea is directly identified with a different object or idea

* *simile* figure of speech in which one object or idea is compared to another by the words *as, than,* or *like*

influence on Shakespeare was significant. More than 50 specific borrowings from Lyly have been identified in Shakespeare's plays. These debts to Lyly are most evident in two of Shakespeare's early comedies, *Love's Labor's Lost* and *A Midsummer Night's Dream*.

Lyly also influenced the English playwright Robert Greene, who wrote the first successful English romantic comedies, notable for their charming, gifted heroines. Greene was among the first English playwrights to successfully weave subplots into the main story. One of his most successful plays, *Friar Bacon and Friar Bungay*, helped prepare the way for Shakespeare's *The Tempest*. In addition to plays, Greene wrote novels, poetry, and pamphlets. In one of his pamphlets, called *Groatsworth of Wit*, he appears to accuse Shakespeare of plagiarism.

During his lifetime Sir Philip SIDNEY was a courtier, a soldier, and a statesman, but he is best remembered as a poet. His narrative *Arcadia* (1590) became a model for later pastoral* poetry. His most famous work, *Astrophel and Stella* (1591), was one of the earliest English sonnet* cycles and contained some of the finest examples of this genre*. Sidney was the patron* of several other writers, including the poet Sir Edmund SPENSER, who became famous for *The Faerie Queene* (1590), one of the greatest allegorical* poems in the English language.

Another writer who sought Sir Philip Sidney's patronage was Thomas Lodge. His poem *Scillaes Metamorphosis* (1589) strongly influenced Shakespeare's *Venus and Adonis*. Lodge also wrote plays, including *The Wounds of Civill War* and *A Looking Glasse for London and England* (cowritten with Robert Greene). He is best remembered, however, for his 1590 novel, *Rosalynde*, on which Shakespeare based *As You Like It*.

Christopher MARLOWE was born in 1564, the same year as Shakespeare. By the early 1590s his plays had earned him a reputation as one of Elizabethan England's greatest dramatists. The success of his first drama, *Tamburlaine the Great*, helped establish unrhymed iambic pentameter* as the standard form for the Elizabethan stage. Marlowe was especially famous for his tragedies, among them *The Tragical History of Doctor Faustus*, which is considered to be his masterpiece. He was also noted for his beautiful narrative poems, such as *Hero and Leander*. Marlowe's work was one of the most important influences on Shakespeare's writing. Shylock in *The Merchant of Venice* was probably modeled on Barabas, the central character in Marlowe's play *The Jew of Malta*.

Thomas Kyd was another Elizabethan dramatist who significantly influenced Shakespeare. Kyd published all his works anonymously, however, so there is no direct evidence that he wrote the plays that have been attributed to him. The best-known play attributed to Kyd, *The Spanish Tragedy*, tells of a father's delayed revenge for his murdered son. This drama almost certainly influenced *Hamlet*, one of Shakespeare's greatest works.

WRITERS OF THE EARLY 1600S. By 1600 George Chapman was ranked among the finest playwrights in England. His first successful play was a comedy called *The Blind Beggar of Alexandria*. Chapman wrote poetry as well as plays, but he is best known for his translations of ancient

* *pastoral* relating to the countryside; often used to draw a contrast between the innocence and serenity of rural life and the corruption and extravagance of court life

* *sonnet* poem of 14 lines with a fixed pattern of meter and rhyme

* *genre* literary form

* *patron* supporter or financial sponsor of an artist or writer

* *allegorical* referring to a literary device in which characters, events, and settings represent abstract qualities and in which the author intends a different meaning to be read beneath the surface

* *iambic pentameter* line of poetry consisting of ten syllables, or five metrical feet, with emphasis placed on every other syllable

Playwrights and Poets

* *satire* literary work ridiculing human wickedness and foolishness

Greek literature, including Homer's epics the *Iliad* and the *Odyssey*. It is evident that Chapman and Shakespeare influenced each other. Chapman borrowed some of the plot for *The Revenge of Bussy D'Ambois* from *Hamlet*. Shakespeare, in turn, drew on Chapman's translations of Greek literature for characters, plots, and even language.

Another prominent writer at this time was Ben JONSON. Known for his satire* and brilliant writing style, Jonson was considered by many to be the greatest Elizabethan playwright and poet. In 1598 he gained fame by writing a highly successful comedy, *Every Man in His Humour.* Over the next 15 years or so, he wrote several other successful plays, including *Volpone, Epicoene, The Alchemist,* and *Bartholomew Fair.* Jonson and Shakespeare clearly influenced each other. Jonson's play *Catiline* was modeled on Shakespeare's earlier Roman tragedies, and Shakespeare's *Timon of Athens* shows traces of Jonson's style. Jonson's contribution to English literature was considered so great that from 1616 until his death in 1637, he received a pension from the crown.

John Marston, one of Jonson's chief rivals, first gained fame as a poet with *The Metamorphosis of Pygmalion's Image* and *The Scourge of Villanie.* His best-known work, however, is a play called *The Malcontent.* An incident in Shakespeare's *King Lear* appears to have been borrowed from this play. Meanwhile in Marston's poem *The Scourge of Villanie* there is a reference to Shakespeare's *Romeo and Juliet.*

Near the end of the 1500s, an English playwright and actor named Robert Armin joined Shakespeare's acting company. Armin played the parts of clowns and fools, including Touchstone in *As You Like It.* It is likely that Shakespeare created several of his comic roles just to take advantage

Shakespeare and several of his contemporaries met regularly at the Mermaid tavern on the first Friday of each month. This literary circle, known as the Friday Street Club, included playwrights Ben Jonson, John Fletcher, and Francis Beaumont.

of Armin's talent. Armin's own plays include the comedies *The Italian Taylor and His Boy* and *Two Maids of More-clack,* both of which appeared in 1609.

The previous year English playwrights John Fletcher and Francis Beaumont began their writing careers by collaborating on the first play either of them had written. Over the next few years Beaumont and Fletcher cowrote at least five more plays, including one called *Philaster.* The similarity between *Philaster* and *Hamlet* shows Shakespeare's influence on their writing. In 1612 when Shakespeare retired as the leading playwright of the KING'S MEN, Fletcher replaced him. It appears that Fletcher then began collaborating with Shakespeare because Beaumont had retired from writing. At least three of the plays attributed to Shakespeare may actually have been written in collaboration with Fletcher: *The Two Noble Kinsmen, Cardenio* (now lost), and *Henry VIII.*

While writing for the King's Men, Fletcher also collaborated with playwright Philip Massinger, and together they wrote several plays for the company. When Fletcher died in 1625, Massinger took over as leading playwright. Many of the plays he wrote were influenced by Shakespeare's work. For example, his best-known comedy, *A New Way to Pay Old Debts,* was influenced by *The Merchant of Venice.* The most memorable character of Massinger's play, Sir Giles Overreach, was probably based on Shakespeare's Shylock. It has been estimated that Massinger modeled the language in his plays on lines from at least 23 of Shakespeare's works.

English playwright and poet William Davenant began his career in the late 1620s. He wrote frequently for the royal court, where he was a favorite of King JAMES I. A number of his plays were adaptations of Shakespeare's works, among them *Macbeth* and *Hamlet.* Davenant rewrote most of the dialogue to eliminate what he considered coarse language and to make the plays easier to understand. Davenant also wrote original plays and several operas. (*See also* **Acting Companies, Elizabethan; Authorship, Theories About; Groatsworth of Wit; Literature and Drama; Shakespeare, Life and Career.**)

SHAKESPEARE'S "SON"

One of the enduring mysteries of Shakespeare's life is his relationship to the playwright William Davenant, who was born in 1606. On more than one occasion Davenant claimed that he was Shakespeare's son. By way of explanation he added that Shakespeare used to stay at his parents' inn, which was on the road between Stratford-upon-Avon and London. Although there is little evidence to support Davenant's claim that he was Shakespeare's child, many historians believe that he was the playwright's godson.

PLUTARCH'S LIVES

* *rhetoric* art of speaking or writing effectively

* *patronage* support or financial sponsorship

Written around the turn of the first century, *Parallel Lives* is a collection of biographies of ancient Greeks and Romans written by the Greek philosopher Plutarch. Commonly known as Plutarch's *Lives,* this work provided source material for several of Shakespeare's plays.

Plutarch was born around A.D. 46 in the town of Chaeronea and educated in the Greek city-state of Athens. He then traveled to Rome, where he became a successful teacher of philosophy and rhetoric*. As his fame grew he received the patronage* of the Roman emperors Hadrian and Trajan. During his years in Rome, Plutarch wrote many texts about religion, politics, and ethics.

After Trajan died in 117, Plutarch returned to Boeotia, where he produced *Parallel Lives,* a series of 50 biographies of Greeks and Romans whom he described as "noble." All but four of these accounts were arranged in pairs, with a brief passage comparing the people in each pair. Plutarch intended the biographies and comparisons to serve as moral lessons, often examining the reasons for the successes and failures of extraordinary people.

Plutarch's *Lives* was rediscovered and highly valued during the Renaissance. A French edition from 1559 was translated into English 20 years later by Thomas North. Shakespeare drew on the *Lives* frequently, using it as his major source for *Antony and Cleopatra, Coriolanus*, and *Julius Caesar*, and to a lesser extent for *A Midsummer Night's Dream* and *Timon of Athens*. (*See also* **Holinshed's Chronicles; Shakespeare's Sources.**)

POETIC TECHNIQUES

* **metaphor** figure of speech in which one object or idea is directly identified with a different object or idea

O ne of Shakespeare's greatest talents was his effective use of poetic techniques to make his characters' speeches more dramatic. Among these devices meter and rhyme work through the sound of lines, while IMAGERY and metaphor* affect meaning more directly. Wordplay and figures of speech use connections between word sounds, phrasal patterns, and meaning to help the language mirror complex human relationships. Other POETS AND PLAYWRIGHTS used these techniques too, but Shakespeare—like any good writer—developed them in his own way. They help make the speeches of his characters more intense and expressive and suggest many further levels of meaning.

METER AND RHYME. A popular meter for Elizabethan verse was iambic pentameter. In this pattern each line normally has ten syllables, with emphasis placed on every other syllable. This creates a line of five iambs, where each iamb, or metrical foot, consists of a weak syllable followed by a strong one. A line of iambic pentameter can be illustrated with graphic marks that show the weak and strong syllables. The symbol / indicates a strong syllable, ˘ indicates a weak one, and syllables marked with \ are intermediate—stressed but not heavily stressed. Individual iambs may be separated by a vertical line—not to suggest a pause but to show how the pattern of stressed and unstressed syllables fits into, or differs from, the basic meter.

> ˘ /   ˘ /   ˘ /   ˘   /   ˘ /
> I could | a tale | unfold | whose light | est word
> (*Hamlet*, I.v.15)

By the time Shakespeare began writing his plays and poems, iambic pentameter was well established as the standard meter for SONNETS, narrative poems, and heroic plays*. Shakespeare followed this convention*, but like other talented poets of his day, he varied it considerably. For example, most lines of iambic pentameter had a break in phrasing near the middle, usually after the fourth syllable. By varying the placement of this break, Shakespeare (and others) created lines that sounded less monotonous and more like everyday speech:

* **heroic play** dramatic work that focuses on a tragic hero or historical leader, such as *Hamlet, King Lear,* or *Richard II*
* **convention** established practice

> To-morrow, and to-morrow, and to-morrow
> > (*Macbeth*, V.v.19)

> Her father lov'd me, oft invited me
> > (*Othello*, I.iii.128)

> If music be the food of love, play on
> > (*Twelfth Night*, I.i.1)

Another way to make iambic pentameter sound more natural is to vary the standard pattern of stressed and unstressed syllables. One common variation is the use of a feminine ending, an extra unstressed syllable placed at the end of a line:

> ˘ / ˘ / ˘ / ˘ / ˘ / ˘
> And all the men and women mere | ly players
> > (*As You Like It*, II.vii.140)

Another variation, called a spondee, places emphasis on an important syllable in a normally weak position:

> \ / ˘ / ˘ / ˘ / \ /
> Bare ru | ined choirs, where late the sweet | birds sang
> > (Sonnet 73, line 4)

Very different from a spondee is a pyrrhic foot, which places a normally unstressed syllable in a strong position:

> ˘ / ˘ ˘ ˘ / ˘ ˘ ˘ /
> My boun | ty is | as bound | less as | the sea
> > (*Romeo and Juliet*, II.ii.133)

Finally, a trochee reverses the basic iambic stress pattern, a stressed syllable is followed by (or precedes) an unstressed one:

> / ˘ ˘ / ˘ / ˘ / ˘ /
> Nothing | will come of nothing, speak again.
> > (*King Lear*, I.i.90)

These variations are found in Shakespeare's poems as well as in his plays. But there is an essential difference between these two kinds of verse. In sonnets or rhymed stanzas*, the rhymes keep showing the verse structure. But a play is constructed of speeches, not stanzas, and speeches need to sound as if real people might actually say them. Because no real person speaks in rhyme, Shakespeare's characters usually speak in blank verse, which is unrhymed iambic pentameter. (They also often speak prose.) As Shakespeare reduced his use of rhyme in the plays, he let the phrasing of his sentences spill over line endings:

> In such a night
> Stood Dido with a willow in her hand
> Upon the wild sea-banks, and waft her love
> To come again to Carthage.
> > (*The Merchant of Venice*, V.i.9–12)

* stanza section of a poem; specifically, a grouping of lines into a recurring pattern determined by meter or rhyme scheme

Poetic Techniques

Short lines created when sentences end in midline are usually completed by another character's words. This makes for lively dialogue. The two characters effectively share the line, creating a musical exchange very different from the stiff speeches common on the stage when Shakespeare began to write.

Shakespeare sometimes made lines longer or shorter than expected, usually for some dramatic purpose. Omitting a line's first syllable may show the speaker's impatience:

> ⌣ /
> Set | it down. Is ink and paper ready?
> (*Richard III*, V.iii.75)

On the other hand, adding a sixth iamb to a line may emphasize some phrasal contrast because 12-syllable lines tend to divide rhythmically in half:

> To have what we would have, we speak not what we mean
> (*Measure for Measure*, II.iv.117)

The long and short lines of Shakespeare's plays are very different from the patterned rhyming of his poems, in which each stanza ends with a rhymed couplet*. In the poems, the rhyme and the thought finish together:

> Were beauty under twenty locks held *fast*,
> Yet love breaks through, and picks them all at *last*.
> (*Venus and Adonis*, lines 575–76)

The development of ideas and the buildup of emotion are also different in the poems. In the plays many characters with vastly different thoughts and attitudes are usually delivering blank-verse speeches, constantly answering one another in a running dialogue. In the predictable verse structures of a sonnet or stanza by contrast, the lyric or narrative voice is basically continuous and uninterrupted, although its tone may vary considerably.

FIGURES OF SPEECH AND WORDPLAY. Writers in Shakespeare's time frequently used classical* figures of speech, techniques of rhetoric* that serve a variety of dramatic purposes. They learned dozens of such devices at school and consciously used them to make the verbal patterning of their lines tense, intricate, and often amusing.

Many figures of speech involve repetition. Stylebooks of Shakespeare's time distinguished between words or phrases immediately repeated, repeated after an interval, or repeated in reverse order. In a passage from *Hamlet* the long-winded Polonius uses all three kinds of repetition when the queen urges him to use "more matter with less art." He replies:

> Madam, I swear I use no art at all.
> That he's mad, *'tis true, 'tis true 'tis pity,*
> And *pity 'tis 'tis true*
>
> (II.ii.96–98)

* **couplet** pair of rhyming lines that appear together, as at the end of a sonnet or stanza of verse

* **classical** in the tradition of ancient Greece and Rome
* **rhetoric** art of speaking or writing effectively

176

Later in the play the king focuses on a cluster of mainly simple words, whose continually varying repetition mirrors the constant circling of his own guilty thoughts:

> *What* then? *What* rests?
> Try *what repentance can. What can it not?*
> Yet *what can it*, when one *cannot repent*?
> (III.iii.64–66)

In addition to repetition, this passage makes effective use of alliteration. This technique involves the use of several words that begin with the same initial sound, in this case *w* (heard in the repeated word *what* and the unrepeated words *when* and *one*. The repetition of the *w* sound heightens the sense of a fixed idea, repeating itself without ever moving forward. Shakespeare constantly employed alliteration and other types of sound patterning, such as the repetition of vowel sounds in the middle of words.

Another form of wordplay is a pun, which is made by placing near each other two words that are similar in sound but different in meaning. Such a play on words appears in Lady Macbeth's lines about her plan to frame two innocent servants for the murder of King Duncan:

> If he do bleed,
> I'll *gild* the faces of the grooms withal,
> For it must seem their *guilt*.
> (*Macbeth*, II.ii.52–54)

METAPHORS AND IMAGERY. One of Shakespeare's greatest strengths was the vividness of his metaphors and similes*. In some speeches, particularly those dealing with love, he used the conventional imagery of his time, as in *The Taming of the Shrew*:

> Tranio, I saw her *coral* lips to move,
> And with her breath she did *perfume* the air.
> (I.i.174–75)

In other cases, he moved beyond convention with the use of suggestive single words, such as "'Tis deepest *winter* in Lord Timon's purse" (*Timon of Athens*, III.iv.15) and with more developed figures of speech:

> If I must die,
> I will encounter darkness as a *bride*,
> And hug it in mine arms.
> (*Measure for Measure*, III.i.82–84)

Whether brief or elaborate, such figures typically heighten the emotion of a passage by bringing another world into the immediate scene and situation—for example, calling affected poetry "the forc'd gait of a shuffling nag" (*Henry IV, Part 1*, III.i.133) or describing soldiers eager for combat as "greyhounds in the slips*" (*Henry V*, III.i.31).

Shakespeare gives tragic characters, in particular, figures of speech memorable for their sharpness, energy, and patterned phrasing. The ghost of Hamlet's father reveals his murderer in a dramatic image:

* simile figure of speech in which one object or idea is compared to another by the words *as, than*, or *like*

* slip type of leash from which an animal's head can be withdrawn quickly

To Fit the Meter

Shakespeare and his contemporaries often heard some combinations of syllables as compressed. It was common to compress such words as *natural* and *general* to *nat'ral* and *gen'ral.* Words such as *flower, power, fire, being,* and *knowing* might be pronounced as one syllable or as two, depending on what the meter required. On the other hand the suffix *-tion,* which in modern English takes only one syllable, was often pronounced as two: *ti-on.* Words such as *soldier, ocean,* and *marriage* could be spoken as three syllables.

The serpent that did sting thy father's life
Now wears his crown.

> (*Hamlet,* I.v.39–40)

Likewise, Macbeth personifies life as "a walking shadow, a poor player, / That struts and frets his hour upon the stage" and thinks of it as "a tale / Told by an idiot, full of sound and fury" (*Macbeth,* V.v.24–27).

Abstractions are often personified in this way, as when Constance in *King John* laments her absent son:

Grief fills the room up of my absent child,
Lies in his bed, walks up and down with me.

> (III.iv.93–94)

A similar personification appears in *Troilus and Cressida,* as Ulysses reminds Achilles how quickly honor and fame decay:

For Time is like a fashionable host
That slightly shakes his parting guest by th' hand,
And with his arms outstretch'd as he would fly,
Grasps in the comer.

> (III:iii.165–68)

Shakespeare's images frequently come in clusters and set up symbolic networks of meaning. In *Richard II* the words *earth, land,* and *soil* appear together, as do *crown, words,* and *breath. Hamlet* is notoriously full of references to disease, ulcers, sickness, infection, weeds, corruption, and maggots. Food, cooking, and disease are linked in *Troilus and Cressida;* Macbeth's ill-fated ambition finds a metaphorical echo in ill-fitting clothes. Still more vividly, the mental agony of King Lear is reflected in images that critic Caroline Spurgeon has described as "a human body in anguished movement, tugged, wrenched, beaten, pierced, stung, scourged, dislocated, flayed, gashed, scalded, tortured, and finally broken on the rack."

POETIC TECHNIQUES IN CONTEXT. Shakespeare often used a variety of poetic techniques within a single speech to reflect the rise and fall of passion within the speaker. An example appears in *Macbeth.* After Macbeth has murdered King Duncan, framed two grooms for his murder, and then murdered the grooms to prevent anyone from questioning them, he tries to explain away this violent act to the Scottish lords:

Who can | be wise, amaz'd, | temp'rate, | and furious,

Loyal | and neu | tral, in | a mo | ment? No man.

The expedi | tion of | my vio | lent love

Outrun the pauser, reason. Here | lay Duncan,

His silver skin | lac'd with | his golden blood,

And his | gash'd stabs | look'd like | a breach | in nature

For ruin's wasteful entrance; there, | the murtherers,

Steep'd in | the co | lors of | their trade, | their daggers

Unman | nerly breech'd | with gore. | Who could | refrain,

That had a heart to love, and in that heart

Courage | to make's | love known?

(II.iii.108–18)

Shakespeare conveys Macbeth's disturbed state of mind by varying the meter dramatically throughout the speech, including many run-on lines. Macbeth graphically contrasts Duncan (pointed to, *"Here"*) with his "murderers" (*"there"*) and almost brutally reenacts the physical act of murder through powerful, stabbing monosyllables* *(skin, lac'd, blood, gash'd, stabs, look'd, breach, Steep'd, breech'd,* and *gore).* The evaluative words, by contrast, often take the rhythm of trochees *(silver, golden, nature, ruin's, wasteful, entrance, murderers, colours),* touching the scene with a ghastly repetitive murmur. The specific references to *daggers* and *breech'd* and *gore* fix the act and its meaning vividly in the minds of Macbeth's listeners. Finally, his opening question *(Who can be wise . . .)* finds a patterned echo in the final one *(Who could refrain . . .).* Together the two questions allow Macbeth to suggest falsely that anyone would have done the same thing.

Through such combinations of techniques, Shakespeare enabled his characters to express forcefully their varied feelings of impatience, anger, regret, love, wonder, puzzlement, suffering, or despair. At the same time, their emotional speeches connect their feelings and situations to larger questions, issues, and perspectives. As a result the specific predicaments and behavior of Shakespeare's various characters in "this insubstantial pageant" have taken on the universal coloring of "the great globe itself" (*The Tempest,* IV.i.153–55). (*See also* **Dramatic Technique; Humor in Shakespeare's Plays; Imagery; Language; Poetry of Shakespeare; Prose Technique.**)

* monosyllable one-syllable word

POETRY OF SHAKESPEARE

Although Shakespeare is best remembered for his plays, he also produced an outstanding body of nondramatic poetry. In fact it was the narrative poem *Venus and Adonis,* not one of his plays, for which he was most famous during his lifetime.

Although Shakespeare's poetry was influenced by the literary traditions of his day, his best poems have qualities that give them a timeless appeal. Like his plays they reveal his brilliant use of the English language and his gift for using literary conventions* in new and unexpected ways. Some images and themes found in the poems echo those that Shakespeare explored in the plays.

* **convention** established practice

USE AND ADAPTATION OF POETIC TRADITIONS

Shakespeare's nondramatic works are *Venus and Adonis, The Rape of Lucrece,* "The Phoenix and Turtle," *A Lover's Complaint,* and the *Sonnets.* Each of these works falls within a literary category that would have been familiar to educated readers of the poet's time. Shakespeare both adhered to and transformed familiar poetic traditions. Scholars often point out that his mature work is characterized by less adherence to the literary conventions of the time.

VENUS AND ADONIS. Shakespeare's earliest published poem, *Venus and Adonis,* which he called "the first heir of my invention," was printed in the spring of 1593. Scholars believe that the poet may have composed both this and his next poem during a period when London's theaters were closed due to an outbreak of plague*, which gave him the time to devote to other types of writing. The earliest recognition of Shakespeare's work that has survived in print came from his contemporaries, who praised the poems.

* **plague** highly contagious and often fatal disease; also called the Black Death

Venus and Adonis is a narrative in 199 stanzas*, each containing six lines. Shakespeare borrowed this six-line form from a poem by Thomas Lodge that also mentioned the classical* myth of Venus, the goddess of love, and Adonis, the handsome youth who is killed by a wild boar. Lodge's poem, which was published in 1589, drew on subject matter he had found in the works of Ovid, an ancient Roman poet whose verses were prominent among Shakespeare's sources.

* **stanza** section of a poem; specifically, a grouping of lines into a recurring pattern determined by meter or rhyme scheme
* **classical** in the tradition of ancient Greece and Rome

Like Christopher Marlowe's *Hero and Leander* (1598), Shakespeare's *Venus and Adonis* belongs to the genre* of mythological-erotic poems, which retold tales of passion from Ovid and later Italian writers. These poems celebrated beauty and the senses and were popular with sophisticated courtiers. Shakespeare dedicated *Venus and Adonis* to just such a courtier, Henry Wriothesley, the earl of Southampton.

* **genre** literary form

Although Shakespeare was revisiting a well-known myth, he changed the story significantly. Instead of having an adoring man pursue the love goddess, Shakespeare shows the passionate Venus attempting to seduce the comely Adonis, who resists her advances. The poet borrowed the idea of a female pursuer from Ovid's story of the nymph Salmacis and the god Hermaphroditus.

THE RAPE OF LUCRECE. Shakespeare also dedicated his second narrative poem, *The Rape of Lucrece* (1594), to Southampton. The poet called *Lucrece* a "graver," more serious work than *Venus and Adonis,* and it belongs to the complaint genre that was popular during the second half of

During his lifetime Shakespeare was admired more for his poetry than for his plays. This image is from the title page of a collection of Shakespeare's poems published in 1640.

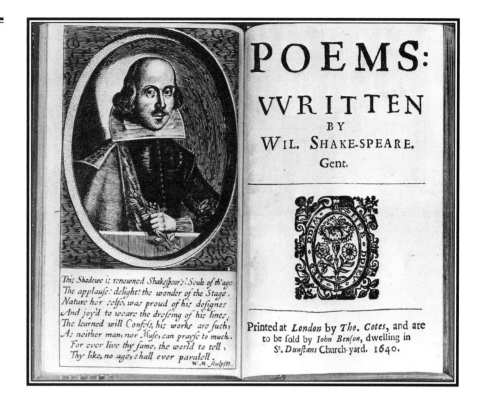

This Shadowe is renowned Shakespear's Soule of th'age
The applause! delight! the wonder of the Stage.
Nature her selfe, was proud of his designes
And joy'd to weare the dressing of his lines,
The learned will Confes, his works are such,
As neither man, nor Muse, can prayse to much.
For ever live thy fame, the world to tell,
Thy like, no age, shall ever paralell.
                                    W. M. sculpsit.

POEMS:
WRITTEN
BY
WIL. SHAKE-SPEARE.
Gent.

Printed at *London* by *The. Cotes*, and are to be sold by *Iohn Benson*, dwelling in St. *Dunstans* Church-yard. 1640.

* **medieval** referring to the Middle Ages, a period roughly between A.D. 500 and 1500

* **evocative** producing an emotional response

the 1500s. Poems of this type were intended to express unhappiness. A highly praised volume called *The Mirror for Magistrates* contained several such poems, featuring the ghosts of famous people who told the stories of their downfalls and grievances. Samuel Daniel's *Complaint of Rosamund* (1593), about the mistress of King Henry II, may have influenced Shakespeare, who used the same seven-line stanza form in *Lucrece* that Daniel had popularized in *Rosamund*.

The Rape of Lucrece is a 1,855-line narrative poem about the ravishing of a Roman wife and her subsequent decision to commit suicide because of the shame brought on her family. The story was well known to English readers from numerous retellings by Ovid and the medieval* English poet Geoffrey Chaucer. It is more a somber and dramatic work than *Venus and Adonis,* but a major virtue of both poems is their polished, clever, and evocative* use of language. Both works were widely admired by Elizabethans. In 1598 poet Richard Barnfield wrote that *Venus and Adonis* and *The Rape of Lucrece* had placed Shakespeare's name "in fames immortall Booke." But Gabriel Harvey, a friend of the poet Sir Edmund Spenser, did not consider the two poems to be of equal merit. He wrote, "The younger sort takes much delight in Shakespeare's *Venus and Adonis;* but his *Lucrece,* and his tragedy of *Hamlet, Prince of Denmark,* have it in them to please the wiser sort."

Shakespeare reworked tradition again in *The Rape of Lucrece.* He abandoned the conventional framework of the complaint genre, which typically included a wailing ghost who told a grievous story. Instead he had a third party, a narrator, recount the tragedy of Lucretia at the hands of the villainous Tarquin. The narrator not only recites events but also presents

181

the reflections of both characters. A large section of the poem consists of Lucretia's woeful speeches.

"THE PHOENIX AND TURTLE." Published in 1601, "The Phoenix and Turtle," a 67-line poem, has been something of a puzzle to critics because it is unlike anything else that Shakespeare wrote. Like earlier poems about assemblies of birds, such as Chaucer's *Parlement of Fowls*, "The Phoenix and Turtle" uses a gathering of various species, including an eagle, a swan, and a crow, each with distinctive characteristics and symbolic meanings, as a starting point for considering a topic of morality. In Shakespeare's poem that subject is the nature of true love, which combines passion (represented by the phoenix, the mythological bird that supposedly dies in flames only to rise again from the ashes) and faithfulness (represented by the turtledove). According to some critics, the complex figures of speech in the work resemble those found in the poems of John Donne. He and other poets writing during the 1600s developed the school of metaphysical poetry that was characterized in part by striking imagery*.

"The Phoenix and Turtle" is unconventional in many ways, especially in its symbolism. The phoenix was traditionally an emblem of immortality, while the turtle, or turtledove, had long been recognized by writers and readers alike as an emblem of female constancy, or faithfulness. Shakespeare ignored the phoenix's association with immortality and made the mythological bird's flames represent passion. The turtle, meanwhile, was presented as male, not female, with the phoenix as "his queen." The two birds perish together in "a mutual flame" that fuses their qualities, passion and faithfulness, into a unified emblem of ideal love.

A LOVER'S COMPLAINT. Published in 1609, *A Lover's Complaint* remains the least known of Shakespeare's poems, and until recently some critics doubted that Shakespeare had written it, even though it first appeared in his volume of *Sonnets*. Like *The Rape of Lucrece*, this 329-line work is, as its title implies, a complaint poem, and it is written in the same seven-line stanza form as *Lucrece*. About three-fourths of the poem consists of speeches by a girl whose lover has abandoned her. She tells her story as she sits by a stream, throwing his letters and gifts into the water.

As he did with *The Rape of Lucrece*, Shakespeare here altered a basic convention of the complaint poem. The girl who makes the complaint against her faithless lover is neither dead nor famous. She is simply a "maid full pale" who is losing her youth and beauty. She mourns an unfortunate love affair and unburdens herself to a passing stranger.

SONNET FORM AND SEQUENCES

One of the literary conventions of Shakespeare's day was the sonnet sequence, a series of poems that explored a theme, told a story, or dealt with related subjects. The sonnet—normally 14 lines with a fixed pattern of

* *imagery* pictorial quality of a literary work, achieved through words

meter and rhyme—was highly popular in England during the 1590s, when Shakespeare wrote his. Shakespeare generally wrote in a form called the English sonnet, and because his poems are among the best-known examples of it, this genre is frequently referred to as the Shakespearean sonnet. Each such poem consists of three quatrains (four lines of rhyming verse) followed by a couplet*.

USE OF THE TRADITIONAL SONNET FORM. The 154 untitled poems known as Shakespeare's *Sonnets* are today his most admired nondramatic work, although they seem to have been considered inferior during his lifetime and for some time after his death. In the best of Shakespeare's sonnets, the formal structure reinforces the subject matter of the poem, which develops in the three quatrains and is summed up—or sometimes surprisingly reversed—in the final couplet.

Shakespeare's sonnets were not published until 1609, although it seems likely that at least some of them circulated among the poet's acquaintances. Sonnets 1 through 126 concern the poet's relationship with an upper-class young man who becomes a beloved friend. The remaining sonnets (127 through 154) tend to focus on his romantic relationship with a woman known to Shakespeare scholars as the DARK LADY. Through the years critics have attempted to identify the male friend and the Dark Lady, but most readers agree that the sonnets are more valuable as literature than as autobiography.

ADAPTATIONS OF THE SONNET FORM. Shakespeare's ability to work within a tradition but to transform it to suit his own purposes is most clearly demonstrated in the *Sonnets*. Sonnet 29 offers an example of how the poet used the formal structure of the sonnet as a framework for expressing a series of thoughts. In the first quatrain, he complains of his misfortunes and his lowly status. In the second he compares his condition to that of others. In the third quatrain, the sorrowful mood of the poem changes when the thought of his good friend lifts the poet's spirits. By the time he reaches the couplet, the poet is so convinced of his good fortune that he would not change places with the highest of mortals: "For thy sweet love remem'b'red such wealth brings / That then I scorn to change my state with kings" (13–14).

Shakespeare generally stayed within the rules that governed the formal structure of sonnets, but he played with the conventional subject matter of sonnet sequences in ways that probably seemed startling and fresh to Elizabethan readers. Typically, sonnet sequences were modeled on the works of Petrarch, an Italian poet of the 1300s. One sequence consisted of a series of lovesick poems addressed to the poet's lady. They praised her beauties and virtues, assured her of the high-minded and spiritual nature of the poet's devotion to her, and cataloged all the symptoms of the poet's passion, such as his inability to eat, sleep, or think of anything but her. Shakespeare's sonnets altered this pattern in several significant ways. For example, the subject of most of Shakespeare's sonnets, and the object of the poet's affection, is a man. Instead of being entirely concerned with love, many of the poems deal with subjects such as time, age,

* *couplet* pair of rhyming lines that appear together, as at the end of a sonnet or stanza of verse

WHO READ SHAKESPEARE'S POEMS?

Shakespeare's plays appealed to audiences of all social classes, including people who could not read. The poems, however, required a literate audience. In the century before Shakespeare, serious writers grappled with the question of whether to write in scholarly Latin or in the languages that people spoke every day. By the 1590s most English writers were writing in English, but literacy was still largely limited to the court, the universities, and the growing middle class. In poems such as *Venus and Adonis*, Shakespeare wrote for an elite audience that would have appreciated the classical references and courtly tone.

death, memory, and the power of poetry to give a kind of immortality to a person, a moment, or a thought.

The sonnets that depict the poet's relationship with his lover, the Dark Lady, present a woman and a relationship that conflict with the Petrarchan ideal. The ladies in earlier sonnet sequences were typically blond and virtuous. Shakespeare's female companion is neither. In Sonnet 130 he pokes gentle fun at the conventions by which women's eyes were always brighter than the sun, their lips redder than coral, their skin whiter than snow, and their hair like golden wires:

> My mistress' eyes are nothing like the sun;
> Coral is far more red than her lips' red;
> If snow be white, why then her breasts are dun;
> If hairs be wires, black wires grow on her head.
>
> (1–4)

The sonnet describes a down-to-earth woman who fails to match up to any traditional standard. In the couplet, however, the poet declares that she is as admirable as any artificial creation.

The most significant difference between Shakespeare's Dark Lady and the ordinary sonneteer's beloved lies not in her coloring but in her character and in the poet's response to her. She is not an airy, virtuous, superior being but a deceitful and lustful creature who may well have betrayed her husband by loving the poet and in turn betrays the poet by loving his upper-class friend. Unlike his contemporaries, the poet who speaks in Shakespeare's sonnets admits that his love for this woman is purely sensual and physical. He also confesses that he is ashamed of himself for yielding to a passion he cannot justify. Such emotional honesty—and the recognition that human character and action are seldom simply good or evil—make these sonnets seem timeless.

CONNECTIONS WITH THE PLAYS. Scholars have traced many links between Shakespeare's poems and his plays. The sonnets, or at least some of them, were almost certainly composed in the early 1590s. Shakespeare was also writing plays at that time, and his experimentation with the sonnet form enriches *Love's Labor's Lost.* Seven sonnets appear in this comedy, some of them in the dialogue and others as songs. Sonnets also figure prominently in *Romeo and Juliet.*

The subject matter of *The Rape of Lucrece,* an overwhelming desire that leads to a tragic rape and its sorrowful and destructive consequences, may already have appeared in Shakespeare's work before he wrote the poem. In the early revenge tragedy *Titus Andronicus,* probably written around 1590, the playwright incorporated Ovid's story of the rape of Philomel by Tereus. Because they deal with similar events and emotions, parts of *Titus Andronicus* and *The Rape of Lucrece* are closely related. Images and phrases in one work often echo those of the other.

The Rape of Lucrece also bears some similarities to *Macbeth,* a tragedy written a decade after the poem. In *Lucrece,* Shakespeare describes Tarquin creeping toward Lucretia: "Now stole upon the time the dead of night, / When heavy sleep had clos'd up mortal eyes" (162–63). These lines are similar to the scene in which Macbeth prepares to murder King Duncan: "Now o'er the one half world / Nature seems dead, and wicked dreams abuse / The curtain'd sleep" (Macbeth, II.i.49–51). The connection between the poem and the play becomes even more evident a few lines later, when the murderer moves toward his victim "with Tarquin's ravishing strides" (II.i.55). The rape that occurs in *Lucrece* is a kind of murder, and Macbeth shares some character traits and actions with Tarquin. Another similarity is that both Tarquin and Macbeth give several reasons why they should not commit their damnable crimes but then commit them anyway.

The Rape of Lucrece is also echoed in *Cymbeline,* written five years after *Macbeth.* Although Imogen is not physically attacked, the villain Iachimo temporarily destroys her happiness by falsely convincing her husband that he has enjoyed her sexual favors.

While hiding in Imogen's bedroom, Iachimo refers to himself as "Tarquin" and notices that she has been reading the story of Philomel and Tereus. These references would have signaled to audiences familiar with Ovid that Iachimo's plot against Imogen—to destroy her virtuous reputation—was comparable to the rape committed by Tarquin.

Such connections are reminders that Shakespeare's plays and poetry influenced each other. As his career developed he devoted more of his time to the plays for which he is most widely recognized. His poetry was a vital part of that career, however, drawing on the same sources, images, and themes as the plays. Shakespeare's poems reveal a writer experimenting with various forms and structures, and they provide an opportunity to view his creative powers from different perspectives. (*See also* **Lover's Complaint, A; Passionate Pilgrim, The; Phoenix and Turtle, The; Poetic Techniques; Rape of Lucrece, The; Sonnets; Venus and Adonis.**)

POLONIUS

Polonius is the lord chamberlain of Denmark, in the service of Claudius, the king in *Hamlet.* He is also the father of two other important characters: OPHELIA, who is the beloved of Prince Hamlet, and Laertes, who plays a part in the prince's murder.

Polonius is a deceptive and hypocritical man, and his character is symptomatic of moral decay in the play. Convinced that Prince Hamlet's love for Ophelia is merely lust, he forbids his daughter to speak to the prince. Later when Hamlet appears to be insane, Polonius uses his daughter to help the king discover what is troubling the prince. He contrives a meeting between Ophelia and Hamlet so that he and the king can eavesdrop on their conversation. Later, hiding behind an arras (curtain) in the queen's chamber, Polonius spies on Hamlet again, this time to overhear a conversation between the prince and his mother. A noise from behind the curtain gives Polonius away, however, and Hamlet, thinking it is Claudius, fatally stabs the king's minister.

Polonius is often regarded as a pompous and somewhat detestable old man. He shows little concern for his daughter, callously using her to

gain information about the prince. In addition, his famous advice to his son, "to thine own self be true, / And it must follow, as the night the day, / Thou canst not then be false to any man" (I.iii.78–80), seems hypocritical, especially when he later instructs a servant on how best to spy on Laertes.

Nevertheless, most critics regard Polonius as comical rather than villainous. They argue that his foolish behavior, such as when he says, "brevity is the soul of wit" (II.ii.90) and then proceeds to give a long-winded speech, softens his character. Consequently, his murder seems to deepen the sense of impending tragedy in the play.

POPULATION

* *plague* highly contagious and often fatal disease; also called the Black Death

Between Shakespeare's birth in 1564 and his death in 1616, the number of people living in England grew from about 3 million to almost 5 million. Although 5 million is less than a tenth of England's present-day population, the increase of almost 2 million people in just 50 years signaled a population boom that would not be seen again until around 1800.

One reason England's numbers grew so quickly during the 1500s was a decline in the death rate, due in part to the country's relative freedom from plague*, typhus, influenza, and other deadly diseases. Many children still died young, however, with about one in seven expiring before their first birthdays. Nevertheless, the increasing survival rates resulted in a growing number of young people. About one Elizabethan in three was under the age of 15.

During Shakespeare's lifetime, England's population was largely rural. Most people lived in villages of fewer than 500 people. Of those who lived in towns, the majority lived in areas of between 500 and 5,000 people. Shakespeare's birthplace of STRATFORD-UPON-AVON was home to about 200 families. Less than 10 percent of England's inhabitants lived in towns of more than 5,000, and more than half of those lived in LONDON. The population of London grew even faster during the 1500s than the population of England as a whole, and by 1600 it had reached more than 200,000. Much of this increase was due to the migration of rural people (including Shakespeare) to the city. Other than London, only three towns—Norwich, Bristol, and York—had populations greater than 10,000 people by 1600. (*See also* **Cities, Towns, and Villages; Geography.**)

POVERTY AND WEALTH

Poverty was a major problem in Elizabethan England. The majority of people were poor by today's standards, working hard all their lives to scratch out a bare living. The rich made efforts to help those less fortunate than themselves on special occasions, such as Christmas, or in times of particular need, such as during a famine. Of far greater concern, however, were the large numbers of people who had no means of

support at all. Perhaps one of every 500 people fit into this category, with most of them concentrated in urban areas. They included people who were unable to work because of disability and people who had been thrown out of work by changes in England's economy.

During the 1500s the number of poor people in England steadily increased. The feudal* system of landownership, which had ensured that those who worked the land could earn an adequate living, was gradually breaking down. Many agricultural workers were now being forced off the lands their families had lived on for generations. At the same time, European ships exploring America were bringing back vast amounts of gold, which led to inflation and made people's small savings worth even less. English monasteries, which in the past had provided charity to the poor, had been closed down by Henry VIII. Finally, severe weather conditions in the 1590s made harvests very poor, leading to widespread famine. By the late 1500s roughly 10,000 people were VAGABONDS—homeless individuals with no legal means of support. Most of these vagrants were concentrated in urban areas, where they often made up as much as 10 percent of the population.

At the time, the main source of relief for the poor was private charity. With the number of poor people in England increasing, however, voluntary contributions from the wealthy were no longer enough. Over time the government passed a series of laws to deal with the growing tide of poverty. Some of these laws seemed to harm the poorest people rather than help them. For example, in 1547 it became legal to enslave vagabonds who

* *feudal* referring to the medieval system of government and landowning based on rank and loyalty

The poorest of the poor in Elizabethan England were vagabonds and beggars, who had no place to live and no way to support themselves. Those caught begging were commonly whipped through the streets and thrown out of town.

could not, or would not, find a way to support themselves. Other laws, however, improved the lot of the poor considerably. Beginning in 1563 those who did not make charitable contributions through their church could be forced to do so. The broadest measure for ending poverty was the Poor Law of 1597, which directly taxed the rich to help the poor. It ensured that there would be sufficient funds to provide basic care for the poor when private charity was inadequate. The law was so far-reaching that it remained in effect until the late 1900s. It is considered to be one of the great achievements of the Elizabethan age.

The passage of the Poor Law did nothing to reduce the amount of private charity. In fact contributions increased dramatically in the 1600s, partly because the influence of Puritans* led to plainer churches that required less money to support, leaving more money available to help the needy. In addition aiding the poor was considered to be one of the most important duties of the rich. Elizabethans saw *liberality* as the mark of true nobility, which meant not only generosity to the poor but also hospitality to guests of all types.

Those who had wealth liked to show it off. It was considered a great compliment to say that a lord and lady kept their household "in plenty," meaning that they maintained a fine house, many servants, rich FOOD, and fine CLOTHING. The desire to display their riches led many wealthy people to live beyond their means, spending more money each year than their landholdings produced. One noble family was so extravagant in its lifestyle that it had to be put on an annual budget of £200—at a time when a typical servant earned no more than £3 or £4 a year. (*See also* **Aristocracy; Country Life; Court Life; Households and Furnishings; Royalty and Nobility; Social Classes.**)

* **Puritan** English Protestant who advocated strict moral discipline and a simplification of the ceremonies and beliefs of the Anglican Church

PRINCE HAL

See *Henry IV, Part 1; Henry IV, Part 2; Henry V.*

PRINTING AND PUBLISHING

In Elizabethan England, books were published, printed, and sold by merchants called stationers. To produce a book, a stationer obtained a copy of an existing text or paid an author to write a new one. Some stationers hired printers to convert manuscripts into typeset pages, while others did their own printing. Stationers sold copies of printed books in shops and in stalls at outdoor markets and sometimes shipped copies directly to customers.

THE LONDON STATIONERS

* **monopoly** exclusive right to engage in a particular type of business

In Shakespeare's time just a few London stationers controlled all the publishing in England, under the close watch of the monarch. This monopoly*

in publishing was due mainly to the formation of the Stationers' Company in the mid-1500s.

SOLE RIGHT TO PUBLISH. The Stationers' Company was a group of about 100 English printers and publishers. A charter from Queen Mary in 1557 gave members of the Stationers' Company the sole right to publish books in England. Queen ELIZABETH I later restricted this right even more by forbidding any press to be set up outside of LONDON, with the exception of presses in the university towns of Oxford and Cambridge. By 1615 only 22 London stationers were licensed to publish books. The resulting monopoly allowed English publishers to become established in an industry that had previously been dominated by continental* publishers. The licensing of a limited number of stationers also enabled the government to keep tight control over what was published. This was important to the monarch, who did not want any works published that were critical of the crown or church.

Surprisingly, the state's regulation of the publishing industry did not lead to the production of fewer books. If anything, it increased the diversity of volumes that were printed. In the mid-1550s, before the Stationers' Company was chartered, fewer than 100 new titles were issued each year. By 1600, after the Stationers' Company had come to monopolize publishing, more than 250 new titles were published each year. The stationers did, however, set limits on how many copies of a work could be printed at a time, presumably to protect the jobs of the skilled workers in the printing industry. Most books were limited to 1,250 copies. Only surefire bestsellers, such as primers*, prayer books, grammars, and almanacs, could be printed in greater numbers.

INFORMATION FOR SCHOLARS. The clerk of the Stationers' Company kept a record of all the works that members of the company intended to publish. This list, called the Stationers' Register, is a major source of information about publishing during the Elizabethan period. It has helped scholars determine the dates of publication for Shakespeare's plays, and in some cases it reveals the nature of the copy that was registered for publication. The register indicates, for example, that Shakespeare's *Pericles* was licensed in 1608 and that the copy registered for publication rights was based on the prompt book* of the play.

NOTABLE ELIZABETHAN STATIONERS. After becoming queen in 1558, Elizabeth I appointed two members of the Stationers' Company, John Cawood and Richard Jugge, as the royal printers. Their appointments were a turning point in the history of English publishing. Not only did Cawood and Jugge publish a large number of books, but their volumes were of excellent quality, with beautiful, detailed illustrations and high-quality type.

By the time Shakespeare was writing poetry and plays in the 1590s, a London bookseller and printer named William Jaggard had joined the Stationers' Company. In 1599 Jaggard published a collection of poetry called *The Passionate Pilgrime.* He listed "W. Shakespeare" as the author,

* *continental* referring to the European continent

* *primer* small book for teaching children to read

* *prompt book* annotated copy of a play, which contains instructions for entrances, exits, music, and other cues

189

although not all the poems in the collection were Shakespeare's. Jaggard went on to publish a number of well-known editions of Shakespeare's plays. In 1619 he and a stationer named Thomas Pavier issued an unauthorized collection of ten plays (all attributed to Shakespeare, though two of the works were actually by other writers). In 1623, along with his son Isaac, he published the famous FIRST FOLIO edition of Shakespeare's collected plays.

FROM DRAFT TO PRINT

In an age without word processors or even typewriters, the route by which a literary work traveled from the author's handwritten draft to the printed page was slow and difficult. Printing techniques and equipment were relatively crude, and working conditions were poor. Great skill was required to produce accurate, readable books.

FOUL PAPERS AND FAIR COPIES. A printed book in Shakespeare's day started with the author's handwritten manuscript, known (because of its messy scribblings) as the foul papers. This manuscript typically contained many corrections, such as inserted lines and crossed out words. Before it could be set in type, either the author or a professional scribe* had to copy it by hand to produce a fair copy, with all the corrections properly inserted. Most often a printer used the fair copy of a work for typesetting. If the work was a play, it often contained notes that the acting company had added about scenery, action, and stage effects to create a PROMPT BOOK.

Shakespeare, who was known for the ease and smoothness of his writing, appears to have completed original drafts of at least some of his plays that required relatively few corrections. As a result printers seem to have worked directly from his foul papers without having a fair copy made. Several plays, including *A Midsummer Night's Dream, Richard II,* and *The Taming of the Shrew,* are thought to have been printed directly from the playwright's foul papers.

SETTING THE TYPE AND PRINTING THE BOOK. The next step in the production of a printed book was setting the manuscript copy into type. A worker called a compositor did this by hand. The compositor placed small metal letters, called sorts, one by one in rows in a large wooden frame. Once the frame was filled with type, another worker, called a dabber, dabbed the letters with ink. Finally, a pressman ran the printing press that brought large sheets of paper into contact with the inked letters. Paper was very expensive, so skilled pressmen who could operate the press without spoiling any sheets were in demand. After the sheets were printed they were folded to form pages and then sewn together. If the sheets were folded in half to make two leaves (four pages), the completed book was called a folio. If the sheets were folded twice to make four leaves (eight pages), the book was called a quarto.

Printing an entire book was an extremely lengthy and difficult process. Although major printers may have had as many as 100,000 sorts for

* scribe person who copies manuscripts

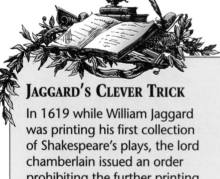

JAGGARD'S CLEVER TRICK

In 1619 while William Jaggard was printing his first collection of Shakespeare's plays, the lord chamberlain issued an order prohibiting the further printing of Shakespeare's plays without the consent of his acting company, the King's Men. To get around the order and continue printing the plays, Jaggard issued the remaining plays with false dates, making it appear that they had been printed before the order was issued. Jaggard's trick was so clever it went undetected until the 1900s.

This engraving shows a busy stationer's shop. Compositors, at the left, arrange letters in rows along a wooden frame while a pressman, at the right, stamps sheets of paper with the inked letters.

their compositors to use in setting type, this was enough for only about a dozen sheets of text. After these pages were printed, the sorts had to be removed from the frames and reused to set the next batch of sheets. This process had to be repeated over and over until the entire text of a work had been set in type and printed. In addition, any illustrations or decorative page borders had to be cut into wood blocks or engraved on copper plates before they could be printed. This work required great skill and was very time-consuming.

ERRORS AND EMENDATIONS

Elizabethan printing and publishing methods left many opportunities for errors to be introduced into books. Compositors made mistakes, and even when they reproduced copy accurately, they were often relying on faulty texts.

COMPOSITOR ERRORS. The way the text was set into type, one letter at a time, made it exceedingly difficult for a compositor to keep in mind the meaning of the words. As a result meaningless passages were sometimes accidentally set into print. The fact that compositors worked up to 16 hours a day, many of them in dim light, increased the chances that errors would occur.

Elizabethan English lacked uniform spelling rules, so compositors felt free to spell words as they wished. Some long works or collections were set in type by several different compositors, each favoring his own version of a particular word. Based on such variations in spelling, it is apparent that the First Folio of Shakespeare's plays was set in type by more than half a dozen different compositors.

ERRORS DUE TO FAULTY TEXTS. In Shakespeare's day there were no copyright laws to give authors ownership of their works. A printed manuscript became the property of the publisher. The author had no further control over the work and earned no additional money from it. As a result any errors that crept into the text of a work were likely to remain uncorrected by the writer.

Acting companies jealously guarded the manuscripts of their plays. They often retained the foul papers of acting scripts, as well as the fair copy used for the prompt book, in order to keep the play out of the hands of rival acting troupes. To obtain the text of a popular play owned by an acting company, a publisher may have paid an actor from the company to reconstruct the play from memory. Obviously a copy of a play that was based on an actor's memory was likely to contain numerous errors. Several of the so-called bad quartos of Shakespeare's dramatic works are now believed to have been based on this kind of dubious reconstruction from memory.

EMENDATIONS. Later editors have tried to correct some of the errors that were introduced into Shakespeare's works when they were first published and printed. Such corrections are called emendations. Obvious misprints, where Shakespeare's original meaning was clear, are easily corrected. Less obvious errors, where Shakespeare's original meaning can only be guessed, are more difficult to correct and are often hotly disputed. In fact two of the most famous emendations of Shakespeare's works—one in *Henry V*, the other in *Hamlet*—are still questioned by scholars today.

In the First Folio version of *Henry V*, Mistress Quickly describes the death of Sir John Falstaff with the words "his nose was as sharp as a pen, and a Table of green fields" (II.iii.16–17). In the 1700s editor Lewis Theobald changed the text to read "'a [he] babbled of green fields," which seems to many readers to make more sense. Most modern versions of the play use this emendation, but some editors have objected to the change. A few have suggested other possibilities for emending the line, such as replacing the word *and* with *on*. The phrase "his nose was as sharp as a pen on a Table of green fields" might make sense to Elizabethan audiences as a sexual pun.

The emendation in *Hamlet* occurs in the opening line of Hamlet's first soliloquy*. In the First Folio edition of the play, Hamlet opens his speech with the exclamation, "O that this too too solid flesh would melt, / Thaw, and resolve itself into a dew!" (I.ii.129–30). The word *solid* was later emended to *sullied*, meaning "contaminated," a word that seems to have been a variant of *sallied*, the form found in the 1604 Second Quarto printing. The idea that Hamlet's flesh is sullied makes more sense in the context of the play, because his mother, Gertrude, has married his late father's brother—a relationship that Hamlet views as incest*. The Folio version, however, fits better with the idea of "melting." (*See also* **Acting Companies, Elizabethan; Censorship, Licensing, and Copyrights; Guilds; Prompt Book; Quartos and Folios; Shakespeare's Works, Influential Editions.**)

* *soliloquy* monologue in which a character reveals his or her private thoughts

* *incest* sexual relationship between family members

PROBLEM PLAYS

See *All's Well That Ends Well; Measure for Measure; Plays: The Comedies; Troilus and Cressida.*

PROMPT BOOK

I n Shakespeare's time the prompt book was the copy of a play that was used for performances by an acting company. Generally, it included more detailed stage directions than other versions of the play. The prompt book typically contained notes for the actors' entrances and exits, cues for music and sound effects, and instructions for changes of scenery. It also indicated any cuts that had been made in the author's original text of the play. In some prompt books, moreover, the names of certain actors replaced the names of the characters in the play.

If a play had already been published, a printed copy might serve as the prompt book after notes and corrections had been added. This may have been the case for Shakespeare's *Richard II* and *King Lear*. The playwright's manuscript was usually the authoritative copy, however. In these cases it was the duty of the company scribe* to reproduce the original so that a duplicate could be used as the prompt book. Before the members of an acting company could receive a license to perform a play, they had to present a prompt copy to the MASTER OF THE REVELS for approval. This was one of the rare occasions when an acting company would have parted with its prompt book. Even lending it to a publisher for printing was considered risky because the prompt book was often the only copy of the play a company had in its possession. Consequently, only a few plays were first printed from prompt books. (*See also* **Acting Companies, Elizabethan; Printing and Publishing.**)

* *scribe* person who copies manuscripts

PROSE TECHNIQUE

A lthough Shakespeare wrote his plays mainly in verse, fully one-fourth of his dramatic output is prose. The proportion of prose in individual plays varies greatly, but nearly all of the later ones contain a significant amount. In his early histories—among the first of his dramatic works—there is no prose at all (*King John, Richard II,* and *Henry VI, Part 1* and *Part 3*) or very little (the dialogue between two murderers in *Richard III,* I.iv). But as Shakespeare's style developed, his use of prose as an alternative to verse became more significant, varied, and revealing. The amount of prose peaked around the middle of his career, then settled to a level approximating 25 percent. Prose in the plays provides not only a stylistic contrast with verse but also a subtle indicator of character and dramatic tone.

FUNCTIONS OF PROSE. Shakespeare's plays, especially the early ones, follow the usual conventions* for the use of prose in Elizabethan drama. Written communications, such as letters and proclamations, are generally

* *convention* established practice

193

Prose Technique

* **exposition** explanation of background information necessary to understand a plot

in prose to distinguish them from the surrounding verse. Scenes involving plot exposition* may also be in prose, as in the opening scenes of *As You Like It* and *King Lear*.

By far the most familiar and telling use of prose in Elizabethan drama is to indicate that a character is somehow incapable of the more sophisticated language of verse. This may be due to madness (as in *Macbeth*, V.i) or drunkenness (*The Tempest*, III.ii), or because a character speaks with an accent (*Henry V*, III.ii). More commonly, characters who speak prose are rustic, such as Launcelot Gobbo in *The Merchant of Venice* and various other "clown" figures. Prose is the language of the many characters who inspire laughter through idiocy or incompetence. It is also that of sharper-witted comic figures whose mocking speeches work against the social order (such as Feste in *Twelfth Night* or the Fool in *King Lear*). In general, prose is the medium for confusion, disorder, and above all humor.

This complements a second major convention: the use of verse and prose to reflect social class. Educated and sophisticated characters express themselves in verse, while the baseborn and ignorant characters generally speak prose. Verse is perceived to be the higher form, appropriate to more noble characters and themes, whereas prose is for commoners and for comedy.

In Shakespeare's early comedies these two conventions tend to coincide. *The Comedy of Errors, The Taming of the Shrew, The Two Gentlemen of Verona, Love's Labor's Lost*, and *A Midsummer Night's Dream* all feature supporting casts of lowborn prose speakers whose function is predominantly comic. Some display a streetwise wit, such as Speed in *The Two Gentlemen of Verona*, but more often these low comic types are ridiculous both to the audience and to the more aristocratic, verse-speaking characters. In *A Midsummer Night's Dream* and *Love's Labor's Lost*, the low characters make themselves doubly ridiculous by attempting to perform serious verse dramas for a noble audience, many of whom find their efforts laughable. The noble characters themselves tend to speak prose only when they must interact with the comic characters, lowering themselves to their level.

In the early histories, which deal with the power struggles of the nobility, there are few such low characters and therefore little or no prose. Where low characters, such as the rebel Cade in *Henry VI, Part 2*, do appear, they speak prose. Cade attempts to use verse, but he cannot sustain it. The contrast between his prose and the verse of his more noble opponents reflects his unfitness to seize the throne. The later histories, *Henry IV, Parts 1* and *2*, and *Henry V*, feature characters from a broader range of social classes. The prose scenes involving Sir John FALSTAFF and his companions provide not only comic relief from the serious verse narrative but also a running commentary on the rest of the action. The sustained counterpoint between verse and prose gives these works greater depth and sophistication than the earlier histories.

SHAKESPEARE'S USES OF PROSE. Although Shakespeare generally observed the convention of using prose to distinguish between upper- and lower-class characters, he did not follow this basic distinction strictly. Rather, he adapted it in a variety of subtle ways. For example, when

higher-class characters "lower" themselves by their behavior, they may drop down to prose, as Prince Hal does in the tavern scenes in *Henry IV, Part 1*. Prose is also the primary medium of expression for any character who is "low" by nature. This includes those who are lewd (such as Pandarus in *Troilus and Cressida*), undignified (Sir Toby in *Twelfth Night*), harshly mocking (Apemantus in *Timon of Athens*), or immoral (IAGO in *Othello*).

Shakespeare used prose not only for contrast or for comic effect but also to achieve a lighter dramatic tone. Relaxed or domestic scenes may be conducted in prose, even between characters of higher social status,

In Shakespeare's plays, prose is generally spoken by commoners or clowns. Because his early plays were about power struggles among the nobility, there were few lowborn or comedic characters and therefore little prose. Shakespeare's use of prose peaked around the middle of his career, when he wrote many of the comedies and featured a broader range of social classes in his history plays.

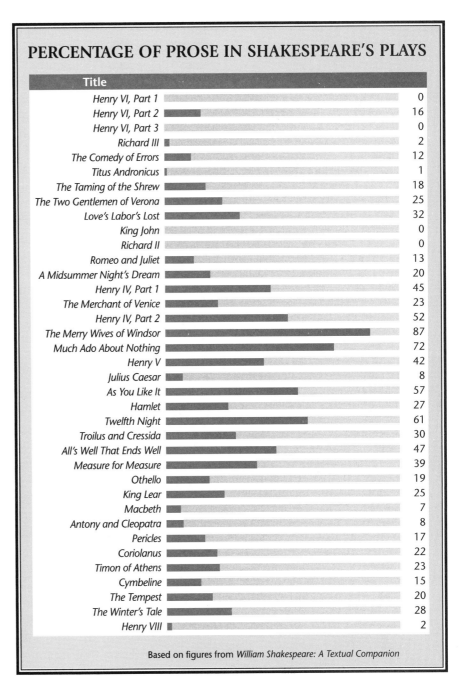

PERCENTAGE OF PROSE IN SHAKESPEARE'S PLAYS

Title	
Henry VI, Part 1	0
Henry VI, Part 2	16
Henry VI, Part 3	0
Richard III	2
The Comedy of Errors	12
Titus Andronicus	1
The Taming of the Shrew	18
The Two Gentlemen of Verona	25
Love's Labor's Lost	32
King John	0
Richard II	0
Romeo and Juliet	13
A Midsummer Night's Dream	20
Henry IV, Part 1	45
The Merchant of Venice	23
Henry IV, Part 2	52
The Merry Wives of Windsor	87
Much Ado About Nothing	72
Henry V	42
Julius Caesar	8
As You Like It	57
Hamlet	27
Twelfth Night	61
Troilus and Cressida	30
All's Well That Ends Well	47
Measure for Measure	39
Othello	19
King Lear	25
Macbeth	7
Antony and Cleopatra	8
Pericles	17
Coriolanus	22
Timon of Athens	23
Cymbeline	15
The Tempest	20
The Winter's Tale	28
Henry VIII	2

Based on figures from *William Shakespeare: A Textual Companion*

such as ROSALIND and Celia in *As You Like It* (I.iii). When Duke Frederick intrudes upon his daughter and niece later in this scene, the shifts from prose to verse mark a heightening of tension. Correspondingly, a shift from verse to prose may be seen as relaxing the dramatic or emotional intensity, as when Romeo banters with Mercutio in *Romeo and Juliet* (II.iv).

In Hamlet's famous confrontation scene with OPHELIA (III.i), by contrast, his shift from verse into prose does not lower the tension of their encounter but signals its disintegration into disjointed abuse. Ophelia's verse lament "O, what a noble mind is here o'erthrown!" (*Hamlet*, III.i.150) describes an alteration in the prince's mental state that has been indicated by his sudden change from verse to prose. In *Othello* another "noble mind" is more gradually "o'erthrown," as Othello comes increasingly under Iago's influence. Othello's moral and psychological collapse in Act IV, Scene i, is signaled by a transition from verse to prose, with the Moor first raving about Desdemona's unfaithfulness and then resolving to kill her. In the murder scene itself, however, Othello returns to verse, which lends some dignity to his violent and irrational acts and shows them to be unnatural to a man of his noble stature.

Shakespeare's prose generally belongs to comical scenes and characters. Even his most complex comedies—*Much Ado About Nothing, As You Like It,* and *Twelfth Night*—contain more prose than verse. In these mature works prose is not reserved solely for fools and comic butts. The dramatic leads, such as Beatrice, Benedick, and Rosalind, express themselves as memorably in prose as in verse. They also use prose in unconventional ways: when there are no "low" characters present and when their conversations are both serious and high in dramatic tension. For example, in *Much Ado About Nothing* (IV.i), Beatrice and Benedick use prose throughout the dialogue in which they confess their love for each other and Beatrice demands that Benedick kill Claudio, his best friend. Similarly, in *The Merchant of Venice* (III.i), SHYLOCK uses prose to condemn the anti-Semitic* prejudice of his enemies. This condemnation scene is not at all comical or relaxed in tone. Shylock's speech does not seem confused or unbalanced; in fact his skillful use of language chillingly suggests exactly the opposite, as he precisely lists his grievances and carefully lays out a series of comparisons and contrasts. Shylock's use of prose could be seen as a reflection of his base or unacceptable intentions, but in this scene his ill will seems entirely justified.

In the later histories the use of prose does not simply provide comic relief or reflect social status. The rebellious Hotspur is described as noble, but in *Henry IV, Part 1* (II.iii) he vents his anger in prose. This shows not that he is low in birth or character but that his feelings here cannot be contained in the formal structure of verse. In *Henry V* the character who speaks the most prose is the king himself. His wooing of the French princess (V.ii) is certainly comic, but his discussion of a king's responsibilities with his soldiers the night before the battle of Agincourt (IV.i) is completely serious. The king's ability to use prose and verse with equal effectiveness shows that he understands the minds of his subjects, commoners as well as nobles, and that he can relate to them on their level and

* ***anti-Semitic*** referring to prejudice against Jews

A Gallery of Prose Speakers

One of the best examples of humorous Shakespearean prose is *The Merry Wives of Windsor.* More than four-fifths of the text is prose, and the assorted characters speak in a variety of gloriously individual prose styles. Two of them—the Welsh parson, Sir Hugh Evans, and the French doctor Caius—speak with broad accents. Mistress Quickly, the hostess of the Garter Inn, misuses and mispronounces words, while the host of the inn is hearty and familiar with everyone. Shakespeare takes full advantage of all the humorous possibilities of prose in one of his broadest and silliest comedies.

in their own terms. But it may also say something about his own mood and state of mind.

PROSE AND VERSE IN PERFORMANCE. Especially in his later plays, Shakespeare's use of verse and prose comes increasingly to reflect the shifting dramatic contexts of his scenes. His characters adjust their manner of speaking according to their situation. Analyzing these choices from an actor's perspective can therefore be instructive. A prominent Shakespearean actor, Janet Suzman of the ROYAL SHAKESPEARE COMPANY, has summarized the difference between verse and prose as follows: "As a general rule of thumb, prose is an outpouring, verse is a distillation." Prose, then, is in general relatively unrestrained, the straightforward revelations of a character's thoughts and feelings. In verse, by contrast, Suzman's "distillation" suggests a more conscious or careful process of trying to contain what may be powerful and even conflicting emotions or to express what may be highly complex thoughts and ideas, in a few well-chosen words. This simple but useful observation complements the generally accepted rules concerning prose usage, helping explain those examples that do not appear to fit the standard categories, such as the Beatrice-Benedick scene described above.

The funeral scene in *Julius Caesar* (III.ii) provides a good example of Suzman's distinction. Brutus uses prose when addressing the crowd in this scene, even though he speaks only verse throughout the rest of the play. Some critics see this use of prose as condescending or as an indication that Brutus is unemotional or insincere, but probably few actors playing the role would agree. It is easier to accept that Brutus's prose speech is an open, direct statement of his views. Mark Antony, on the other hand, addresses the crowd in verse. His oration is carefully crafted to draw first sympathy, then anger from his audience. His choice of words is more calculated, accordingly, and he suppresses his own feelings where necessary to gain the maximum effect from his words.

Actors who apply Suzman's observation can use the shifts between prose and verse to emphasize how the changing dramatic context affects their characters' expressions of their thoughts and feelings. In verse the meaning of the lines may conflict with their form; that is, the punctuation may not coincide neatly with the verse line endings. In such cases (which are increasingly common in Shakespeare's later plays), the actor may make use of this when speaking the lines. He may use the shape of the verse, as well as the midline pauses created by punctuation, to break up the text and produce a more controlled but natural-sounding flow of words. This can help make the text sound more spontaneous, as if it were being invented within the developing action rather than quoted or recited. In other words the actor will seem to "distill" language from the character's thoughts and feelings.

In prose the sense of the words coincides with the form. It invites more of a straightforward "outpouring" of the character's thoughts and feelings. Characters may "pour out" their ideas in prose for a variety of reasons. In some cases they are not mentally or emotionally capable of "distilling" them into verse. In other contexts the nature of the scene may

be such that the characters feel no need to choose their words carefully because there is an openness or trust between them. Such apparent honesty may be deceptive, however. In *Othello,* for example, Iago uses prose to manipulate Roderigo, pretending that he is expressing his feelings without reserve (III.i). By contrast he uses verse to deceive Othello, who is not as simple and naive as Roderigo. It is precisely because Iago seems so cautious and so guarded in his choice of words that Othello believes him, assuming that there is "some monster in [his] thought / Too hideous to be shown" (III.iii.107–8).

One of Shakespeare's greatest achievements as a dramatist was his mastery of two contrasting forms of expression. The range, wit, and expressive power of his prose make it a powerful alternative to verse. By keeping Suzman's observation in mind, actors can use either to their advantage. (*See also* **Fools, Clowns, and Jesters; Humor in Shakespeare's Plays; Language.**)

INDEX

Index

Index

Index

Index

Index

Index

Index

Index

Index

Iago as, 2:14, 133–34
influence on tragedies, 2:169
in morality plays, 2:138–39
Richard III as, 3:17
Shylock in tradition of, 2:104
as stock character, 2:99
villainous characters and, 1:49–50
Village life, 1:72–74
Virgil, 3:118
Viscounts, 1:23, 3:27
Vision through madness, 2:77–78
Visual effects, 1:92
Vogel, Paula, 2:136
Voltaire, 2:55, 3:134–35
Voss, Johann Heinrich, 3:136

W

Wages, 1:62
Wake, 1:48, 87
Walker, William, 1:136
Walking, 3:138
Walsingham, Sir Francis, 3:97
Walsingham, Thomas, 2:87
Wanamaker, Sam, 1:150
War games, 1:141
War of the Theaters, 2:152, **3:154–55**
Warburton, William, 3:58
Ward, John, 3:49
Wardle, Irving, 2:95
Warfare, **3:155–60** *(illus.)*
    arms and armor for, 1:23–27 *(illus.)*
    foreign relations and, 1:91
    military life, 2:112
    naval, 3:84, 95–96 *(illus.)*
    Spanish Armada and, 3:95–96 *(illus.)*
    tournaments and, 3:127
Warhorses, 3:158
Warkworth Castle, 1:45
Warner, David, 3:15
Warner, Deborah, 2:36
Warning signs, 2:82
Wars of the Roses, **3:160**
    castles during, 1:44, 45–46
    Henry VI, Part 1 on, 1:176–79 *(illus.)*
    Henry VI, Part 2 on, 1:179–81
    Henry VI, Part 3 on, 1:181–84 *(illus.)*
    Richard III and final events of, 3:15–18 *(illus.)*
    sources on, 3:75
    television production on, 3:112

Washington Shakespeare Company, 3:107
Watchword to England, A (Munday), 2:139
Water supply for London, 2:59
Water transport, 3:132, 139–40
Watteau, Antoine, 3:115
Wealth. *See* Poverty and wealth
Weaponry. *See* Arms and armor
Weather and the seasons, 1:124–26 *(illus.)*, 2:126–28, **3:160–61**, 3:165
Weddings, 1:48
Welles, Orson, 1:167, 2:28, 74, 135, 3:50–51
West, Benjamin, 1:28
West Side Story, 3:52, 69
Westminster, 2:58
Wet nurses, 2:129
Wheel of fortune, 2:100, 168–69
Wheeled vehicles, 3:139, 140
Whetstone, George, 2:92
Whipping, 1:82
White Tower, 3:128
White, Willard, 2:136
Whitehall Palace, 1:57
Whitsunday, 1:125–26
Wieland, Christoph Martin, 3:135
Wilhelm Meister (Goethe), 2:54
Will. *See* Shakespeare's will
William Shakespeare's Romeo + Juliet, 3:52
William the Conqueror, 1:46, 3:128
Windsor Castle, 1:75
Wine, 1:130
Winter festivals, 1:124–25
Winter's Tale, The, 2:156–57, 165–66, 3:48, **3:161–66** *(illus.)*, 3:161
Witches and evil spirits, 3:100–101, **3:167–68** *(illus.)*
    dangers after childbirth from fairies, 1:47
    ghosts and apparitions, 1:149
    in *Henry VI, Part 1*, 1:178
    in *Henry VI, Part 2*, 1:179
    in *Macbeth*, 2:70, 71, 72
    spirit conjuring, 2:80–81
Woman's Prize, or The Tamer Tamed, The (Fletcher), 3:106
Women
    boys in roles of, 1:5–6
    clothing for, 1:60
    in comedies, 2:156
    death during childbirth, 1:87
    disguised as men, 1:98–99
    education of, 1:108–9

friendship between, 1:139
healers (wise women), 2:98
herbal remedies concocted by, 1:188–89 *(illus.)*
place in family, 2:88
roles in Elizabethan society, 1:145
roles in plays for, 1:121–23
on stage, 1:2, 8, 9, 10, 93, 3:55, 57
work of, 1:73, 78, 3:168, 169, 170
See also Feminist interpretations; Gender and sexuality; Marriage and family
Women's Part: Feminist Criticism of Shakespeare, The (Lenz, Greene, and Neely), 1:120, 121
Woodlands, 1:134–35
Woodward, Henry, 1:14
Wool industry, 1:12, 39, 40, 3:130–31, 169–70, 170–71
Woolf, Virginia, 1:95
Word abuse and misuse, 2:10–11
Wordplay, 2:42, 119, 174, 176–77, 3:150
Wordsworth, William, 3:94
Work, **3:168–72** *(illus.)*
    country life and, 1:72, 73–74
    craftworkers and, 1:76–80 *(illus.)*
    farm labor and products, 1:11–12
    guilds and, 1:155–56 *(illus.)*
    in medicine, 2:96–98
    unemployment with agricultural changes, 1:73
World Shakespeare Bibliography, 3:74
Wriothesley, Henry, 2:141, 180, 3:45
Writ, 2:45
Writers inspired by Shakespeare. *See* Literature inspired by Shakespeare
Writers. *See* Playwrights and poets
Wyatt, Sir Thomas, 2:48, 3:92

Y

Yeomen, 1:11, 23, 3:87–88
Yong, Bartholomew, 3:149
Yorkist tetralogy, 2:2, 3–5. *See also Henry VI, Part 1*; *Henry VI, Part 2*; *Henry VI, Part 3*; *Richard III*

Z

Zeffirelli, Franco, 1:162, 3:22, 51, 69, 106
Zelauto (Munday), 2:139
Zoffany, John, 1:28

216